ALSO BY BRUCE FEILER

Learning to Bow

LOOKING FOR CLASS

LOOKING FOR CLASS

Seeking Wisdom and Romance
at Oxford and Cambridge

Bruce Feiler

RANDOM HOUSE

NEW YORK

The events described in this book are real, although the names and identifying characteristics of all students and faculty have been changed. A few of the characters are composites, including Peter and Susanna.

All rights reserved under International and Pan-American Copyright Conventions. Published in the United States by Random House, Inc., New York, and simultaneously in Canada by Random House of Canada Limited, Toronto.

Library of Congress Cataloging-in-Publication Data
Feiler, Bruce S.
Looking for class : seeking wisdom and
romance at Oxford and Cambridge / Bruce Feiler.
p.   cm.
ISBN 0-679-41492-4
1. University of Cambridge—Students—Anecdotes. 2. University of
Oxford—Students—Anecdotes.   I. Title.
LF129.F45 1993
378.426'59—dc20   93-18156

Manufactured in the United States of America
24689753
First Edition

Book design by Oksana Kushnir

For
Aleen Wolf Feiler,
who taught me when to bunt
and when to swing away,
and who gave me the gift of travel

Tut-tut, it looks like rain.

—A. A. Milne
Winnie-the-Pooh, 1926

CONTENTS

AFTER CLASS

The year ended, as it started, with a sacrificial death. The victim, in my case, was shoes. All during the year that I lived in Cambridge, I had worn only American shoes—sneakers, flip-flops, tasseled loafers, and other insults to the Crown. But when I came home at the end of the year, I didn't even unpack my drab menagerie but left it buried in my duffel bag like some opinion I'd outgrown. And then in my first weekend at home I went to the oldest store I could find to buy a pair of pure British bucks.

In the store a salesman was lacing my feet when a young man sat down beside me. "Excuse me," the salesman said to the man. "Are you two together?"

"No," said the man, whose face was quite pale.

"Sorry," said the salesman, turning back toward me. "He and I spoke earlier. . . . And, well, you two have the same accent and all."

"The same accent?" I turned toward the man, who was dressed in dark blue, and said in what I thought was my unaccented English: "Excuse me, where are you from?"

"Now, I live here," the man said. "But I was born in England."

"England?" I said, alarmed: I didn't mind having British taste on my feet, but I didn't want it on my tongue as well. "That's odd. I just spent a year in Cambridge, and—"

"Were you *at* Cambridge?" the man interrupted, which is Cambridge-speak for "Did you really attend the Greatest University on Earth or did you merely dabble at one of the many language schools that scrounge on Our Good Name?"

"I was at Cambridge," I answered.

"Oh, really," he said, barely crinkling a smile. "Perhaps we were the same class."

Surely he had meant to say year, I thought. Surely he had meant to suggest we might have been there at the same time. But then again, he did say class. And, after all, it did make sense. For those who wander through its halls, Cambridge, like Oxford, is much more than a school; it is a social badge of honor. Many I knew there, when they get out, will wear that badge with pride. But two I met didn't want that badge: each of them, in a way, had killed to get in. And because, in the end, their stories inspired me, my story begins with theirs.

PROLOGUE

COMING UP

Rivers and Roads

It was a dreary morning when the wheels
Rolled over a wide plain o'erhung with clouds,
And nothing cheered our way till first we saw
The long-roofed chapel of King's College lift
Turrets and pinnacles in answering files,
Extended high above a dusky grove.

—William Wordsworth
The Prelude, 1850

A young man stepped forward into the bleached morning light and drew a sword from a sheath at his waist. His mouth, like the sky, was dry. All around him, from the shops, the sheds, and the terra-cotta fields of the arid Indian town, whispers streamed through the dusty streets and settled before the shrine. Up above, the sun stood still, as if bowing to a moment in the passage of youth. While far below, faces peered toward the boy in front of the altar and blushed the shade of baked red earth as they first inhaled the divine perfume of a lamb about to die.

Moving cautiously, the boy gripped the sword around its gilded handle and lifted it slowly to a peak above his head, using both his hands, both his eyes, and the amalgamated strength of the town's congregation. The boy, barely a month past twenty, was royally dressed in a white cotton gown, a scarlet cap, and black canvas slippers. His stringy hair was matted to his brow by a delicate lace of perspiration. Feeling the drip of his anxiety, he steadied his stance, redoubled his grip, and awaited the signal from God.

As far as anyone in town could remember, the sword had never failed to attract the needed signal. A generation earlier, after World War Two, the boy's father had used the blade to consecrate his country's independence; later his older brother had used it to gain good fortune for his marriage; now he was required to use the sword to guarantee safe passage on a voyage—one that many others would take that day, but few would observe in its ritual glory. For this son, the second son, was leaving home for a journey that would take him to a higher world, to the world of poets and kings, to the world of England. Rana Patel was going to Cambridge.

For a quarter of an hour he awaited the signal—his arms outstretched, his breath held tight, his face as still as stone. But the message didn't come. The lamb continued to wander about, and Rana began to squirm. Years earlier, his older brother had successfully decapitated the lamb with one blow from the sword and anything less on his part would augur misfortune for the rest of his life.

Then suddenly, when Rana thought he could remain poised no longer, the lamb drooped its head and began to drift, first forward, then back, with the subtle sway of an empty cradle. Beginning with its cloven feet and stretching through its sinewy legs to the hunch of its infant back, the lamb began to shiver, to quake with the force of a tender shrub seized by monsoon winds. Rana knew this was the beacon he sought. Closing his eyes and arching his back like the callow lamb he was destined to slaughter, he pointed the sword toward the heart of the sun, summoned a resolve from the depths of his person, and sliced the blade toward the woolen flesh he would transform into parchment.

When Rana finally opened his eyes, he could see a prayer on the lips of the town and hear the blood that began with a drip, eased into a stream, and flowed inexorably down toward the sea. From this river he had built a bridge. And at that moment, when the whispers began to bask in the glory and Rana began to shine, somewhere on the other side of the sun it began to rain. . . .

. . .

A young woman stepped up to the antique sink and turned on the water to hide her distress. Her climb—so thorough—seemed about to collapse. True, Peter's father, all through the evening, seemed not to notice the remains of her northern accent. His mother, who surely noticed her roots, acted as if she didn't care. But Susanna still knew that they didn't approve. Even though she and Peter would be returning to Cambridge the following day, no degree of education—no change of accent, no bleaching her hair—could completely bury her lowly background. And then, after dinner, she made her misstep, excusing herself for a trip to the toilet with the line "I'll just go and wash my hands." Peter's mother—was it on purpose?—had given her directions to the washroom, which, as customary, was removed from the toilet. Eager not to admit her faux pas, Susanna opted for the only solution. Moving as silently as possible, she slid off her shoes and climbed onto the basin. She hiked up her skirt, slid down her stockings, and was just about to relieve herself when the sink, overwhelmed, relieved itself first: crashing to the ground, smashing the pipes, and spoiling Susanna Greely's return to Cambridge by spilling her onto the washroom floor and spewing tap water, in a mock fountain of youth, all across the polished tile and all over her borrowed dress. . . .

I stepped to the curb, dilated my umbrella, and stared as far as my eye could see. The road was a river, reined by the sky. The river was crowded, dammed to the bridge. From Long Island to Manhattan, all along the arteries, cars were clogged in an endless stream. Bobbing, I stood at river's edge on Broadway, waving at occupied yellow cabs and drawing behind me like a pontoon bridge a suitcase, a camera case, a backpack, a duffel bag, a laptop computer, and a masticated paper sack containing two weeks of unread *New York Timeses*. From all accounts the president seemed tense: the Crisis was growing darker, he said, and men and women were being shipped to the East in the middle of the night. History, it seemed, was moving west to east, while I, fresh from Japan, was moving east to west.

"Where you going?" said a driver as he splashed to my side.

"Camelot."

"Is that in Brooklyn?"

"It's in England. I'm going to JFK."

"Uy," he said in a Queens English accent. "That's a long ride. 'Fraid I'm gonna have to stop along the way. I gotta go. Know what I mean?"

"Sorry," I said as I slid through the door. "I'm afraid I don't have time to wait."

He humphed, squeezed his legs, and took off with a start, while I checked my watch time and sank back in the seat. It was a little over an hour before my plane would take off and with it my quest for the perfect English grail—the driest wit, the densest fog, the ultimate degree. For most of the next half hour, however, every time my driver would round a corner and draw me closer to the start of my pursuit, a small orange light would cry out from his dash, CHECK EXPECTATIONS, at which point he would slam on his brakes and I would slink down in despair.

A little under an hour later we finally arrived. I handed the driver my last remaining dollars and hurried off with my hundred pounds of luggage to try and catch my flight. Dripping, I made it down the vertical escalator and along the underachieving horizontal one as well, before being stopped at the security gates, where I was asked to open my suitcase, take a picture with my camera, and, for counterterrorist-typist purposes, write a simple sentence on my laptop computer: "I gotta go. Know what I mean?"

With the engines already humming and the British papers long since distributed, I stumbled down the gangway at the appointed departure hour. I offered the attendant my luggage with an apologetic bow and lugged my three carry-ons down the aisle. Once they were stuffed overhead and underfoot, I leaned back on my flotation device, shielded my eyes from the last NO SMOKING sign I would see for a year, and released myself to the soothing voice of "my captain," who said that the rain had caused such a river that our road to London would be delayed, happily ever after.

"Mummy, mummy, look, the wings are falling to bits."

Phillida McClosky, aged seven-and-a-half, was pounding on the double window at the end of my row as our plane approached Heathrow International Airport a little over ten hours later, following a three-hour weather delay in New York and a seven-hour flight to London.

"They are not," comforted her mother.

"No, no!" Phillida insisted, now turning to me for support. "I'm telling you, the wings are falling to pieces. They're all mucked up."

"Mucked up?" I said.

"Sure," she said. "They look like this." She held her arms askew like an awkward bird. "We'll never land with wings like that."

Phillida and her family were just returning from a holiday in America.

"Granny fell down and hurt her leg, so we had to go visit her," she explained. "Then she got all dressed up to meet us at the airport and fell down again. Poor Granny."

"Did you eat well in America?" I asked her.

"Well, once we went to a restaurant and I had a hamburger. It was pretty good."

"So what do you want to eat first when you get home?"

She thought for a second, then clasped her hands together and stuck out her moistened tongue. "I want a huge plate of sausage and beans."

"Phillida, dear, look," called her mother. "You can see the M-4."

"You will be pleased to note," said the captain over the loudspeaker, "that we will be experiencing no unforeseen delays this morning during our final descent into London. Down below you will find a pleasant view of the River Thames and the M-25 motorway."

"Everyone seems to know all the roads," I observed.

"We have to learn them in school," Phillida explained, still looking at London below. "I can tell you how to get from Brighton to Edinburgh without a map. . . . Hey look!" she cried. "I can see Waterloo Bridge. That's my favourite."

"Do you know all the bridges, as well?"

"Of course," she said, turning back toward me. "This is Britain. You can't go anywhere in this country without crossing a lot of bridges."

Inside the terminal, where everything strikes the new arrival as a metaphor, various illuminated signs stood out on the chrome-and-plaster walls as I carried my luggage toward the "Disembarkation Lounge." One, a red sign with white lettering, seemed like a declaration of independence from a unifying Europe: 100 FLIGHTS A WEEK TO PARIS AND AMSTERDAM (AND 100 BACK AGAIN). Another, a wry slogan over a close-up of club soda on the rocks, seemed a national anthem of sorts: THIS MAY APPEAR STRAIGHT, it said, BUT THE DISCRIMINATING EYE WILL NOTICE A TWIST.

After disembarking through the well-named lounge, I approached a lone policeman wearing an ice bucket–shaped helmet and asked if he could direct me to the bus station.

"Buses depart from across the street," he said, pointing his machine gun at a sign above his head that showed, indeed, a pictogram of a bus with an arrow pointing across the street. "Be sure and look both ways," he said.

Thanking him, I stepped into the street and glanced to my left, where I immediately noticed a message painted on the pavement that said, politely, PLEASE LOOK RIGHT. Chastened, I looked to the right, then to the left, and even to the right again before pulling my bags across the street and through the station door.

"I would like to take a bus to Cambridge," I said to the woman behind the counter.

"Sorry," she said, "there are no buses to Cambridge."

"Are there trains?"

"Sorry, no trains."

"Surely there must be some way to go."

"Perhaps you should try the coach station."

"What's a coach station?"

"It's where the coaches depart."

I looked at her. "I realize that, but what's a coach?"

"It's a bus."

"But I thought this was the bus station."

"It is, but buses travel only short distances and coaches travel further."

"I see. And where, may I ask, is the coach station?"

"See that bobby across the street?"

"The policeman."

"The copper. Go past him, down the hall, up the lift, and out to the right."

I took a deep breath and began gathering my luggage.

"By the way," I said. "How much does it cost?"

"About ten quid," she said.

"Thank you very much."

"Thank *you,* sir. And don't forget to look both ways."

For the next fifteen minutes, as I redragged my gear past the bobby-copper, down the hall, up the lift, and out to the right, I tried to determine precisely what a "quid" was and whether I had ten of them or not. I had exchanged money before departing—at two dollars a pound—but could not remember receiving any quids. Frankly, I could not remember even hearing of a quid. At this point, suffering from physical exhaustion, not to mention linguistic deprivation, I briefly considered dropping my hundred pounds and catching one of Heathrow's hundred flights to Paris: at least there I could speak the language.

Regaining my composure inside the elevator, I opened my *Pocket Guide to London:* "The unit of currency in Britain is the pound sterling," it said, "which is divided into 100 pence (p). There are coins for 1p, 2p, 5p, 10p, 20p, 50p, and £1." All very courteous, I thought, but not very helpful. Next I looked in my pocket dictionary: "Quid, *n,* from Middle English *quide,* a cut or wad of something chewable." This sounded more like tobacco than money, and I knew I was out of luck.

"Luton, Stansted, Cambridge," said the loudspeaker as the elevator opened its doors and I stepped cautiously to the right. "Last call . . ."

I sprinted the last few steps to the coach.

"Hurry along," the coach driver said. "Bring your bags inside. I'll get your fare after I start."

Using three trips and three sets of seats, I eventually loaded my luggage into the cabin of the National Express Luxury Coach oft-stop service to Cambridge and went to pay my fare.

"That'll be twelve quid," the driver announced.

I leaned down nonchalantly so as not to appear out of place and pretended to be occupied with my wallet.

"By the way," I said, "how much is a quid these days?"

"Are you American?" he said.

"Yes," I mumbled.

"Well, son, a quid equals one pound sterling, always has, always will. It's the one with Her Majesty, the Queen of England, on the front."

"I see. And why doesn't it say that on the note?"

He took his eyes off the road and for the first time looked at me. "It doesn't have to, my boy. We have a long memory in this country. We English don't easily forget."

·   ·   ·

I had rediscovered England in Columbus. About a month before departing for Britain I attended the wedding of some college friends in the capital of Ohio. Late Sunday evening, following three days of prenuptial and postnuptial festivities and three nights of little sleep, I found myself in a conversation with two other guests, one of whom—like myself—had just returned from living in Tokyo, the other from living in Cambridge.

"So I hear you just finished a book on Japan," said Jennifer. "I can't wait to read it. Don't you just love the way the Japanese go to sing-along bars and get drunk every night."

"The British do that, too," added Daniel. "Except the pubs all close at eleven."

"Then what does everybody do?" she asked.

"The nobs catch a taxi," he said. "The yobs catch the bus, and the lager louts just go outside and sing themselves silly in the streets."

And so it went, back and forth until four in the morning, first a story from Japan, then a tale from Britain. In the course of that evening I learned the English terms *nobs* (snobs), *yobs* (toughs), *fags* (cigs), and *getting pissed* (the process of putting stout, ale, lager, or some other liquid into someone to make them drunk or taking it out of them to make them disgraced. As Daniel explained, a typical pub-sentence goes something like this: "Last night I went to the pub and got pissed, then I met this bloke who pissed me off, so I took the piss out of him.") More important, as the night progressed and the conversation flowed east and west across the oceans, forward and backward in time, I began to see in this triangle the odd constellation of my own odyssey.

When I first went to Japan five years previously, while a student at Yale, I was wholly ignorant of Asia. In two decades of a supposedly great American education, I had managed to learn only about Europe. When I graduated from high school, I could have named all six wives of Henry VIII but not one Japanese emperor. As a history major at college, I could have listed causes for the

Glorious Revolution, the French Revolution, and the Russian Revolution, but would not even have known which century spawned the Meiji Restoration. In over three years of living, working, and traveling in Asia—one as a student, one as a teacher, and one as a reporter—I aggressively and often naïvely tried to throw off the yoke of my European bias. I studied Japanese, read only local writers, and trekked around the rising world of the Pacific Rim. On one typical evening near the beginning of my Asian awakening, I argued with my brother, then a graduate student at Oxford, that Europe was passé, beyond the mend, and no longer worth our attention. The frontline of history had moved to Asia, I said, and Europe was in decline.

Several years later, on my way home from Asia, I spent a summer in Europe, backpacking around France, studying in Scandinavia, and traveling for the first time behind the sagging Iron Curtain. Whereas Europe before had seemed sclerotic and fossilized, the entire continent on that trip seemed to be shedding its lethargy following a generation of Cold War. With talk of greater union in the West and newfound freedom in the East, people from the Baltic to the Mediterranean were whispering excitedly about a New Europe. Even more important for me, the Old Europe that I had so defiantly scorned seemed to reach out and draw me home like a displaced son. The weathered stones underfoot, the towering columns overhead, even the faded chiaroscuro in the grand drawing rooms of erstwhile dukes, tasted as sweet and warm as a gingerbread house after a three-year diet of salted soy delights.

The final stop on my tour that summer was London. England seemed dimmer than other places in Europe, more weathered and grey. But it also seemed more familiar. After an absence of several years, during which the closest I had come to British culture was an outrageously expensive pot of "high" tea in the Peninsula Hotel on Hong Kong Bay, the details of English life reminded me at every turn of stories and songs I had long forgotten or never even heard: Paddington, Buckingham, Bloomsbury, Canterbury, London

Bridge, still falling down. What I remembered most from that trip were the rooms of books—the dusty grandeur of the London Library, the musty allure of second-hand shops on Charing Cross Road, and a single almond-shaped lamp in the Radcliffe Camera at Oxford that glowed through a tinted pane. Six months after that trip, halfway through writing my book about teaching in Japan, I applied to become a student in Britain.

During the time I lived in Japan, I learned to respect the vital role that schools play in the success—or failings—of a nation. In Japan the key to the country's postwar success has been its secondary schools, which systematically, deliberately transform students into hardworking citizens. As a result, Japan's secondary schools today are arguably the most respected and envied in the world, and Japan at century's end enjoys a burgeoning role in world affairs.

Britain, on the other hand, has had a difficult century. In 1890 the land of Queen Victoria enjoyed the world's largest empire, the world's mightiest navy, the world's strongest currency, and the world's largest city. In the last hundred years British monarchs have seen the empire seized by upstart nationalists, the navy lose control of the seas, the pound lose much of its value, and London—the national pearl—become transformed into a giant museum on the one hand and a Third World relocation center on the other. When Britain ruled the world a century ago, the key to its success was not its secondary schools but its elite universities, which systematically, deliberately transformed students into members of a ruling class. As a result, Britain's best universities were then, as now, arguably the most respected and envied in the world. But what role, if any, have they played in the less grandiose recent century in British history? More important, what role are they playing now as Britain struggles to throw off its own yoke of anti-European bias and join a unifying Europe? Finally, are Oxford and Cambridge at century's end models of the academy as it was meant to be or anachronisms of a bygone era? These questions, among others, were on my mind as I wrote my application.

For reasons more practical than romantic, I chose Cambridge over Oxford. For close to seven hundred years the two universities, known together as "Oxbridge," have been like siblings, twin rivers drawing strength from the same tributary, crossing similar terrains, and discharging their students into the same hallowed bay of the British master class. But in the area of postgraduate programs, the two schools have taken different paths. Oxford, fifty miles northwest of London, has built on its strength in the humanities, while Cambridge, fifty miles northeast of the capital, has opted for more practical programs, such as engineering, law, and, the program to which I applied, international relations.

The application itself, due in mid-February, was fairly straightforward, containing no existential questions like "What was the most meaningful piece of advice you ever received?" or "What three items would you remove from your house if it was attacked by nuclear weapons?" Instead, the questions were more formal: surname, forename, military rank, and proposed topic for a twenty-five-thousand-word thesis to be completed by the end of the year. The catch, however, was that every time I sent my application to Cambridge via Federal Express, the Board of Graduate Studies sent back a letter by sea mail indicating that I had failed to include a copy of some document such as my high school diploma or my last will and testament.

Months passed—April, May, June—and with the exception of these periodic form letters, I received no word from the Board. I decided to telephone. Calling Cambridge from America, I soon discovered, is like walking through one of those giant shrubbery mazes behind antique country estates: it takes half an afternoon to get through to the other side, and once you do you are back where you started.

"Sorry, Mr. Feiler, the Board of Graduate Studies have not seen your application in some months." (The British, in deference to their Royalist past, still use plural verbs for collective nouns.) "It must be at the Centre of International Studies."

"Sorry, Mr. Feiler, the Centre of International Studies are not able to inform you of our decision. We have sent your application back to the Board of Graduate Studies."

At last, in late July, six weeks before the start of school, I received a letter by air from the Board of Graduate Studies informing me that the Centre of International Studies had formally accepted my application but that I would not be admitted to the program until a college had accepted me as well. Cambridge, unlike universities in America, is composed of over thirty privately owned colleges that provide room, board, and a residential community to the twenty-thousand students and teachers affiliated with the university. It was back into the maze for me.

"Sorry, Mr. Feiler, the Board of Graduate Studies have not seen your application in some weeks. It must be at King's College, your first choice."

"Sorry, Mr. Feiler, King's are not accepting Americans this year. Your application has been sent to Clare, your second choice."

Finally, in early August, I spoke with the director of graduate studies for Clare College, the estimable Dr. A. B. Jones, or rather *Dr* A. B. Jones (the British generally don't use periods after abbreviations, but they do usually use them after initials, and in either case they don't call them periods, but "full stops"; that said, in this book they will be included), who informed me that he had one position left, for which he would like to interview me.

"Now?" I asked.

"Or never," he said. He cleared his throat and ruffled through some papers as I straightened my nonexistent tie.

First, he wanted to know why exactly it was that I had received a B+ in French during my sophomore year at Yale. "Clare College is accustomed to receiving only the top students from American universities," he said, "and this blemish is most troubling."

"Well," I stammered. "As you probably know, college in America involves a lot more than studying. I was probably out saving the world or something."

There was silence on the other end. Perhaps it was now *and* never, I thought. Moving quickly to cover my mistake, I told him I was not embarrassed about the blemishes in my transcript, since they were, after all, acquired five years ago. He moved on to the next question.

"I notice from your vita," he said (*vita*, I learned from my dictionary, is Latin for "résumé," which of course is French for "exaggerated list of what you've done in your life that's designed to impress other people"), "that you've done a lot of traveling in your life. Is Cambridge just another stop in your world tour?"

Naturally, the obvious answer to this question was "Yes," but I decided to play my role a little more gracefully and issued some interview humble-babble about the virtues of the program being greater than the virtues of the place.

"I wouldn't care if the international relations program was in Duluth instead of Cambridge," I said. "This is the right course for me."

As soon as I said that, I wondered if Dr. A. B. Jones had ever heard of Duluth, but it was too late: I had already revealed myself to be a boorish American who couldn't speak French very well and who, in any case, was foolish enough to want to spend a year living in Minnesota instead of England.

"I have one more question," he said. "In Cambridge we consider our academics to be of utmost importance, far more significant than what you Americans call 'saving the world.' I would like to know if this thesis of yours is a serious academic endeavor."

At this point his condescension was driving me—and my phone bill—through the roof.

"Dr. Jones," I said. "Everything I do is serious. I would not consider spending a year on a project if I did not think it worthwhile."

"Well, Mr. Feiler," he said, "I regret that your application has reached my desk rather late in the year, and I'm afraid that you will find all other colleges in the same difficult position as we are. But considering the interesting things you've done in your life, and that Clare College prides itself on having interesting students, I am minded to offer you a slot. . . ."

There was a pause as I tried to interpret what he said—regret, filled, *minded?*—but all I could muster was an image of weeks passing by, with no word from Clare, and my application trapped in the maze.

"Excuse me, sir," I said. "What does that mean?"

"Well, son, that means I will inform the Board of Graduate Studies to inform the Centre of International Studies that you have been admitted to Clare College."

And just like that, after forty-five minutes of questioning and twenty-five weeks of anxiety, I was finally accepted to Cambridge. Six weeks later, with my manuscript recently completed and Columbus Day fast approaching, I traveled for a day from Savannah to New York, flew for a night from Kennedy to Heathrow, and rode for an afternoon on a bus, called a coach, from the banks of the Thames to the Backs of the Cam.

WELCOME TO CLARE COLLEGE, read the sign on the gate where the polished black taxi dropped me off with my bags. NO DOGS, STROLL-ERS, BICYCLES, OR PICNICS. NO MOORING ON THE BANKS.

The Cam is a lazy sort of river. Not a river of mythic dimension on which slaves rode to freedom or hunters sought their prey; not a river of epic proportions on which nations thirst for being or crops depend for life; and not a river of geological significance that carved canyons out of stone or valleys out of peaks. The Cam is a sluggish, rather lackluster stream that rises from the chalk hills northeast of London, eases north through the fens of East Anglia, and empties into a wash at the base of the great North Sea. Despite its distinctly high-minded air and unfortunate low-life smell, the Cam has the good sense to wend its way through the grassy banks and cobble-stone streets of one of the most picturesque medieval towns in Europe. Here the river is narrow, often no wider than a horse can jump; it is tame, perfect for late afternoon strolls, bicycle rides along its banks, picnics on its shores. Here, in the Middle Ages, an enterprising resident resolved to join one shore with the other and set out to build a bridge.

Why did the road cross the river? No one may ever know. The person or people who built that bridge, even the person or people who paid for it, drowned in their own anonymity. The earl of Sandwich had a meal named for him; King George a colony; even the English ox has a city named for it in the one place where an ox could ford the Thames. But the chap who built the bridge across the Cam made no name for himself and only his construction lives on. In fact, the locals liked his structure so much that they named their town after it: Cantebrigge in the eleventh century, Caumbrigge in the fourteenth, and finally Cambridge from the sixteenth century until today.

These days no one seems to know how Cam, which rhymes with *dam* became Cambridge, which rhymes with *rain ditch,* but everyone knows how that town changed geography forever. Rivers are supposed to go up and down—up toward their origins and down toward their demise. But Cambridge defies this classification. When one comes to the school that was named for the town that was named for the bridge that crossed the river, no matter if one comes from north or south, from Edinburgh or Brighton, one always comes "up."

I dragged my bags inside the nagging gate and dropped them before a small office at the bottom of a three-story archway. Inside, a middle-aged man sat hunched behind a counter with a squint in his eye, a scowl on his face, and a Sherlock Holmes pipe that drooped like a treble clef from between his frowning lips.

"Good afternoon," I said. "I'm here to register."

"What's your name," he said, dropping his pipe derisively to his lap and appraising me with a practiced stare.

"Feiler," I said with a slight buck in my voice, like a private at boot camp.

"Mr. Feiler," he said, now rising from behind his desk, gathering his glasses, and flattening his waistcoat around his stomach, which mirrored in size and shape the bowler that hung over the back of his chair. "This is Clare College, the second-oldest college, in the second-oldest university, in the Greatest Country on Earth. We like to maintain a certain dignity here, but also a certain friendliness. What, may I ask, is your Christian name?"

"I don't have one," I said. "But my first name is Bruce."

"Good," he replied. "I'll call you that."

"And what," I asked, "do I call you?"

"Well," he said, now ambling toward the waist-high counter that separated me from him. "You should know that I'm the deputy head porter of this college. I'm the one who decides what gets through that gate, and what doesn't. Who comes in, and who stays out. Some people call me a son-of-a-bitch, but my friends call me Terry."

"Good," I said. "I'll call you that."

He bowed. I reciprocated and extended my hand. "I can always change later, can't I?"

He chuckled and shook my hand. "You're from America, I take it."

"Yes, sir," I said.

"I thought so. We've had a few Colonists at Clare over the years, but I won't hold that against you. In fact, my friend, I'll take it as a challenge. I'm going to make an English gentleman out of you, even if it takes all year."

For several minutes we ambled through the routine of registration, as I exchanged my signature for a set of keys and my honor for a set of sheets, a blanket, and a dictum not to put tape on the antique walls. As I did, several female students gathered in the Porters' Lodge behind me and waited to complete the same procedure.

"I've been traveling for a long time," I said when the process seemed to be over. "Can you tell me where my room is?"

"Your rooms are in V," he said, holding up his fingers in a victory sign à la Winston Churchill. "That's a famous entryway."

"Rooms?" I repeated hopefully.

"Oh, there's only one room," he said. "It's a bed-sit. But in Cambridge we call all our lodgings rooms. It's the way we've always done it."

"I see. And why are these rooms so famous?"

He paused for a moment, running his finger down his sideburns. "Let's just say they're famous for love."

He snickered and waved me out the door.

"Just don't forget Old Terry's three rules," he called. "First, thou must be friends with Terry. Second, thou must come to the May Ball. And third, thou must let Terry flirt with your date on the night of the ball."

The students behind me giggled. I believe I saw one person write the rules down.

"Now get out of here, you dirty old Yank," Terry said. "I'd much rather speak with these young British ladies."

Under the archway I gathered for the final time my suitcase, camera case, backpack, duffel bag, laptop computer, and the ramshackle sack of *New York Times*es that had crossed too many datelines and too many time zones to be of any use, and headed through the college courtyard to the infamous climbs of V Entryway. Under the sign VIVENT PER OMNIUM MEMORIAM 1939–1945, I found my name painted in white calligraphy on a black slate panel: V10 B. S. FEILER. I climbed one flight of wooden stairs and opened the door underneath my name, which was again painted on the wall in Latinate script—genus and species—as if I were an exotic animal or a tenured professor.

Inside, I dropped my luggage in the center of the floor and reached for the light. It didn't work. I reached for the lamp. It also didn't work. Glancing around in the pale evening haze, I detected in a space barely larger than my New York taxicab a bed, a desk, two chairs, and, rather optimistically I thought, four empty bookcases. It

occurred to me in my sodden haze that this bed-sit should actually
be called a bed-chair or a sleep-sit, but I decided that in a land where
a bus is a coach, a pound is a quid, and the left lane in many pedestrian crossings is painted with a sign that says PLEASE LOOK RIGHT, this
was hardly the right time to start bucking the language—especially
when I had more luggage than lamps and very little sleep.

Exhausted, I left my bags in a puddle on the matted floor and
went, as instructed, to *sit* on the bed, which sucked me into its liquid
arms. Unable to sit in my new bed-lie, I closed my eyes in a wave
of sleep and dreamed that I was swimming upstream, to a mythical
place in some glorious past, where words flow like rivers, and rivers
run like roads, where young boys sacrifice the blood of youth for a
chance to drink the water, and where young girls come to escape
their past and climb to a higher class.

MICHAELMAS TERM

I

MATRICULATING

Town and Gown

§♭

Down in the town off the bridges and the grass,
They are sweeping up the old leaves to let the
    people pass,
Sweeping up the old leaves, golden-reds and browns.
Whilst the men go to lecture with the wind in
    their gowns.

          —Frances Darwin
          "Autumn Morning at Cambridge," 1898

*K*nock, knock, knock. The pounding door rattled me from my dream like a rock being skipped across my forehead and sinking to the sludge of my sleep. Knock, knock, knock. Kick.

"Who is it?" I called from the seat of my bed.

"It's me," came a muffle that began in the hall outside the door and without as much as waiting for an invitation stormed through the lock and into my rooms like a tempest bearing tea. I looked down at my watch—seven-fifteen—and when I looked up, I saw staring down at me an elderly woman dressed in pale pink whose disapproving glare and proprietary stare reminded me of the Little Old Lady Who Lived in a Shoe.

"I'm your bedder," she said.

"But I'm in bed," I said.

"Not to worry," she said. "I don't make your bed. I just take out the bin." She marched to the far wall between the two windows, reached beneath the desk, and retrieved my metal litter bin, which was devoid of any litter but strewn with stacks of still-soggy *New York Times*es. "My name is Edna," she said. "How about you?"

"I'm Bruce."

"Are you American?"

"Can you tell?"

She looked at me sprawled on the unmade bed.

"I've met a few over the years. . . . Now let me just tell you a few of the rules in V Entryway."

Edna was a short, sturdy woman with thinning white hair and a bulging pink apron. On this morning, like a hundred hence, she smelled more of smoke than disinfectant.

"I arrive every morning at seven," she said. "Have me a cup of tea downstairs with the ladies and then go round to the rooms. I should be arriving here around quarter past. I empty the rubbish every day, wipe out your sink in the corner when I have time, and Hoover the floor mat once a week. . . ."

If I did not wish her to come into my rooms every day, she continued, I could leave the bin outside the door as a sign for her not to enter. Which reminded her, fresh milk would automatically be delivered to the door every morning in pint-sized bottles. If I would like to stop this service, I should notify the housekeeper immediately. Did I have any questions?

"Well, yes, actually. Is there a shower?"

"Oh yes, the shower. I'm afraid there's only a bath. There was meant to be a shower in this entryway last year. I had already made the fitting on the tub. But it was during exam time, you know, and the students"—she glanced down the arch of her nose, mustering as much reverse snobbery as she could—"well, the students did not approve." Anyway, she would see what she could do. In the meantime, there was a shower in U Entryway.

"But be careful," she warned. "My daughter is the bedder over there and she will get on you if you don't clean up after yourself." She glanced at my clothes in a pile on the floor, and tiptoed over them toward the door.

"Well then, see you tomorrow, Bruce."

She slammed the door with a migrainous shock and dragged my bin along the plaster walls until she arrived at the rooms next door and banged her fist dictatorially on my neighbor's nameplate: H. L. YANG.

"You look like you need a cup of tea."

When I knocked on her door an hour later, Halcyon Yang was sitting quietly with a book in one of two grey corduroy armchairs, sipping tea with milk and nibbling a biscuit, which she said was a scone and which she pronounced, royally, as "skahn."

"Very British," she said with an exaggerated, self-mocking roll of her tongue. "Would you like a taste? Edna lent me the tea. . . . What a card."

As I stepped into the room, Halcyon marked her place with a bookmark from her lap and pursed her lips in a piercing grin. She was striking, poised, Chinese—much less pale, and much more attractive than I had dared anticipate.

"I'm warning you," she said. "Edna doesn't stop talking. Has she told you about her husband?"

"Not yet."

"Well, it seems he's been having insomnia problems. So Edna makes him sleep on the sofa so she can get some rest. By the way," she said, "won't you have a seat."

I bowed reflexively, then stopped myself, almost tripping on my way to the bed to sit down. She watched bemused, her body lithe like a sparrow, then tossed her head back and laughed like a princess flattered by my boyish fluster. As I steadied myself, Halcyon slid the book from her lap onto the floor. As she did, I noticed the title: *Holy Bible*.

For the rest of the morning Halcyon and I sat around introducing ourselves to each other. A magazine editor from Hong Kong whose father had gone to Oxford, Halcyon was returning to university after a ten-year absence to fulfill a lifelong dream and study archaeology. She was, she confessed, an unrepentant Anglophile.

"Do you have your gown?" she asked me as we carried the dishes to our shared kitchen, which was called, after the personal servants who were assigned to up-coming students, a gyp.

"What for?" I said.

"We have to take the matriculation photograph this afternoon and everyone must wear the proper gown."

"I have one that my brother used at Oxford. Will that do?"

Halcyon turned around and stared at me with a disbelief verging on pity.

"*Oxford?!*" she cried. "Did you say *Oxford*? My dear boy," she intoned with a schoolmarmish tweak, "in sport Oxford wears the dark blue and Cambridge wears the light blue. In school their gowns are sleeveless; ours are full-cut. It has been that way for seven hundred years. It will be that way for a thousand more." She stepped forward and took me by the arm. "Now you must forget about that other place. And before you make another mistake, I must take you into town this instant and turn you into a proper Cambridge man."

Fifteen minutes later, dressed in sneakers and faded blue jeans, led by the arm, I set out with Halcyon to redress my improper hemlines. Cambridge on the first day of Michaelmas Term—the first of three terms in the academic year—was full of all sorts of proper men and women, scurrying about town, seeking light bulbs and jasmine tea, gathering books and gowns. In addition to the students, the town was also full of equally proper men and women preparing the various Cambridge heirlooms for the beginning of the year. In the

Memorial Court of Clare, a four-story, caramel brick château built around a grassy quadrangle the size of a tennis court, several bedders were huddled around the glass-paneled doors polishing the brass hand plates. A gardener was striping the grass with a mower— moving back and forth as on a putting green—and Terry the Porter, decked out in three-piece suit, pocket watch, and bowler, was bowing at mothers accompanying their darlings and scowling at dads who were walking on the grass.

Clare College, located in the city center of Cambridge, is arranged like a giant barbell, with large mansions on either side of the river, linked by a narrow hundred-yard-long footpath and a stone bridge across the Cam. Memorial Court, on the side of the river farther away from town, was built after the First World War, then expanded after the Second. Part palace, part barracks, it is neo-Georgian in design, with an eighty-foot archway leading onto the lawn, multipaned windows looking over the town, and a terra-cotta roof that artfully conceals a slew of undesirable attic rooms. In the center of the courtyard, like a day-old garnish, sits what must be one of the most awkward nudes ever sculpted by Henry Moore.

Leaving Memorial Court, the building relegated to first-year students, Halcyon and I strolled along the tree-lined path toward the famous footbridge. The path runs alongside the Fellows' Garden, with its banks of exotic flowers, plots of manicured grass, and a sunken stone pool in the center, where one member of the college—after shouting to me—would jump from the top of the Grand Marquee eight months later on the night of the May Ball. The garden is part of the famed stretch of Cambridge known as the Backs, since the backs of many colleges look over the river to this Elysian strip of land.

"Did you hear the story about the Bridge?" Halcyon asked as we stopped on the summit of the 350-year-old footbridge, the oldest one still spanning the Cam.

"Which one?" I said.

The Bridge—the pride of Clare—was constructed out of squared stone slabs, arched underneath like three setting suns, and lined above with a waist-high balustrade. Along the top were fourteen stone spheres about the size of bowling balls.

"Terry told me that several years ago some undergraduates wanted to play a practical joke," Halcyon said. "They made a Styrofoam ball, painted it to look like stone, waited for a group of tourists to come by in a punt [a flat-bottomed recreational vessel the size and shape of a canoe], then tossed the ball over the edge with a horrifying shriek. The tourists—a bunch of Japanese with long lenses and video cameras—started screaming for their lives and leapt out of the punt into the Cam."

"That's funny," I said. "Terry told me the same story, but he said the tourists were Americans."

Stepping into Old Court, the central building in college, the aura of natural elegance quickly gives way to an air of Shakespearean antiquity. Clare, which is believed to be the Solar Hall in Chaucer's *Canterbury Tales,* was founded in 1338 by Lady Elizabeth de Clare, granddaughter of King Edward I. The present building, about the size and shape of a Gothic theater-in-the-round, was built over the course of two hundred years beginning in the seventeenth century. A pert, four-story structure looking down on four squares of carefully checkered grass, the court is open, with a common façade of warm ocher stone. Behind the veneer, Old Court contains some of the most important buildings in college, the Chapel (for weekly praying), the Hall (for formal dining), the Buttery (for daily eating), and the Bar (for nightly drinking).

Leaving Old Court, we emerged into a labyrinth of cobblestone paths and Gothic buildings in the heart of Cambridge. Clare is situated in the sacred core of Cambridge colleges, along with St. John's, Trinity, King's, and Queens' (King's is named for one king, so its apostrophe precedes the *s;* Queens' is named for several queens, so its apostrophe follows). These five colleges are lined up along the showcase part of the river like a row of boastful boys showing off their morning coats to bashful girls at a plush Victorian ball. While the backs of these colleges face the river, their fronts face onto the town. Outside of Clare, we walked in the shadow of Trinity to our left—home of Byron, Tennyson, and lately Prince Charles—and King's to our right—home of E. M. Forster, Bertrand Russell, and the ever-famous Boys' Choir. Across from King's, near the outdoor market in the central square, we found a small corner shop called Ryder & Amies, "Suppliers to the University of Blazers, Scarves, Ties, Sweaters, Tee Shirts, Cuff-Links, Sweatshirts, and Gowns."

"May I help you?" asked a gentleman in a double-breasted suit as I stepped up to the worn wooden counter.

"I would like to buy a gown," I announced.

"Are you a student?" he asked.

Halcyon grinned.

"Yes," I said.

"Are you an undergraduate?"

She laughed out loud.

"No."

"Are you over twenty-four years old?"

The process of applying for a gown, I discovered, was almost as labyrinthine as applying for admission. Not only was I asked my name and rank, but I was carded as well. Cambridge, it turns out, has as many gowns as it has degrees. There are gowns for undergraduates, others for those who have their B.A., still more for those who have their M.A., and the ultimate gowns lined with fur for those who have their Ph.D. As if this were not complicated enough, Cambridge does not give mere degrees to its graduates, it gives everyone *honours* degrees, even those who merit no discernible *honour*. As proof of their rarefied status, graduates of Cambridge colleges are entitled to swap their *honourable* B.A. for a humble M.A. three years after they leave. Thus, while all other students all over the world must study and sweat and go into debt for their master's degrees, Cambridge graduates (and those from Oxford as well) can simply receive theirs by post when they turn twenty-four at a cost of only five quid.

After I produced some identification and a letter from my department, which he called a faculty, the proprietor announced that I was entitled to purchase an M.A. gown. I should be pleased by this status, he informed me, since as late as the 1960s the university refused to recognize B.A. degrees handed out by other institutions, including those elsewhere in Britain and especially those upstart universities in America. He pointed out that on the letter from my faculty the name of the assistant director was followed by the title Ph.D. and in parentheses, like the snub of a nose, Oxford.

"And what's the difference between these gowns?" I asked.

"A couple of inches in the hem and sleeve and more than a couple of degrees in respect."

"And the cost?"

As soon as I said that, I knew it was crass and oddly American, somewhat like an M.B.A. degree.

"Well, son," he said with visible restraint. "I'm not sure how to answer that question. In this country status can't be purchased, you know. You should be grateful to receive it."

With the help of Halcyon, I flipped through a long rack of limp black gowns. Once in the proper section, each gown was roughly the same size, with a hem as low as a monk's habit and sleeves as swingy as a maiden's kimono; but each was cut from a different cloth. I sampled natural fabrics from various former British colonies, including India and Egypt, before settling on the least expensive one, a synthetic fabrication of 100 percent polyester, "Made in America." My gratitude cost me one hundred pounds.

"By the way," I said as I walked out the door, now in line with the Cambridge class code, "what do I wear beneath the gown?"

He pursed his lips and closed his eyes. After close to an hour of relating the rules that govern everything from the proper cock of one's nose (perpendicular to the ground) to the way to brush one's hair (straight in front with a rabbitlike tuft in the back), the salesman looked at me with the impatient smile of an overworked baby-sitter. "You're at Cambridge now," he said. "You're an adult. You should be able to make up your mind. Just do us a favor and don't wear white shoes."

White shoes were nowhere to be found that afternoon when I appeared in a blue suit and penny loafers in the grand Old Court of Clare, but white socks were aplenty. Dozens of begowned students swarmed around the squared columns and triangular pediments like bats in a Gothic belfry. Most of the women wore high-necked white shirts and knee-length black skirts; most of the men wore grey trousers, white shirts, and their outgrown blue blazers from school. The ties ranged in color from dawn to dusk, with more originality being reserved for the socks, which brightened the otherwise fune-real air with outbursts of argyle, lime green, and pale blue, as well as an ample serving of Wimbledon whites.

After several moments a nervous young photographer began hurrying around the huddled groups and taping signs on the win-dowsills: A–F, G–L, M–R, and S–Z. The bats began flocking to their caves. There were 120 in all, and each one would be formally admitted to the college by signing a red leather book, being photographed in a flowing black gown, and eating a gravy brown meal.

"Students, students, may I have your attention, please?"

The shaky photographer climbed atop the scaffolding that had been erected across the courtyard from temporary bleachers set up for the occasion.

"I am going to begin calling your names in reverse alphabetical order."

On the far side of the alphabet about three dozen students were just gathering under the A–F sign.

"Where are the F's?" I asked at the door.

"I am the F's," said a baby-faced freshman with the silken, ironic tone of a British upperclassman.

". . . Winstanley, Walpole, Turnball, Teasdale . . ." the megaphone echoed off the cavernous stone.

"What's your name?" I asked.

"Farrady," he said.

"I'm Feiler," I said. "And I guess that means we're stuck next to each other."

"At least for the afternoon."

". . . Starling, Siddons, Rimmington, Prime . . ."

It turns out we were stuck next to each other for much longer than that. Simon Farrady had the room, née rooms, directly above mine, and for most of the next three terms the only thing between him and me were the creaks, cries, and plaintive sighs of his under-lubricated, overstrained bedsprings. Simon was dashing—a young British thoroughbred—who, like his father, had gone to an elite public school (the British, holding fast to their euphemistic past, still call private schools "public") and who, unlike his father, had chosen Cambridge over Oxford.

"Where did you go to school?" I asked.

"Marlborough," he said. "Just like the cigarette, with *u-g-h*."

"Did they teach you to smoke?"

"They taught me to charm. The rest I learned on my own."

". . . Martin, MacAndrew, Killick, Holmes . . ."

The "rest," as I learned in countless cocktail hours and nightcap sparring sessions in the course of the coming year, he learned on the road. After graduating from the Marlborough School, Simon in-dulged in the great British tradition, born of the upper classes now trickled down to the mean, of a "year out" to see the world. Cam-bridge students speak of this "year out" as if it were an inalienable right of passage, rather than the luxury it actually is. "What did you do in your year out?" one hears over supper. "I sailed Scotland," one student responds. "I trekked India." Simon first "trained" to Germany, where he worked as a minion for Mercedes-Benz and commuted on the weekends to the home of his German girlfriend in the Black Forest. Next he sailed to Australia, where he posed for numerous snapshots, which would grace his rooms in Cambridge, of various tourist spots over his shoulder and various girls in his arms. Finally, he planed to Tokyo, where his parents were working and where he handed out towels to British expats at the American Club and went out all night to practice his charm on moonstruck Japanese girls.

"What did you think of Japan?" I asked.

"Brilliant," he said. "But a little uptight. I challenged my father's boss to a drinking contest, and my father almost spit up his whisky. He said if I didn't lose the contest he could lose his job."

"*. . . Higham, Grocock, Gill Leech, Frye . . .*"

Simon did indeed lose the contest and thus won over his Japanese hosts. They set him up for tennis matches, took him to tour a Toyota plant, and even invited him to drink with them on an all-night trek to the top of Mount Fuji.

"*. . . Flannigan, Feiler, Farrady, Deeks . . .*"

"We better get going," I suggested.

As we moved toward the sixth tier of bleachers, Simon warmed to his audience. He was cocksure and proud, taller than I by just the wisp of his greased brown hair and the polished way he straightened his back so it looked like the sterling handle of an antique knife.

"*. . . Ladies and gentlemen, may I have your attention? Please stop talking. Cross your arms in front of you, look directly at the camera, and, whatever you do, don't move. . . .*"

"Yes, Japan is fascinating," Simon said as we turned our attention to the wide-angle lens. "You should really go there sometime. Of course, most of your countrymen over there never stop talking. They don't know how to behave. But you should try it anyway. I'm sure you could learn a lot."

"I know—"

"*Are you ready? Three, two . . .*"

"I lived there for three years."

"One."

As soon as I spoke, Simon turned toward me and dropped his jaw in embarrassment as the camera before us winked into the eyes of all the bats except for one. While the rest of us were dining on mutton that evening, Simon Farrady was still digesting his foot. A friend-ship—a duel of wits—was born.

II

ROWING

Trumpeters and Swans

You may tell the sweet raptures of courting a lass,
And shooting a bolt from a lover's quiver,
But what in the world can these pleasure's surpass
That we boating gents find on the river?

—John Leavis
"A Boating Song," 1849

The cream had yet to be skimmed from the milk and the bedders had yet to stir when Halcyon knocked on my door at a quarter to morning and dragged me into the fog. I searched for my sweats, which my crew called kit, and slipped them on outside in, then found my sneakers, which they called trainers, and dragged myself from upstairs down. In the basement room of Memorial Court we boarded our bikes, which had recently been dredged from the Cam before we bought them at a police auction, then pedaled over the public bridge next to Clare and headed into the mist.

At that hour Cambridge was shrouded by clouds of fog and had the unearthly feel of a neverland trapped in the daze of time and reborn as a mute, medieval everytown. Farmers in the marketplace were busy unpacking racks of pheasant and legs of lamb, crates of carrots and barrels of cheese. The scent of boiling hops from local breweries lingered in the air. Up above, red brick chimneys and ginger stone spires faded into the woolly sky, which was punctured in various balding spots by silhouetted cruciforms reaching toward heaven and charcoal gargoyles lunging toward hell. Down below, the one-way warnings and no-entry beacons were thoughtfully covered over by the lawless haze as we made our way through the maze of college halls to the far side of the Cambridge myth. Here, at a wide-open pasture called Midsummer Common, cyclists from across the university converged like supplicants to a biblical feast and streamed in a silent crusade to the open cathedral of the Cam. The students had come to immerse themselves in the last surviving religion of the Oxbridge elite. They—and we—had come to pray in the Holy See of rowing.

"Gentlemen, on your knees!" cried the coach as the anxious eight gathered before the two-story, Tudor Clare Boat House on a slope leading down toward the river. "From this day on, you'll worship only me. That's the only way to win. . . . Now give me fifty push-ups while I flirt with your cox."

A week earlier, in a fit of youthful bravado and Olympian delusion, Halcyon and I had ducked into the Clare Boat Club Fresher Squash, a highly disorganized convocation at which drunken Old Boys from the "largest club in college" tried to squash as many freshers (the sexless term for freshmen and -women) into an unventilated room and hoax them into getting up at five-thirty every morning, strapping themselves feet first into a banana boat built for eight, and breaking ice with their blistering hands while frostbite grew on their hungover noses, all for the chance of bringing glory to the house of Lady de Clare. "We don't care about your politics or your physical condition," they said. "Anybody can make the team."

The first promise proved to be dubious, the second an absolute lie. Even though Cambridge has a special competition in the fall reserved for novice rowers (both graduate and undergraduate), the competition among the neophyte boats is as great as that in the veteran divisions. The next morning, when I arrived for the tryout with several dozen other dupes, I had to prove first that I could row by tugging on an oar in a floating bathtub, then that I could get in shape by chasing a coach on a bicycle for several miles, and finally that I could pull my weight by sitting on a seat and yanking on a stick that turned a wheel that triggered a machine—called an ergometer—that measured my physical condition, and, for all I know, my political beliefs. Upon seeing this, Halcyon decided to forgo the rowing and become a coxswain, or steerer, instead.

When the results were announced at the end of the week, I had been placed in the Second Boat in the number-five position—the seat in the center that is usually reserved for the person with the brawniest arms, but in this case had been misassigned to the person with the boniest legs. Halcyon had been chosen as the cox for our boat.

"What have we done!?" she cried after reading the announcement. "We have sentenced ourselves to go out on the river before dawn every morning with a band of overzealous seventeen-year-olds."

"Don't worry," I kept saying as her eyes stretched wide and she pretended to pull out her hair. "It's only for one term; it's only eight weeks. And besides, you get to go along for the ride. We have to do all the work."

"Get up off the ground, lads. That was pitiful. If you even hope to touch the First Boat, you'll have to do better than that. Now pair up with a teammate and give me fifty sit-ups."

At Clare, teaching the new recruits was a job coveted by senior members of the Boat Club, for it offered free reign over first-year men and free access to first-year women. Our coach was a third-year geography student named Peter, who had during the course of his college career attained two of three prizes most coveted by Cambridge men: a "Blue" and a "Babe." He earned his Blue, an official blazer in Cambridge baby blue that is the local equivalent of a varsity letter, by rowing against Oxford in a lightweight crew. He earned his Babe, a slightly less official but more desirable distinction, by flashing his blue-blood smile and princely good looks and bedding the most beautiful girl in college. He failed, however, to earn a First, the most official badge of all, by not scoring in the top 10 percent of his class. Instead, he scored a Third on his second-year exams, the academic euphemism for "Nice try, son. Better marry money."

On our first day of practice, still a day before classes began, Peter came prepared to assert his prowess. He started off dressed in a sweater and sweats, befitting the crisp autumn chill that skipped across the flue of the river and swirled around the crowded Boat House, but as he led us through a battery of exercises and warm-up drills, he slowly began to shed his clothes until he stood before us—and all others on the river—in a citrus yellow short-sleeved, short-legged spandex body suit that bulged in every conceivable place with his well-toned majesty.

"Hey, coach, aren't you cold?" asked Andy, the smallest rower in our boat, who had curly black hair, a Charlie Chaplin mustache, and none of the evident virility of Peter de Clare.

"No," he said. "And you should take after me. I want this crew to be stylish and mean."

"Stylish and mean," Halcyon repeated, barely concealing a giggle. "That can be our motto."

After we completed our wake-up call, Peter summoned us all together in a circle and issued our battle plan.

"Lads," he said, in a tone he had evidently practiced in front of the mirror. "Welcome to the hardest six weeks of your life. You should not worry that you haven't made the First Boat, but there are a couple of things you should know. First, there's a tradition that the Second Men beat the First Men in a boat race at the end of the year. It has happened three years in a row, and I expect it will happen again. They are bigger than you are, so you have to work harder."

Some of the boys shuffled their feet, but they were captivated by his charm.

"Second, you are going to have to get up early. About five times a week, I reckon. When I was a novice, we were on the water at five forty-five. There is still ice on the river at that hour, so we may have to send a small barge to break it. Also, it's dark, so some of you will need to buy portable bicycle lights we can attach to the front of the boat. The final thing is that if you're late for practice, you have to buy everyone—including me—a pint. If you miss practice altogether, then the penalty is two pints."

This rule brought relieved applause.

"But you can't drink them yet," Peter warned. "The highlight of the year is the Crew Meal with the Ladies' Second Boat. All bets must be paid that night."

"Look out, ladies. Here we come!" burst a particularly mealy redhead behind me.

"One last item," Peter said. "I'll try to arrange some weightlifting sessions and some fun runs—about four miles."

The elation turned to groans.

"That's what it takes to win, I'm afraid. Everyone has to do it."

"Even the cox?" Halcyon asked.

"Even the cox," the lads shouted together.

"Now," Peter said, "hands on the boat."

Inside the darkened Boat House about a dozen boats were stacked upside down on the shelves like caskets in a mortician's shop: fiberglass for the upper classes, mahogany for the middle, and layered oak for the underclasses, including the Second Novice Men. On command from our coach, relayed through our cox, we heaved the heaviest shell onto our shoulders, quivered down the concrete ramp to the edge of the river, flipped the boat right side up, and laid it to rest in the water with a gentle slap on the surface. One by one, we retrieved our oars—giant wooden poles with yellow blades, roughly the shape of iced-tea spoons and the height of walking stilts—and locked them into the riggers. With the sun now winking off the river and other crews careening around the bend, we were finally ready to board.

"Stroke side, hold the boat. Bow side, in."

Starting from the bow of the boat and counting every other seat, those of us with bow-side blades sat down on the sliding seats and strapped our shoes to the back of the trusses that supported the seat directly in front.

"Bow side, steady the boat. Stroke side, in."

As we tried to balance the tottering boat, the other four rowers assumed their seats.

"Madame, take your seat and push off from the bank."

Halcyon slid into her perch at the stern of the shell and grabbed the ropes that controlled the tonguelike rudder. The boat wobbled back and forth as it eased toward the center of the river. Wobbling along with the boat, we waited in anticipation as Peter boarded a borrowed bicycle and prepared to follow us on a path along the river and bark instructions at every stroke.

"Gentlemen, are you ready?" he shouted. "Count off."

"Bow, Two, Three, Four, *Five,* Six, Seven, Stroke . . ."

"Cox!" Halcyon punctuated at the end in a slightly anxious British accent.

"All eight," Peter cried in cadenced staccato. "At backstops. Stern four, sit in the boat. Bow four, follow your stroke. Full slide, half pressure. Are you ready? Row!" As soon as he issued the command, Peter jumped atop his bicycle and began pedaling as fast as he could down the path. "Hurry up, lads!" he cried. "Concentrate!" But when he looked over to check on our progress, he noticed that we were not moving quite as fast as he. In fact, we were not moving at all. At the sound of his nuanced, crew-hip command, all nine of us had frozen in utter ignorance and erupted into unifying laughter.

"Hey, coach," called Charlie Chaplin when Peter returned. "I hate to be the one to tell you, but we ain't understood a word you said."

"Bloody hell," he cried. "You boys are daft. Let's take it from the beginning."

Like many new students, especially those from afar, I arrived at Cambridge with stars in my eyes. I had reviewed the list of distinguished alumni—Milton, Byron, Newton, Darwin. I had rented the twelve-part televised homage to Oxbridge, *Brideshead Revisited*. I had even filled my suitcase with random books about England: *Return to Albion, The Glittering Prizes,* and, from Cambridge alumnus A. A. Milne, *Now We Are Six*. Arriving with even more expectations than luggage, I vowed to *do* Cambridge the way it was meant to be done. Along these lines I had three goals: I wanted to row, to debate at the Union, and to have a date for the ball. By the end of the year I had achieved all these desires, but by then my stars had already faded. The fade began on the river.

From long before I came up to Cambridge, I viewed rowing as an upper-class sport. In England, after all, where the sport was born, the greatest clubs were at Oxford and Cambridge; in America, where it was replicated, the greatest practitioners were at the likes of Harvard and Yale. I assumed in my middle-class naïveté that rowing, like fox hunting or polo, was somehow passed down through the blood and thus genetically denied to me. But when I began to row for Clare, I soon discovered that the story of rowing, like that of the universities that raised it to an art, is a far more scrambled social tale.

According to legend, the first organized rowers were not kings, but slaves—like Charlton Heston in *Ben-Hur*. The Romans used banks of indentured servants to propel their double-decker war boats, called biremes, by chaining rowers to their thwarts and whipping them to greater effort. Julius Caesar probably utilized such a crew to propel the biremes that he used to invade the island of

Britannia in the first century before Christ. The small size and numerous rivers of Britannia assured that rowing would be a popular method of travel for both traders and invaders for the next two thousand years. In the great Stourbridge Fair, for example, which was held every Michaelmas season in Cambridge from the thirteenth to the eighteenth centuries, all manner of goods—from Scandinavian herring to German wine—were rowed up the Cam from the Continent and rowed down again when the trading was done. But what was good for the merchant was well beneath the gentleman. When the lord mayor came to the fair, which later inspired the fictional Vanity Fair, he often arrived by boat—but he never touched the oars.

Like its most popular sport, Cambridge itself was not always an exclusive upper-class retreat. The earliest students may not have been slaves, but they were not all gentlemen either. During the first five hundred years of the university, students were divided into three classes: a majority were fee-paying members, a few paid higher fees for the right to eat with fellows, and a third group paid no fees at all. These students, among them Spenser, Wordsworth, and other icons in the Cambridge Hall of Fame, were known as sizars, because their sizes, or meals, were given to them in return for waiting on their wealthier classmates. Ironically, the reputation of Cambridge as a place of privilege was not sealed until sizars were eliminated in the nineteenth century, at almost exactly the same time as rowing became an organized sport of leisure.

Following the lead of the exclusive public schools, Oxford and Cambridge set up rowing clubs in the early 1800s. The two universities first competed against each other in 1829 in a widely publicized race that ended underneath the bridge at Henley-on-Thames. The shift in rowing from work to sport coincided with the shift in commerce from river to rail. With the waterways freed of commercial barges, rowing quickly spread as a recreational activity and trickled up from red blood to blue. During those formative years the sport was not simple: boats were a cumbersome six hundred pounds; oars were long and difficult to rotate; seats were narrow and stationary, forcing participants who wished to increase their leverage to grease their leather shorts with oil or smear their hind ends with oatmeal. Regardless, the sport still flourished, with professional leagues on both sides of the Atlantic and, in 1900, a berth in the Olympiad.

Modern times, however, were much less kind. Like Her Majesty's Empire itself, rowing was unable to retain the glory it enjoyed at the end of Victoria's reign and continues today mostly in the few elite schools and universities where tradition is most coveted. But even there the tradition has changed. The devastation of World War One brought an end to the gilded age of Oxbridge. By the 1930s, half the students required scholarships; by the 1950s all students received free sizes from the state; and by the 1990s over half the student population came from state-sponsored secondary schools. Today rowing remains the most popular sport in Cambridge, but like so much else it seems to be a case of the pampered middle classes trying to recreate a faded past. The rowers at Clare were the sentimentalists, chasers of a bygone dream. Like me, they could easily join the Boat Club, but the true-blue members of the university had already moved far upstream where they could stay well out of the way of the reckless up-and-coming.

As the morning progressed, our technique improved, with Peter teaching us in pairs the elements of the stroke: hands away, back bent, slide to the front . . . feather with the left hand, pull with the right, push from the balls of the feet. Unable to stick together, we practiced in twos, then in fours, shifting from the pairs in the bow of the boat down to the ones in the stern. We learned to straighten our arms, stiffen our wrists, lengthen our slides, loosen our grips, and focus our eyes on the back of the neck of the person directly in front. We were told not to swat the ducks on the river and not to catch a crab, the act of snagging an oar in the water that is the rowing equivalent of dropping a relay baton. All the while, Peter pedaled along the bank, shifting from one side of the river to the other, and barking orders in his roughneck style and his stiff-lipped accent.

"Hey, Charlie Chaplin, keep your head still."

"Number Seven, Goofy with the red hair, keep your mouth shut and your head still."

"Who's that—one, two, three, four, five. Five, what's your name?"

"Bruce."

"Bruce, straighten your back, you look like you've fallen over like a sack of potatoes."

As we drilled, moving past the boathouses to the long reach and circling back again, the river gradually became more and more congested, like sinus passages succumbing to the flu. Novice boats from two dozen colleges lurched forward in two opposing lines—down the river to the right; up the river to the left (the opposite of British coaches and pedestrian crosswalks). The boats were indistinguishable from one another, except for the colors of each college painted on the blades: gold for Clare, violet for King's, red for St. John's.

At nine o'clock, as our session neared its end and the river began to decongest, Peter announced that he wanted us to try our first informal "piece." In a piece all eight row at once along a set course and attempt to simulate strenuous racing conditions. For us it was an effort to capture some of the magic of rowing after several hours of drills. We positioned ourselves under the railway bridge, heading back toward the line of boathouses near Midsummer Common. Peter dismounted from his bicycle and stood like a fleet-footed, gold-plated Mercury ready to sound a trumpet.

"I want to do this piece until you get knackered," he said. "Cox, take your commands from me. All eight . . ."

"Eight."

"At backstops . . ."

"Backstops."

"Half pressure. Full slide. Are you ready?"

"Ready."

"Row."

"Row."

In a fit of adrenaline, we stormed up the slides as fast as we could and dropped our oars in the darkened water, pulling, pulling through the muddy river until our blades sprang free at the end. The lunges were grossly uneven at first, with blades springing free bow-and-stroke in an unsyncopated dog-paddling style that was neither stylish nor mean.

"Stick together," Halcyon pleaded.

"Slow the slide," Peter cried. "But don't give up the work."

Within several strokes of the awkward start, the boat began to steady with pride and a rhythm began to emerge. Away with the arms, forward with the back, up with the wrists, through with the legs. Back with the blade, ahead with the slide, in with the catch, out with a feather. With each stroke the separate components of each maneuver began to give way to the collective will of the crew. *E octopus unum:* Out of eight, one.

"Keep up the work, lads," Peter called from behind. "You're almost there."

"Almost where?" Halcyon cried. She turned her head to search for our coach, who had begun to climb a bridge and switch sides of the river. "Peter, Peter," she called. "Where are we going?"

In that moment of indecision, the octopus lost control. Peter had been left in the wake and Halcyon left alone at the helm. The lads, meanwhile, kept paddling away, streaking toward the footbridge several strokes away where the river curved abruptly to the left and narrowed to a stream.

"What's wrong?" asked Max, the stroke of our boat who sat directly in front of the cox.

"We've lost our coach," Halcyon said.

"Well, tell us to stop," somebody shouted.

"What do I say?"

"Ahead Eight!"

The cry came from our rear, which was really our front.

"Stop your boat, Clare."

"I'm trying," Halcyon whimpered. "Stop. Help! Pull in your blades."

Just as she cried, our blades slapped against an oncoming boat with the deafening patter of a giant castanet. As the boat lunged toward a willow weeping over the bank, my oar plunged breathlessly into my gut, and a blade behind me snapped off at mid-stem, somersaulting in the air and landing with a splash beside Charlie Chaplin, who was bobbing at mustache level in the middle of the Cam. And in that chaotic moment, as some of the boys began to curse and others began to laugh, as all of us turned toward the other boat and recognized the terrified faces of the Clare Second Novice *Ladies'* Crew, a four-foot swan with a fire-hose neck burst from its haven beneath the willow tree, flapped its wings in a frightened fury, and skipped across the water with a trumpeter's squawk because it, as we, was unable to fly since its wings had been clipped.

"Good day, ladies," said Charlie Chaplin when the swan had settled back on the water and our oars had come to rest. "Would you like to join us for a Crew Meal next month? We promise to make this up to you. We'll even buy all of you pints."

"I hear you went swan hunting on the Cam today."

Simon came to my door later that evening snickering about our misfortune. Since our meeting beneath the alphabet signs, he had begun to stop by my rooms regularly—usually offering a presupper cocktail, or seeking a postpub nightcap. Though tall enough to visit pubs from age twelve, Simon had the kind of fuzzless face that would make it difficult for him to order drinks until well past the age when he would be eligible for his M.A. degree.

"You must know that you need a license to hunt birds in this country," he said, "and nobody—not even you—is allowed to touch the swans: they belong to the Queen."

"Practice is at six tomorrow," I said. "We'll be glad to find you a spot."

"I'll leave the swanning to you . . ." he said.

"And keep the sharking to yourself."

He looked at me with bemused surprise as he flopped down in one of my grey easy chairs, stretching his flare-bottomed, blue-jeaned legs halfway across my bed. "How do you know that word?" he asked.

"Sharking, you mean? It's all the boys in the boat talk about. Who sharked who, and what sharks do, and how to exploit our status as rowers to shark a ladies' boat. I'm telling you, rowers catch much more than crabs. You ought to give it a try."

"I've already got my hands full, I'm afraid. But I see you've had some success in the sharking department."

"What are you talking about?" I said.

"Your lovely Chinese neighbor."

His remark caught me off guard. When I first met Halcyon, I had considered sharking her. She was attractive, un-Britishly friendly, and she had an accent so captivating that during our earliest days at Clare I would often keep my door open when she was in her room and even keep my mouth shut when she was in mine. Gradually, however, I relinquished the idea of coming on to her as she began actively coming on to me first. I first became concerned about this otherwise appealing idea, when, just days after we met, Halcyon asked me why I had sat with Simon at dinner instead of sitting with her. Several days later, she asked me why I hadn't come home until one o'clock in the morning. And finally, just a week into October, she asked me if I would agree to be her date to the Clare May Ball. Faced with the prospect of this long-term shark, I suddenly wanted "just to be friends."

"Halcyon?" I said to Simon. "I'm afraid you're mistaken. Besides, you should know better than to get involved with the girl next door."

He smiled. "I wouldn't be so sure." Turning away, he quickly surveyed my room but seemed disappointed by what he didn't find. "Mind if I have a drink?" he said.

"Don't tell me you're a lush as well."

"There's no sin too great for me," he said, producing a bottle of whisky from underneath his baggy navy blue sweater. "I am lost in a sink of depravity."

"Those are pretty big words for an engineer," I said.

"I know, but I don't know what they mean, so I can use them."

I put down my copy of Clausewitz's *On War* and went to fetch a glass from the gyp. Simon kicked off his scruffy black brogues and unscrewed the top of his bottle. A product of an English public school—a kind of boot camp for the elite—Simon carried himself in the slightly disheveled but still preppy manner that makes little old ladies and their pubescing granddaughters go weak in the knees. Like most boys who come of age in these all-male nunneries, however, Simon's sexual education was anything but genteel. Arriving at Marlborough at age thirteen, with a warning from his father to avoid buggery, Simon was thrust into a world of adolescent fantasies and porn magazines, hormonal surges and communal showers. In one common stunt Simon told me about, a group of boys stand half-naked in a circle and masturbate over a piece of bread, which the last person to ejaculate onto is then forced to consume. Many graduates of these schools come out terrified of sex; others, like Simon, come out consumed with it.

"Aren't you drinking?" he said when I returned.

"I'm in training," I said, laughing before he could. "Anyway, you sound like you're the one with the trouble."

"I just got a letter from Japan," he said.

"From your mother?"

"From my girlfriend."

"I didn't know you had one."

"Neither did I." He took a gulp. "But now I seem to have more. She says that we're engaged."

While he was in Tokyo preparing to come up to Cambridge, Simon indulged in the principal expat hobby and picked up a Japanese girl. With other girls in other stops on his round-the-world

Grand Tour, Simon was able to pursue his fancy with complete discretion. In Japan, however, he was living at home. "My mum would die," he said. "She idolizes her son. She's something out of the last century."

One day, about a week after the affair started, his father came to his room.

"Son," he said, "I think we should have a chat. Your mother and I think you are looking very tired lately. You've been coming home about—what did you say?—two o'clock, and then you don't emerge until midday. Well, that's about ten hours of sleep. Your mother is concerned that you're on drugs."

"I took a deep breath," Simon said, "and stretched my arms just like you do when you're about to tell a big lie."

"Dad," he said. "There's a reason why I look so tired. There's a girl living in my room."

"Well," his father said. "That's better than we expected. Is she on the pill?"

"Of course, Dad, of course."

"Is it serious?" his father asked.

"I guess not," his son answered. "We went to bed on the very first date."

Simon had broken off the affair when he came to Cambridge, but with this letter it became apparent that she did not understand. In fact, she had broken off an arranged betrothal to devote herself to him.

"I guess I have this problem," he said. "Girls fall in love with me."

"Some problem," I said.

"I know, but my father advised me to have casual affairs while I was at Cambridge."

"I suppose he doesn't want you to settle down too quickly."

"But when you move around as much as I do, you begin to wonder if you can only have casual affairs. You begin to wonder if you can ever fall in love. I've already had this happen to me several times at Cambridge. I go to the pub, consume large amounts of alcohol, and have a really great conversation with someone—you know, 'true love' and all that—then we go home and have it off. I'll see them several days later and they won't remember."

"So it's not exactly true love?"

"Guess not. They're just casual affairs at the pub on the way to a wife, two-point-three kids, and a commuter train to London. My life is so programmed. I wish I had more stimulating conversation. This is Cambridge, after all, the cream of the crop."

"Aren't you impressed with your classmates?"

"Not really."

"They're not smart?"

"Oh, they're plenty clever. They're just not interesting. We all came here expecting to talk about world politics and philosophy, but in truth all we talk about are the shows we watched on the telly when we were three. I haven't found anyone here that I like as much as Emiko."

"Well then, maybe that means you can fall in love."

"I hope not," he said. "I can't stay celibate until Christmas. After all, I'm only human."

Simon took a last sip of whisky, doffed his imaginary cap, and lumbered out the door. Seconds later he was back with a knock.

"Mr. Feiler," he said, employing the mock deferential tone he used to remind me I was almost old enough to be his father, "I hope you enjoyed our little conversation."

I assured him that I did.

"Good," he said, "because I blew it. There was a note on my door upstairs."

"What was her name?"

"I don't know and it doesn't matter. I'll probably forget by to-morrow."

"Well," I said. "You can't complain. You asked for conversation."

"Wrong," he retorted. "I can complain. I asked for stimulation."

III

TOURING

Cons and Dons

This royal throne of kings, this scepter'd isle, . . .
This happy breed of men, this little world
This precious stone set in the silver sea, . . .
This blessed plot, this earth, this realm,
    this England.

—Shakespeare
Richard III, 1592

On the first day of Michaelmas Term the weekly student newspaper *Varsity* led with the sensational headline, HOAX LEAVES FRESHER NO PLACE TO GO: MYSTERY RECRUITER CONS AMERICAN STUDENT OUT OF $5,000. The story, written with a dramatic flair verging on the tragic, told how "Cynthia Shepard," a twenty-three-year-old American from Miami, arrived in Cambridge at the beginning of term to study English literature at Corpus Christi College, only to find that officials at the college had never heard of her.

Distraught, the teary-eyed Floridian explained that she had been approached the previous spring by a man claiming to be a recruiter for Cambridge University. He produced "official-looking brochures" and a "curriculum prospectus," she said, and even made her sit a two-hour entrance examination. When the man announced she had passed the exam and produced a letter of acceptance, Cynthia gladly paid him five thousand dollars to secure her place.

"Duped into payment from her own savings by the smooth-talking American," the newspaper reported, "she gave up the chance of a $20,000 scholarship at the University of Miami to chase her dream of studying at Cambridge."

Unlike *Varsity,* the university itself was not moved by Cynthia's plight and insisted it could not find her a place.

"Really?" editorialized *The Sun,* one of the nation's largest tabloids. "All Cambridge University cannot find room for ONE girl. Cambridge bombards American alumni with appeals for money. It should show it has a heart as well as a begging bowl."

The university, however, showed no heart. Ignoring the national crusade and the potential international scandal, it refused to alter its regulations and Cynthia Shepard was sent back to Florida with no degree from Cambridge.

"It can't be helped," Terry the Philosopher-Porter said to me when we discussed the story. "I'm afraid we have procedures up here. If the young lady would like to understand how we do things here at Cambridge, she should sign up for the tour."

"Good afternoon, ladies and gentlemen. Welcome to Cambridge. It's up to you to make clear to me how I can make your afternoon most enjoyable and edifying. My name is Roger and I'm here to please you."

Roger Alabaster, Esq., was a veritable vision of tweed. His limbs were long, his neck was narrow, and his nose was twisted like a banister. His thinning hair hung over his pedimental forehead with the wisp of a schoolboy awakened from a class-time nap. At Terry's suggestion, nay insistence, I decided to take the "Official Blue Badge Tour of Cambridge" before I got caught in a social faux pas

and before I had become such a "Cambridge man" that I would be
embarrassed to be seen with a pack of tourists mispronouncing
Magdalene, which sounds like *maudlin,* and complaining that the
beer was warm. Halcyon, my fellow outlander, asked if she could
come along.

"We want to see the most historic spots," blurted an American
woman dressed in tennis shoes and a brand-new sweatshirt from
Madame Tussaud's Wax Museum.

"The most historic spots?" Roger repeated. "You're asking for
trouble. I thought there would be a shower of cries for the well-
known frothy stuff: King's College Chapel, Trinity College, perhaps a glimpse of Clare College. But these are in fact not the most
historic spots. You see, the oldest college is only thirteenth century,
but the oldest part of town is twice as old as that. . . ."

He paused to let the effect linger.

"I think what we'll try to do is get the famous buildings out of the
way and see if we have time for more. But don't fret, you will get
to see some history as well, although I warn you, you need very
skilled eyes to spot the really interesting parts of our history, the
really obscure signs. That's why you're lucky to have me as your
guide."

At the sound of the two o'clock chimes, Roger led the group of
two dozen to a small medieval church beside the central market.
When we arrived, he began an extended paean on the nuances of
construction materials—the buildings in town were built from rub-
ble, he said, so they had fallen into disrepair; the ones in the university were built with stone, so they still stood for viewers to enjoy. As
he spoke, clearly enjoying himself, Roger rocked back and forth in
place in a manner that resembled a wobbly lectern. His vowels
echoed upward, his r's genuflected, and he enunciated every poly-
syllable of his polysyllabic vocabulary.

"By now," he said, when he had finished his speech and fallen
back on his heels, "you will have noticed that I have the tendency

to talk rather a lot. I want to remind you that this is not meant to be a lecture tour. If I do go on too long, just tug on the end of my raincoat and I'll stop talking straight away."

"Did you notice his coat?" a lady whispered to her husband as we filed toward our next destination. "It's a Burberry."

"Did you notice his coat?" Halcyon whispered to me at almost the same time. "He has it facing inside out so we can see the label."

After shuffling down the main street, which the British call the high street and which in Cambridge is called King's Parade, we stepped through the double-breasted black gates that lead into the courtyard of King's College.

"Now take note," Roger began when we had assembled on a cobbled sidewalk in front of a miniature sign that said, in triplicate: PLEASE KEEP OFF THE GRASS; NE MARCHEZ PAS SUR LES PELOUSES S.V.P,; BITTE NICHT AUF DEN RASEN TRETEN. "This is King's *College*, not King's University. It isn't Cambridge University either. Here I want to introduce you to an important distinction between the *colleges* and the *university*."

A college, he went on to explain, is a small, independent community of its own, with space for eating, drinking, reading, writing, sleeping, and studying.

"In principle," he said, "as soon as you enter through the gates of a college, you are in a private space. It's noisy and public on the outside; quiet, closed, and contemplative on the inside. The second principle is that colleges are basically square in their plan. Each one has a chapel, a hall, and other buildings to accommodate the senior members of the college. Here, let me begin to draw a few strands together. . . ."

The group squeezed together and its collective eye widened.

"The arrangement of the buildings is a remnant of the disciplined life of a medieval monastery. When the university was founded, being a student was almost the same as being a monk. Do you know why?"

"Because all you did was eat, sleep, and study," said the American wax woman, who seemed to be drooling on Roger's lapel.

"But wait, you've missed the most important part: pa-rayer. And believe it or not, prayer was an exceedingly important part of college life. Why? you ask. Because hundreds of years ago, if you asked in Europe what's the truth, the first answer that would come to mind was that the truth was something arranged according to the principles of the *Hand of God*."

With this comment Roger thrust his hand into the air like a Shakespearean actor, then dropped his voice to a whisper.

"When you are dealing with the truth," he said, "you are dealing with something that's divine. In Cambridge, as elsewhere, there has always been a very close connection between study and prayer. That's why the college faces inward, like a cloister . . .

"But!" he suddenly boomed, "times change. You see that building over there? He pointed toward the towering drip castle cathedral that King's College calls its chapel. "Henry VI, the founder of this college, designed that chapel in the fifteenth century to symbolize the greatness of God. He wanted it to be plain, with little decoration—a place for private worship. But he died before it could be completed, and by the time it was finished, by Henry VIII, the spirit of the age had changed.

"Now this is extremely important," he urged, his voice rising to the level of indignation as the organ inside began to wail. "If you look closely at the building, you will notice that at the very summit the decorations aren't religious, they're political: roses and gates. What you are seeing are symbols of the King's power in a building designed to honor God. The message is, and I'm drawing several strands together here: God is great, but so is the King of England. A sacrilege for Henry VI, who believed in the papacy, but appropriate for Henry VIII, who broke away from Rome to start the Church of England. If I were an art historian, and thank God I'm not, I would say that this college is a medieval construction, but one that comes so late in the development of the Middle Ages that it contains flashes of the modern spirit. And that, my friends, is the essence of Cambridge. The King is the Country; the Country is the Church; and the Church is the University."

He ended his speech fully raised on the balls of his feet, with the organ climaxing as if on cue and several of the tour members retrieving their cameras to snap an image of the chapel with its grand explicator spread-eagled in front. Letting out his breath and coming down to earth, Roger looked at the group with a satisfied smile and gave his raincoat a tug.

"We'll take a five-minute break right now and meet again at the gate."

"Walking around Cambridge is like walking around a museum."

Halcyon and I were ambling around the King's College grounds, peeking into various beech-shaded courtyards and rubbing our fingers along the braille of the well-read stones.

"I see what you mean," I said. "But with all the tourists roaming the walks and all the students locked in their rooms, sometimes it seems like a zoo."

She peered through a stained lavender window into the library. "At least the students don't bite."

Halcyon and I had one overwhelming thing in common. We both came to Cambridge awed by its architecture and intimidated by its reputation. Not only was Cambridge widely believed to be one of the Seven Academic Wonders of the World, but it had been that way for almost eight hundred years. For us, as perhaps for Cynthia Shepard, coming to Cambridge was fulfilling a dream; specifically, it was a chance to absorb the time-honored "Renaissance" view of the world. But as we discovered, and discussed, in our earliest days at Clare, the reality of Cambridge is much less glowing than its myth would suggest, and much less broad-minded than it first appears.

If anything, the university today seems trapped by its past. Even more than the numerous anachronistic handicaps—the lack of adequate showers, the one pay telephone for every hundred students, the multitude of signs that lord over the college grounds (NO WALKING ON THE GRASS UNLESS ACCOMPANIED BY A SENIOR MEMBER OF THE COLLEGE; PLEASE DON'T FEED THE STUDENTS)—Cambridge is governed by a set of conventions that were established for the most part in the Middle Ages, when the colleges were first constructed to be monasteries of the mind. There are numerous examples of this legacy. The academic year, like the agricultural calendar around which it was based, begins in the fall. The three terms of the year are named for religious occasions: Michaelmas, the feast of St. Michael that usually coincides with the start of fall term; Lent, the forty-day fast that overlaps most of winter term; and Easter, which usually falls at the beginning of the spring session.

Even more than these structural antiquities, however, the intellectual life of the university today is still surprisingly monkish. As graduate students, Halcyon and I were expected to complete our work almost entirely on our own. In my case, the requirements for the M.Phil. (master of philosophy) in international relations were to pass an exam at the end of Lent Term, turn in a twenty-five-thousand-word dissertation (about a hundred pages) at the end of Easter Term, and sit for an oral examination after that. Beyond a few optional lectures in the mornings, however, the directors of the course left us to our own devices. At the introductory meeting for the sixty members of the program, the director, Mr. R. C. B. Langley, M.A. (no Ph.D.), distributed a six-page, single-spaced reading list, announced the dates of our exam, and declared, dismissively, "You're adults now; get on with it."

My first encounter with my thesis supervisor was no different. In the second week of term, I wandered over to a section of campus called the Sidgwick Site, climbed to the fourth floor of the Faculty of Oriental Studies, and knocked on the closed door at the end of the hall: R. R. LONG, PROFESSOR OF JAPANESE HISTORY.

"Come in . . ."

Inside the tiny room, about the size of a confessional, bookshelves climbed from floor to ceiling, manila folders crawled from wall to wall, and note cards tiptoed skyward from every square inch of a rolltop desk, at the back of which sat an embalmed computer and in front of which stood a bespectacled technophobe.

"Sherry?" he said, without turning around.

"No, thank you," I said, with no place to sit down.

The back of Dr. Richard Long, hunched over an inchoate man-uscript, was slightly stooped in the shoulders of his brown woolen jacket, slightly rumpled at the seat of his grey flannel trousers, and slightly frazzled at the ends of his white wiry hair that stuck out of his head in a frenzied Einsteinian style. After several moments spent rearranging the cards on his desk, Dr. Long turned around to greet me, apologized for having lost my C.V., and suggested that I re-move some books from a chair and tell him a little about myself.

As I briefed him on my background, my biography, and my idea of writing a dissertation on the Allied Occupation of Japan, he nodded quietly to himself, began to pull some books from the shelves at both sides of the room (no need to leave his seat), and scribbled some notes in his calendar book.

"Very well," he said, when I had dribbled to a stopping point. "I'm afraid your topic won't do; it's been done. But not to worry; look through these books, find an alternative, and come back to see me at the start of next term. In the meantime, try to stay out of trouble and learn to drink sherry—semidry, I recommend."

Undergraduates at Cambridge follow a similar pattern of inde-pendent study, and it was meeting them that ultimately shattered my ideal of a Renaissance education at work. Cambridge rather fussily requires its students to study only one academic subject dur-ing their three years at college—no language requirement, no inter-disciplinary balance, no well-rounded view of the world: just a single subject. Like graduate students, undergraduates attend lim-ited numbers of classes and take no tests at all during their first two terms, only at year-end. This policy has distinct repercussions on the life of the college. First, since students have no assignments or tests for two-thirds of the year, they go out of their way during the early terms to squeeze in as much extracurricular activity as humanly possible, such as rowing, rollicking, and getting pissed. Second, and more telling, one of the most comic aspects of life at Cambridge is that students no more than eighteen years old refer to one another by the career titles of the academic subjects they study, as in "He's a second-year engineer"; "She's a third-year medic." They even call law students "lawyers," even though real-life lawyers spurn this term in favor of the even more hierarchical ones, barrister and solicitor.

Finally, and most debilitating of all, the limited course of study has unfortunate social consequences as well.

"They can't carry on a conversation!" Halcyon shouted one night after returning from dinner with a scientist. "All he understands is country music and astrophysics."

"So what did you talk about?" I asked.

"Safety precautions in the lab."

I had the opposite problem with my first date, a woman who read philosophy at King's and who was active in a discussion group called, oh-so-cleverly, Philosopher King's. When she found out that I had not read Plato "in the original," she gave up on me halfway through the soup and spent the rest of the evening looking over my shoulder for some Real Men of Letters.

"What did you talk about?" Simon asked.

"The defects of translation."

Despite our desire for well-rounded companions, the university still seems to prefer rough-edged squares. As an institution, Cambridge has abandoned the requirement that all students speak Latin (1950s), it has slackened the requirements that all students dine in gowns (1960s), and it has even overturned the requirement that all students be male (1970s), but it has refused to alter its long-standing course requirements. The university today still stakes its reputation on the old-fashioned premise: You are what you read.

. . .

"You will notice," said our guide as we huddled in Trinity College, "that I have been talking about where students are praying, where they are eating and drinking, but that I have neglected one of the most interesting questions: where are students studying?"

Several of the tour members nodded their heads as they surveyed the Great Court of Trinity, with its large platters of pristine grass, oversized wedding-cake-shaped stone well, and stained glass gingerbread Hall.

"Well," he said. "Let me answer that question by explaining to you a typical day in the life of the college: Between eight and nine, students and teachers come pouring out of the little staircases into the court and disappear into the Dining Hall. Three hundred years ago they went first to the Chapel, but now they go straight to breakfast. An hour later they come back into the court and go up the little staircases and back into their rooms. Then the students, but not the teachers, come out again. Down those little staircases they come, carrying books and papers. For several minutes there is frenzied activity as the students come out of their own staircases and disappear into others. Then, and this is the beauty of it all, quiet descends on the college. . . ."

"What has happened?" cried one of the men.

"Aha!" the guide shouted. "What has happened is that the students have gone into the rooms of their teachers. That, my friends, is where the teaching takes place. It's all done in sets of two, you see: a teacher and a pupil. That is what we call supervision. Every student has supervisions, usually once or twice a week, and that intensive form of learning is the most important element of the Cambridge education."

There was a slight mumbling among the group.

"I see a couple of frowns," the guide said. "Do the colleges have so many teachers that they are able to provide individual, one-to-one tuition? The answer to that question is yes."

The mumbles turned to aahs.

"How can this be afforded? you ask. It is extraordinarily expensive, certainly. But remember what I have been saying, and here again I would like to draw a few strands together for you. While these are academic institutions, they are also a bit like monasteries. People give presents of property to these colleges, in the same way as people once gave gifts to monasteries."

"But wait," cried the American lady, who had pulled a chocolate bar from her purse. "If every college is a separate institution, then what is the university?"

"That's a very handy question," Roger said like a satisfied teacher who had led his class to his principal point. "At last I'm ready to answer the question 'What does the university provide for the colleges?' In 1209, when a group of renegade academics from Oxford first came to Cambridge, *university* was the word used to describe a group of scholars. Naturally, the group divided over time into smaller groups, which eventually became the colleges. They decided that those who completed their course of study at this college would apply to the university to be certified. The college provides the education; the university grants the degrees."

"But how do students get in?" she asked. "Is there a test?"

"Yes," he said. "It's called the A-Levels. Schools all across the country prepare their students for these. The results are graded nationally, and when the results are published, the universities get to look at them and pick their students. Cambridge and Oxford like to pick those who get straight A's, which are quite difficult to get on these exams. . . ."

The bells of St. Mary's tolled four times just as the sun dipped behind the Trinity Hall and Roger ascended to his final point.

"But take note," he warned. "Before they're admitted, students have to take another exam and be interviewed by a college. Students are questioned with two criteria in mind. First, is the student really as bright as he or she seems to be? And second, is he or she a nice person? Very bright people are often not nice, and those people are not admitted to the college. Cambridge, you see, is more than just an academic environment; it's a communal way of life."

"And what happens to those who don't pass the interview?"

"Well," he said, "I must say again that you are very lucky to have me as your guide because I have a remarkably objective view of the place, since I was trained at a rather *older* university than this one, and one that is *not* normally mentioned around here. . . ."

There was a slight chuckle of recognition as our "Official Blue Badge" guide finally divulged himself to be a dark blue traitor.

"You see, there is a view at *that* university, which as I said is not normally mentioned here, that people at Cambridge do not have a sense of humour. Well, I can assure you that just isn't true. If one of the colleges at Cambridge, say Trinity College, dislikes a student slightly, they may say, 'Well, we think you ought to apply to St. John's College.' "

A tittle began.

"But, if they dislike a student *quite* a lot, they may say, 'Well, we think you ought to apply to Awxford.' "

It built to a rumble. Roger mounted his toes and thrust his pointer finger high into the sky.

"But if they dislike a student a great deal, they might say, 'Well, we think you should apply to some provincial school. Why don't you think about Harvard?' "

The congregation burst into applause. Their catechism was confirmed: Oxford is Cambridge; Oxbridge is Britain; and Britain is forever quaint.

A week after the story on Cynthia Shepard appeared in *Varsity,* the rival newspaper *Weekly Revue* ran a front-page article headlined THE AMERICAN SWIMMING POOL FRAUD: WAS SHE TRICKED OR IS SHE THE TRICKSTER? The story, written with a cynical tone verging on the xenophobic, described how the supposedly unsuspecting American told Cambridge authorities she eagerly gave up her twenty-thousand-dollar scholarship to Miami University and paid five thousand dollars to the "clean-cut and respectable" agent for a seat at Corpus Christi. But was the affair really what it seemed? the paper wondered. Where were the other duped students? And was Miss Shepard really "so naïve that she did not even ask for a receipt?"

In a crusading effort to find the truth and preserve the good name of the university, the *Weekly Revue* actually contacted Miami University and discovered that it in fact offered no scholarships of twenty thousand dollars. The "first national student newspaper" even contacted the English Department at Miami and learned that "no one had ever heard of Cynthia Shepard." In the end, the valiant journalists saved the name of their national treasure and concluded that the American was probably the trickster, trying unsuccessfully to bluff her way into the Greatest University on Earth. The moral of the story, the paper suggested, was that substance always triumphs over style, and all the smooth talk and cunning plots of Hollywood-America are not enough to dupe the lords of the realm and keepers of the plot at the University of Cambridge. "Arriving with such a sorrowful, heart-rending story, how could anyone possibly refuse her a place?" the *Revue* wondered in its *coup de grâce*. "Well," it boasted. "Cambridge did."

IV

LOVING

Cold Sharks and Scorpions

Though I am young and cannot tell
Either what Death or Love is well,
Yet I have heard they both bear darts,
And both do aim at human hearts.

—Ben Jonson
"Though I Am Young," 1641

"*B*ruce, you wanker, come inside. Wait till you see what I
got."

Ian Zahir opened the door of his top-floor rooms in the Old
Court of Clare and pulled me inside by the lightweight sweater one
seems always to need in Britain.

"What is it?" I said.

"A letter," he gushed.

"From whom?"

"I'm in love."

He spread his arms like an opera singer and arched his back in
crescendoing glee. Collapsing back on his unmade bed, he plucked

a guitar from beneath a pile of open Penguin Classics and began to strum a song: "I'm beautiful, she's beautiful, we're going to fall in love. . . . I'm sexy, she's sexy, we're going to frolic in the mud." It wasn't poetic, it hardly even rhymed, but in the ardor of the moment it was the most romantic song that Ian had ever heard. He let out a joyous, deep bass laugh and rushed forward to embrace me. "I'll write it down, I'll call her. I'll sing it beneath her window. . . . Do you want to hear it?"

"I just did."

"Not the song, fool, the letter."

He dropped his arms from around my waist, stuck his hand down his faded jeans, and pulled a card from the band of his bikini undershorts.

"Listen: 'Dear Ian, Sorry I haven't returned your phone calls recently. I have been working very hard on a paper on Hobbes. I have to meet my supervisor late next week, maybe we can meet after that. . . .' " He closed his eyes and swooned.

"That hardly sounds ravishing to me," I said.

"No," he snarled. "It's the end. Look at the signature." He turned the card toward my face and pointed to a mass of wide loopy letters with an occasional curlicue hovering over the clutter like a halo trying desperately to dot a wandering *i*.

"It's very elegant," I said, "but I can't read it."

"Neither can I," he admitted. "But you see that mark there, it matches the first letter of her name. And this one here, it must be an *o*, because it's got the same shape as in 'Hobbes.' So I did a little work." He pulled from his pocket a wad of tissues, pen caps, and cash-machine receipts, along with a college housing memo on the back of which was a complex cryptographic chart. "I figured out that these three letters must be the same, along with this one here. So that if you turn the letter to the light and if you squint your eyes just a little, then—yes, then—you can read her signature: 'Lots and lots of love, Louise.' "

Ian Zahir, a graduate student in SPS—social and political science—would break any code or cross any bridge for a chance at falling in love. A recent alumnus of Clare, he would also burst either one of his lungs for a chance to tell his tale. If Simon was charming in his youthful thoroughbred, slightly lanky gait, Ian was passionate in his full-bodied, leonine, slightly menacing prowl. Half-Persian, half-British, and native of a wholly rich suburb of London, Ian was more than commonly vain and wore his generous golden locks moussed with a sculptor's care so they framed his face like the mane of a sphinx.

In sport Ian was a fencer. Having taken up saber at age thirteen, he had earned a Cambridge Blue by competing against Oxford, and was currently spending several days a week training for the British Olympic team. In play he was a dartsman. Even though he rarely drank, never smoked, and hadn't even sampled drugs, Ian was obsessive about two things: showers, which he took four times a day, and darts, which he played incessantly until he started to perspire or began to lose. Usually these occurred at about the same time. For despite his athletic condition, Ian was self-consciously skinny, and in an effort to disguise what he considered to be his only discernible flaw, he constantly wore several baggy T-shirts next to his body, several baggy lightweight sweaters over those, and at least one baggy camel-hair blazer on top of all that, so that he looked perfectly mastadonic in size and was perpetually hot.

I first met Ian at a port-tasting party for new members of the Clare MCR—the Middle Common Room, where graduate students can drink grown-up drinks and make childish jokes without competition from freshers or fellows. I was sitting on one of the tattered grey sofas sharing obligatory chitchat with several members when Ian plopped himself down at one end of our circle, turned his back, and glared out the window at King's. For several minutes he was silent, almost brooding, until he heard me mention the word Japan, at which point he spun himself around, threw his hair into our ring, and, without so much as introducing himself, began to fire nonstop questions directly from his outstretched finger into my withdrawn face.

He was a classicist, he said, and wondered if I knew about the similarities between ancient Greece and modern Japan.

Yes, as a matter of fact, I did.

This was important, he observed, not some casual notion. Had I realized, for example, that both classical Greece and contemporary Japan had arranged marriages?

Yes, it so happens, I had.

No, wait, he said, there's more. Was I aware of the fact, for instance, that ancient Greece and modern Japan were both shame cultures, ones in which social groups were so powerful they shamed their members into following their rules?

Yes, it turns out, I was.

One by one, the other guests retreated as Ian, point by point, became more animated, hunching his back, pinching his thumb and forefinger together, and jabbing them together into my eyes. Finally, after about a dozen such questions, he leaned back, finished off his glass, and declared, "Good. Now that I know what you believe, let me tell you about me."

He didn't shut up for a year.

"So you see," Ian said, flinging Louise's letter high into the air and jumping, boots first, onto his unmade bed, "she finds me irresistible."

"I think maybe *unavoidable* is a better word."

"Let's go sing her my song."

"We can't," I said.

"Why not?" he insisted.

"She's trying to write a paper on Hobbes and you're supposed to be cooking me dinner."

"Oh, *shite*," he muttered. "I almost forgot. Did I tell you Dr. Kramer is coming? I'd better take off my jacket, I'm sweating like a pig."

. . .

It is a truth universally acknowledged, Jane Austen might have written, that a single student in possession of a good education must be in want of sex. Cambridge, for all its high-minded pretensions, is no exception to this rule. The image of celibate student-monks scurrying up and down staircases, meeting with learned dons, and engaging in one-to-one tuition of the most enlightened kind may be fine for tourists and parents but would come as quite a surprise to the bedders and porters who see the underside of an undergraduate's life, not to mention the inside of his bed-sit chamber. If anything, Cambridge today is a sexual melting pot where the inexperienced meet the idealistic, the promiscuous meet the repressed, and where classical Aristotelian notions of love meet modern sexual perversions of a type of which Jane Austen never dreamed. It is, in short, a laboratory of love—one into which I plunged headfirst and out of which I emerged tongue-tied, with a fatal attraction, a modern melodrama, and a fairy tale, all to my name.

Traditionally, Cambridge has had an uneasy attitude toward love and sex. For much of its history abstinence was the norm, the result of the three axioms that guided university admittance for all but the most recent century: a student had to be English, had to be a member of the Church, and had to be a man. Dons, for example, were forced to remain celibate if they wanted to keep their posts. To be sure, Cambridge students got around these limitations in all manner of ways that reflect in retrospect the sharpness of their minds and the dullness of their social lives: Samuel Coleridge, for one, was corresponding with one woman in London while engaged to another in Oxford; Rupert Brooke invited Virginia Stephen (soon to be Woolf) to go skinny-dipping with him in the Cam. For the most part, however, Cambridge men dealt with their forced isolation by saving their love for formal balls after term and savoring one another in college with drinking bouts, sporting matches, and an occasional experimental fling. In *Brideshead Revisited*, Evelyn Waugh's classic evocation of Oxbridge innocence, Charles Ryder and Sebastian

Flyte enjoy a blissful coexistence during term that is only made grander by the plush surroundings and nameless freedom of their *amor platonicus*. (Homosexuality is not mentioned in the book; it was illegal until the 1960s.) After graduation Charles turns to art, marriage, God, and finally to love in the person of Sebastian's younger sister, but is never able to recapture the romance of his collegial youth.

With the arrival of women in recent times—first at affiliated colleges a century ago, then at Cambridge colleges in the 1960s and '70s—love moved from the department of abstract philosophy to the associated faculties of chemistry, biology, linguistics, and geography (your rooms, or mine?), as well as, in more recent years, international relations. According to old university hands, particularly Terry the Matchmaker-Porter, the arrival of women has coincided with a decline in the quality of rowing, a rise in the price of a haircut, a reduction in the amount of studying, and a rise in the cumulative grade point average (women tend to score higher than men). In the late 1980s, when Magdalene became the last college to admit women, it immediately saw its standing in the academic ladder jump from its perpetual contentment near the bottom to a dizzying perch near the top, thereby aggravating in many of its lager-loving, male-chauvinist alumni an acute agrophobia.

Academic performance notwithstanding, the university elders were not pleased with the decline of morals that accompanied the arrival in recent decades of so many fresh parvenues. On one of my first days in Clare, I went into the Porters' Lodge with Halcyon to register our bicycles with the college. Terry was giving us instructions on how to mark the bikes with a security code: C468190. "What does the *C* mean?" Halcyon asked. "Why, Clare College, my dear," he told her. "Only a girl would ask such a question. About the only thing they're good for is dancing with and looking at."

To guarantee that the only thing Cambridge "boys" do with Cambridge "girls" is dance with them and look at them, colleges instituted a variety of neo-Victorian rules to restrict every other conceivable alternative. *The Clare College Student's Guide*, for example, enumerated one full page of restrictions covering parties. "Parties are defined as lively gatherings of more than ten people," the guide informed. "If the number does not exceed 25 it is a 'small party' and may be held in your own rooms in College." If you want to have more than twenty-five people, the guide said, your gathering must be classified as a "large party" and may *not* be held in your rooms. Music, defined by implication as "lively sound," may be played at small parties provided the following conditions were met: 1) it is played on Friday or Saturday night; 2) it ends by 11:45; and 3) it is not unduly loud. The key to the college's chaperoning command was that if you wanted to have any kind of party, be it large or small, be it for sipping or for sharking, you had to get *written* permission from the head tutor of the college. Moreover, if you wanted to use your room (i.e., a small party), the tutor would require you to get a *written* release from every member of your entryway, a process which in effect nullified the entire enterprise since most entryways had more than twenty-five people and since college etiquette demanded that you couldn't very well get someone's written permission for a party you didn't invite them to attend.

Totalitarian regulations notwithstanding, the college eventually realized that rules against lively gatherings might restrict the mingling of more than twenty-five people but would have little effect in deterring the even more pernicious mingling of only two. A new set of regulations was in order. "Guests may enter and leave College at any time up to midnight," the guide instructed. If members wished to have a guest spend the night, they could rent a visitor's accommodation from the college. Failing this, students could put guests up in their rooms, but 1) only for one or two nights, 2) only on a "camp bed" rented from the porter, and 3) *caveat cupid!*—only with *written* permission from the tutor. In all the annals of the college this rule was undoubtedly my favorite. The potential ramifications were endless: "Just stare into the candle a little longer, darling, while I run tell the tutor I picked you up in the pub." Of course, this approach would not be possible either, I discovered, because candles are also forbidden. Unwittingly, I had discovered the sacred heart of the *familia Cantabriggiensis*. For generations of Cambridge students—past, present, and future—the mark of maturity in a man's life is when he brings a girl home to meet his tutor. And if a young man chooses to ignore this rule and invite a girl to his rooms for some untutored, unpermitted repose, then some colleges in Cambridge might still charge the offender a two-pound, term-end "brothel fine," for inordinate wear and tear on the bed.

The cumulative effect of these regulations is often like a giant prophylaxis on the lifeline of the college. Sex is a common topic for discussion at Cambridge, but, with a few glaring exceptions (notably Simon, above my head), seems not to be a common activity. From the opening days of term, for example, university periodicals began dishing out advice to lovelorn undergraduates. "Stress-Relieving Tip of the Week," wrote *Varsity* in its Week 2 edition. "ALWAYS MAKE IT A ONE-NIGHT STAND." "If someone invites you back for 'a nice cup of coffee,' " the newspaper advised, "do not reply 'but I thought we were going to have a shag [screw],' as the two are synonymous. If a 'non-sexual' cup of coffee is on the agenda, this will be clearly specified. Once you are 'chez them,' do not immediately look around for the kettle." Instead, "a favourite tactic is to remove one item of clothing, saying 'Oooh, isn't it hot in here,' and insist on sitting down on the bed. According to our extensive research, a good snog [necking] should follow shortly."

At Clare this advice seemed to have little effect. HAPLESS SHARKS SEEK HELP FROM UNEXPECTED SOURCE, whimpered a headline in *The Procrastinator*, the weekly gossip rag. "The Clare Sharks are suffering from their worst start to the season in living memory," the paper reported. "It was always going to be a tough game for the lacklustre lads, up against one of the toughest defences in the league, but they continue to be plagued by poor finishing as numerous scoring opportunities went begging." The article, which singled out the particularly poor efforts of Coach Peter de Clare ("perhaps he needs a little technical refinement despite being built for the game"), ended by sounding this humiliating warning knell: "Time to wake up, sharks! The other teams in the league are beginning to capitalise on Clare's stunning lack of success, as sharks as far apart as Trinity and even Oxford scored away wins over the weekend."

The bawdy report did not go unnoticed, and a week later an outraged letter appeared in *The Procrastinator*. "I was sorry to read last week about the lack of success of the Clare Sharks 1st XI," wrote a third-year historian who was head of the Cambridge Lesbian and Gay Campaign. "I'm not surprised they're not getting much sex, though, as I think women generally prefer to have sex with people who acknowledge them as human beings. Perhaps the sharks can't do this because they've got a massive collective castration complex, and have to channel their deep fear of women into rampant misogyny." Back and forth the two sides went, the future leaders of the Western world, with the detractors accusing the original writers of homophobia ("I suppose the sharks can't bear the thought that gay men might be having a better sex life than they are") and the writers accusing the detractors of distorting the truth ("He assumes knowledge of people's motivations based on erroneous assumptions; he was not possessed of all the facts pertaining"). Finally a letter appeared after several weeks that seemed to sum up the entire episode: "It seems incidents like these are one of the consequences of living in a goldfish bowl . . . albeit a fairly large and comfortable goldfish bowl with thirteenth century architecture."

What struck me about this exchange was how much it reminded me of my own undergraduate days: clever, sophomoric, and tasteless jokes on one side compounded by clever, radical, and trendy rage on the other. One group of undergraduates so craves sexual bliss that it develops a childish obsession; the other so wants to transcend the act that it descends into an ideological temper tantrum. Perhaps Clausewitz was onto something, it occurred to me, and love is just the continuation of politics by other means. Indeed, at Cambridge—as elsewhere—love *is* like war for many people, and sex is its chief battleground. And as I watched the battle unfold, I couldn't help wondering why there appeared to be so little correlation between performance in academics and proficiency in love. If anything, there seemed to be a conflict between the two. Clare students, for all appearances, could pass rigorous entrance exams but not get dates for Saturday night. They could read romantic poetry and incite chemical attractions, but not translate these abstract ideas into actual practice. In the laboratory of love these days, the public discourse on relationships is emphatic and impassioned, while in private the conversation is much less dogmatic and much more deeply felt.

"Then, just as he landed in the water . . ."

A little over an hour later I was telling a story on the bed in Ian's rooms with a plate of Chinese noodles on my lap and a glass of Irish stout in my hand. Ian was busy fiddling in the gyp and fussing like a nagging host: Are the noodles warm enough? Is the broccoli cut too large? That left me alone in the spotlight, building as I usually do toward the climax of the story, waving my arms as I also do when blessed with a responsive audience. "It spread its wings, opened its beak, and . . ."

It cannot be said that Dr. Cyprian Kramer would strike the casual observer as responsive. He was tall, almost gangly, his face was thin, ascending from the curb of his rounded chin to a pair of spectacles affixed to his nose like academic training wheels. When I finished my story, Dr. Kramer did respond.

"That was pretty funny," he said without so much as a grin. "Let me guess: Scorpio?"

"Close. Swan."

"Even funnier. You *must* be a Scorpio."

"What, my sign?"

He nodded, jiggling his blond shoulder-length ponytail that hung from the rear of his balding head.

"Well, yes, I am a Scorpio."

"I thought so. Of course, you won't believe me, that's why I never guess anyone's sign in public, but I knew that."

I stared at him. "How?"

"From the way you told that story. It's the same way I would have told it—the pauses, the gestures, the climax. Indeed, you're a typical Scorpio, as am I."

Dr. C. P. Kramer ("Call me Cyprian: it's Greek for 'prostitute' ") was a classicist and a former don of Ian's in ancient philosophy. Like Ian, his junior by ten years, Cyprian was born in London, had attended the prestigious St. Paul's School, and had been an undergraduate at Clare. Unlike Ian, Cyprian came from a middle-class family, attended St. Paul's on scholarship, and stayed on at Cambridge not merely for his master's but also for a Ph.D. After receiving his doctorate, Cyprian was invited to become a fellow at Clare, a position which entitled him to free rooms in Memorial Court, free meals at High Table in Hall, and free reign to walk on the grass, unaccompanied. His area of expertise was an unsung Roman writer named Marcus Annaeus Lucanus, or Lucan, who wrote an epic poem two thousand years ago that has been mostly ignored by scholars. Cyprian, on the other hand, adored its twisted humor and exotic style. The reason, he said, was that he and Lucan shared one vital sign: both were Scorpios.

"You've got to be kidding," I said.

"Why?" he replied.

"You mean to tell me your academic career is based on what day of the year you were born?"

"Your love life is based on that," he said. "Why not your professional life as well?"

Eventually, inevitably, when the serving was complete, the conversation settled onto the semiotics of love. The laboratory was in session.

"So tell me," I said. "I'm engaged in a kind of quest. Is Cambridge a good place to fall in love?"

"Yes," Cyprian quickly answered.

"Of course," Ian agreed.

"Well . . ." they began to reconsider. "Maybe it's not so simple."

Ian had come to Cambridge yearning to fall in love. If Simon was the type of student who left public school consumed with sex, Ian was the type who left petrified. During Ian's first term at Clare, a beautiful girl from his entryway came to his door at two in the morning, dressed only in a nightgown, and asked for a cup of coffee. "She was the most beautiful girl in our year," he remembered (Cambridge students, like the porters, still use the term *girl*). "All my friends wanted to snog with her—I slammed the door in her face." After that trauma he moved slowly, sitting across from girls in Buttery—the cafeteria underneath the Hall—and starting conversations with them in the JCR, the Junior Common Room underneath the Chapel. Halfway through his second year, Ian's preparations finally paid off: she was blond, a historian, a horseback rider, and a tender influence on Ian's rapacious soul. Her name was Miranda.

"I fell in love with her eyes," he recalled. "She had the most vulnerable look in the world. Also, she was good. The ideal of good. She could walk into a storm and calm it with her grace. I made her laugh; she made me weak. I never let her out of my sight." He shut his eyes and swooned.

"You should have seen them together," Cyprian said. "They would yell and scream and curse the day they met, then melt into each other's arms and kiss away the tears. She was definitely an Aries."

"And a whore," Ian snapped.

The previous summer, after two years of tumultuous romance, Ian and Miranda traveled to Sardinia to celebrate their graduation. For two weeks they frolicked in the sand, went skinny-dipping in the surf, and then three days before the end of the trip, while Ian was upstairs taking a shower, Miranda danced with another man, who kissed her goodbye on the lips.

"I was destroyed," Ian remembered. "I had given her my heart,

I had shared my soul, I had even showed her my foreskin, the most sacred possession I have, and she abandoned me." Ian flew back to London the next day and decided to postpone a legal training course for another year of philosophy at Cambridge.

"She says she wants you back," Cyprian reminded Ian, who had stopped eating altogether and picked up his guitar again. "It was only a kiss."

"It was a violation," he declared. "We had a pact. Love is much more than sex: it's an understanding. Call it sappy, but I have this extraordinarily traditional opinion that the highest form of love requires exclusivity. It is special because it's particular. I don't accept this idea of human frailty. If you say, 'I'm only human,' you can never achieve greatness. Kant said if you believe in love you can achieve it. The act of following a certain moral code can transform it into law."

As philosophical as Ian was about love, Cyprian was providential.

"I don't believe you can make laws out of words," Cyprian said after Ian had drifted off into a self-pitying silence. "There is a certain amount of fate involved. I haven't had many relationships, but when I find a match that fits my chart I'm not going to let some philosopher tell me what to do. What you don't understand, Ian, is that the stars are wiser than all the sages put together, the planets are more powerful than Plato."

He reached over and lit a Marlboro cigarette and unsuccessfully offered one to me. Ian waved at the smoke in the air and rolled over on his bed. Then Cyprian told a story with Scorpion finesse about a woman he recently met in line at the buttery of the History Faculty. She was drinking coffee by herself, she was French, and she was looking for someone to teach her Italian. Buoyed beyond his sheepishness by the remarkable chance, Cyprian, doctor of Latin, offered to help. But first he asked her a question.

"I couldn't believe it," he sighed. "She was a Gemini. If only she had been born twenty minutes later, she would have had some water in her."

"Water?" I said. "What's that?"

"Bruce," he said, "you disappoint. It means she would crave love and protection—"

"Which only Scorpios can provide."

"We *are* passionate and deep, you know."

"I'm learning," I said. "And what do we match?"

"Water. Cancer, Capricorn, Pisces."

"But not Gemini."

"That's air."

"That's bollocks," Ian shouted from the bed.

"That's not the only problem," Cyprian retorted. "There's the matter of her name, Sophie. Oh, Sophie, my least-favourite name, after, of course, the obvious choices of Sharon and Lisa. And she likes clothes. I mean really likes clothes. She wears a different outfit every time I meet her. Usually, I don't recognize her, or it takes me several minutes to find her. It's rather embarrassing."

"And she wants you to like clothes as well."

"Me?" he glanced down at his standard-issue Cambridge uniform—baggy grey trousers and black turtleneck. "I can't, it would ruin my image as a slouch. Last week I said, 'Okay, I trust your taste. Let's buy a pair of shoes for me.' We couldn't. All she wanted me to buy was a pair of Italian patent leather loafers. I wanted a pair of sandals. 'You can't wear those,' she said. So I bought nothing."

Ian could no longer contain himself. "Cyprian," he blurted, "you're a loser."

Cyprian was unfazed. "Then there's the problem of food. This is one of Sophie's favourite subjects. She hates English food. I kind of like it. She's a vegetarian. She keeps offering to cook dinner to show me how wonderful a cook she is. She wants to cook me fish. I hate fish."

"So let me get this straight," I said. "She likes Italian clothes, and you don't. You like English food, and she doesn't."

"It's worse."

"How?"

"She likes France, and I don't."

"You wanker!" Ian cried.

"She wants to teach me French. I hate French; I even hate the French. It was my first foreign language, but I don't like it anymore. It's probably because of the French officials who were rude to me in Paris. I prefer Italian."

"That's perfect," I said. "That's what she wanted all along."

"It's not perfect," he insisted. "In Cambridge, English is the language of love."

With that remark Ian popped up and slammed his befisted arms on his knees. "Then why do you see her?" he demanded.

"Because it's rare," Cyprian said without lifting a finger. "It's rare to meet someone with whom it is possible to have a conversation. I don't believe in all your philosophical constructions, all your educated guesses. There's something terribly English about it. Education is such a controlling thing, and I believe love is much more basic. I remember when I was young, very young—about six or seven. I used to take a bus to school, and there was a woman who took the same bus. I became infatuated with her. Later, five or six years later, when I knew what a film star looked like and had seen porn mags and the like, I happened to take that bus and the same woman got on. I realized then that she was ugly—amazingly ugly, in fact. And I have been questioning ever since. Perhaps I fell in love because it was my naïve self before I had learnt what beauty, or sex, or love actually is. I think education corrupts the heart."

"You're a traitor," Ian said when Cyprian was done. "You're a traitor to everything you taught me. What about the classical notion of love—that there is a higher ideal out there that we must strive to achieve. Education is not a burden, it liberates us from the tyranny of our bodies and opens up new worlds. . . . Bruce, don't you agree?"

With this last question Ian turned in my direction, and he and Cyprian paused in their spat to hear my mediation. I was fully prepared to equivocate. On the one hand, I could see Ian's point about the virtues of high ideals. On the other hand, I could sympathize with Cyprian's fear of losing a love to some philosophy. Faced with these conflicting urges, I was going to say instead that maybe a university was a bad place to look for love, since all we seemed to do was talk about it.

But they didn't want to hear me at all.

"I don't agree with you," Cyprian insisted.

"Then you're wrong," Ian shouted back.

"No," Cyprian responded, relishing the exchange though never raising his voice. "You're wrong, and I'm right. You should appreciate what you had with Dominique and grab it before it disappears."

"I can't. I won't." Ian stood up and started pacing the room. He plucked a dart from his circular board and spun it in his fingers. "Don't you see? I'm young, and if I don't experiment now, I'll never know if it was right. Miranda is dead. Louise is my pursuit, my *agon*." He paused for a minute over his Greek mandate and lifted the dart to his eye. "I'll push myself harder. I'll test her devotion. Love must be the strongest emotion. I have to know: Would she die for me? Would I die for her? Would I die for love?" He aimed the dart at the heart of the board and propelled it toward the target. The dart bounced off the thin metal ridge around the center and landed on the floor.

"Bull's-eye!" Ian shouted with Pyrrhic glee.

"Sorry," Cyprian retorted with Roman acumen. "If it doesn't stick, it doesn't count. Those are the rules of the game."

V

DRINKING

Bottoms Up and
Trousers Down

This place [Cambridge] is the Devil, or at least his principal residence, they call it a University, but any other
appellation would have suited it much better, for Study
is the last pursuit of the Society. . . . I have only supped
at home 3 times since my arrival, and my table is constantly covered with invitations.

—Byron
Letter, 1805

I bought my first bow tie the day before the dinner. The invitation
made me do it:

The gentlemen's 2nd novice eight with cox
cordially invite
the ladies' 2nd novice eight plus cox
for a
CREW MEAL
of chili, rice, and casual sex
followed by coffee and mints
at 8 P.M. Thursday
Memorial Court
Smart Dress

RSVP   PBAB

I knew that PBAB, the four most important letters to any Cambridge student, meant "Please bring a bottle," but I didn't know the meaning of "Smart Dress"; so I asked.

"It means a DJ," said Max, the toniest member of the boat and also the most out of shape.

"A DJ?" I repeated, unenlightened.

"You know, a dinner jacket."

"A tuxedo, you mean."

"That's right. A black jacket, a white shirt, and a bow tie. You have one, of course."

"Of course," I said with exaggerated aplomb, being suddenly thankful for having been invited to my cousin's wedding on Long Island the previous year. At that time, after receiving some sartorial advice from my father, whose fashion tastes were freeze-dried in 1947 at the apogee of the British Empire, I purchased my first tuxedo. I had made it through four years of Yale University without once trying on a tuxedo, but I would not finish my first month at Cambridge without donning my DJ. At Cambridge, it seems, a curious dress code applies: the more dressed up the guests must get, the more debauched a party becomes.

So that afternoon I trekked off to the shop called A. E. Clothiers, across the street from King's, and asked for a Clare bow tie.

"What kind of Clare tie would you like?" asked the man behind the counter as he lifted his nose from a stack of scarves, smiled, and gingerly laid one hand atop the other, like a pastor before a corpse.

"You mean I have a choice?"

"Why, yes," he intoned, "you can have the Regular tie, or the Rugby tie, or the Boat Club tie."

"I'll take the Boat Club tie."

"Which one?"

"There's more than one?"

"Well, you have the yellow ones for the first boat, but I don't imagine you've got that far." He smiled; I coughed. He continued.

"Or the yellow ones with the black stripes, or the white ones with the—"

"That's all right," I interrupted. "I'll just take the Regular tie. The black one, with the yellow stripes."

"Very well," he agreed. "Will there be anything else? You have the hooded sweatshirt, of course."

"Of course." I reached for my checkbook, in England a cheque-book.

"How about cuff links, a tiepin, a money clip . . ."

"That will be all, thank you."

"Very well. Come back anytime."

Now that I had my tie, I needed someone to teach me to knot it. On the night before I left for England, in the hopes of averting embarrassment, I had asked my mother to give me a lesson. I had stood dripping wet in the late summer heat staring into a mirror as my mother, the Anglophile, stood on a stool behind me and tried to show me how to fasten a tie around my shirtless neck.

"It's just like tying a shoe," she kept saying.

Not only is it not like tying a shoe, I concluded after two hours of lopsided, floppy-eared knots, but it is also not like riding a bicy-cle, because in the interim between shirtless summer and wing-tipped fall, I had forgotten how.

At first I sought out Simon. He was a prep school boy, I figured, so surely he had learned how to dress smartly for tea.

"I don't know how to do that," he smirked. "My grandmother always did it for me."

Then I asked Cheryl from Canada, K.K. from Malaysia, and Halcyon from Hong Kong—all people from places that were at one time under the British Empire—but none of them could tell me either.

"It's just like tying a shoe," Halcyon said, though she couldn't seem to demonstrate on me.

Finally, I asked Bill, from Northern Ireland. We were sitting in the Buttery the day of the dinner and he assured me he could explain. He took a napkin, rolled it from corner to corner, and started to knot it around an egg-shaped salt shaker—empty, like most, from overuse.

"That's it!" I shouted.

"That's what?" he said.

"You've got to make the loop before the knot."

"That's right," he said, "but where do you put it?"

"That's easy," I said. "You put it through the hole."

And so it came to pass that I locked myself in my rooms that evening just hours before the crew meal, stood cursing before my closet mirror—this time in shirt and no shorts—-and sold my soul to the fading Empire by rendering my neck like a shoe.

"Hey look," Max called as I arrived with Halcyon at the attic rooms on the far side of Memorial Court. "Brucie's got a Clare bow tie."

"Nice tie," cried John—Number Two—as he stirred the chili.

"And look at this outfit, lads," cried Max—the Stroke. "Spot on. Where did you get it?"

"America," I said, to his clear disappointment.

"And these grey trousers, what are they made of?"

"Denim."

"I like them, Brucie, but why didn't you wear your whole DJ?"

I glanced at the chili on the stove, the bread on the counter, the wine in Max's hand. As I did, I recalled the story Ian had told me about the annual dinner of the Clare soccer team where half the members, after getting totally sloshed, climbed to the roof of Gonville and Caius College (usually called simply Caius) and tossed chunks of lamb kebab at the other half of the team, who had jumped across the ten-foot chasm to the roof of the Senate House.

"Because," I said, "I know what you're like when you're pissed."

"Clever lad," Max said, vacuuming up the last contents of his glass and flashing a burgundy smile.

The rules for the Crew Meal were quite simple: the boys do the cooking, the girls bring the liquor, and no one walks past the Porters' Lodge dressed in his or her smart Sunday duds. The reason for this precaution is that with at least eighteen people in attendance, a Crew Meal would be classified as a "small party" and therefore would require written permission from the head tutor and disbandment before eleven o'clock. The gentlemen of the Clare Second Novice Boat had no intention of observing these rules.

"Hey, Bruce," said Oliver—Number Six—"do you mind whipping this cream? I have to stir the rice."

For the next half hour I stood in the gyp in my DJ and jeans whipping cream with a fork and a spoon. With the arrival of the Crew Meal, we had reached the halfway point of term and my life was settling into a rhythm. Our crew would practice four or five times a week, usually beginning before 6 A.M. After rowing I would bicycle back through the yawning town, hurriedly gulp down my bottle of milk, and pedal off to sleepy lectures on the Sidgwick Site: "Neo-Realism and the Second World War," "U.N. Peacekeeping in a Bipolar World," "International Relations in a Somnolent State." After lectures, I would drop off for lunch in the Buttery, then head back to V Entryway and nap away most of the afternoon with an open book spine-up on my chest. Before dinner Simon would drop by my rooms on his way to Old Court; while afterward he and I, or I alone, would meet up with Ian for a game of darts, a round of pool, or a conversation on the virtues of Louise Rogers, a discussion that never proceeded past the theoretical but which invariably proceeded past "last call" at the pubs, at which point we would head down to the Clare Late Bar, since it was one of the few places in town open past 11 P.M.

As the cream began to thicken in the bowl and my arm began to ache, the ladies began to arrive in the attic, toting their wine in brown paper bags and gripping their shawls around naked shoulder blades. One of the last guests to poke her nose in the kitchen was Susanna, the third-year coach of the ladies' boat, who was draped half-naked herself on the arm of Peter of Clare.

"Is that his girlfriend?" whispered Charlie Chaplin—the Bow—who was busy pouring low-grade vodka into a cherry gelatin mold.

"Since last year," responded Max. "Since she dyed her hair."

After spreading the whipped cream on a rum-soaked cake and arranging a can of mandarin oranges in a pattern around the top, I slid the intoxicated cake into the refrigerator and joined the others in the room, where a penciled looseleaf sign on the door read, PARTY HERE NOW.

"Have a drink," Oliver said as I entered the room, shoving into my hand a miniature blue brandy glass with two fingers of amber spirits inside.

"What is it?" I asked.

"An aperitif," he said. "A blend of wine and whisky. Sort of like sherry, but better."

"What's it called?"

"I don't know, but don't worry, it's a *real* drink, we didn't make it ourselves: it came from a bottle."

I took a sip of the sweet-and-sour drink, which reminded me of children's candied cough syrup, then traded it for a glass of red wine. The rooms, which belonged to Number Seven, had the angular, somewhat cramped feel of an antique cedar chest, with exposed beams jutting out from overhead, dark paneling on the walls, and two windows carved into the roof to let the rain drip in. The thin metal shelves were overflowing with typical fresher fare: A-Level notes for chemistry, stained coffee mugs, and a bag of granulated sugar slightly torn at the top and dribbling onto the floor. The grumpy countenance of Winston Churchill stared down from the wall like a porter on patrol.

Despite the abundance of alcohol, the party had not advanced past the sock hop stage by the time I arrived. Peter was working one side of the room teaching the lads how to drink. "Think of the glass as a woman's body," he said, "then plunge your face right in." "Should my nose get wet?" asked Number Six. "Never your nose," the prof professed. "The proof is in the lips."

Susanna, for her part, was goading the girls on the other side of the room.

"And what do *you* do?" she said upon arriving at me, wiggling her purple miniskirted hips and twisting her obviously bleached-blond hair.

"International relations," I said.

"Oooh!" she spewed with inebriated intensity. "That sounds *serious*, what does it mean?"

"I don't know," I said. "I'm still trying to figure that out."

"Well," she said, "when you find out, please let me know. We could sure use some of that around here right now." She released her finger from her hair, spilling it loosely from her head and dribbling it down the front of my shirt. "But don't wait too long. I might be too pissed to remember."

With sixteen rowers, two coxes, and two super-intoxicated coaches, the original nine bottles of wine were soon emptied and snogging one another on the ground. The boys in the boat had anticipated this problem, and on the morning of the meal it was decided to inform all the girls that they should each PB2B, assuring us a supply of eighteen bottles—at least one per person. But after a little more than an hour, and long before the boil-in-the-bag rice would be ready for the chili con carne, the expanded liquor stock had nearly run dry.

"Ladies, ladies, could I have your attention, please." Susanna stood atop one of the low white tables and smiled down at the party. "Ladies, it seems we have run out of wine, and it is our responsibility to provide it. So if I go out and buy some wine, I need your promise to pay me back."

There was some general discussion about how much wine (two cases), what color (red), and what grade (low), before Susanna went off with Peter to the nearby liquor store, called an off-licence.

"Save us some of the food," Peter shouted from the door. "And don't take your clothes off without us."

·　·　·

In retrospect, I suppose I shouldn't have been so surprised by the drinking I found at Cambridge. After all, in addition to attending college in America, I had also studied at several universities outside the United States: a semester in Osaka, a summer in Oslo. Each of those places, like each of those countries, had its own elaborate drinking rituals. Still, when I arrived in Britain, both the amount and the type of drinking I discovered overwhelmed me at every turn.

To begin, students at Cambridge are virtually bombarded with occasions to drink and excuses to get pissed. Even before I arrived at Clare, I received a letter, by air, from Dr. A. B. Jones inviting me to have sherry with him before the matriculation dinner. After I arrived, I got more invitations from tutors (teachers), boaties (rowers), ruggers (rugby players), and even the rectors of the Christian Athletic Club, who served port alongside their orange juice. Liquor was everywhere in college. Clare, unlike King's and Trinity, did not have its own winery, but it did have its own wine cellar for fellows, its own bar for students, and even its own staff of full-time bartenders. At the university level, myriad clubs exist for organized drinking, including the infamous True Blues Society, whose initiates must dress up in breeches, waistcoat, bow tie, and tails and down an entire chalice of claret in under half a minute. Closer to home, Clare boasted an all-male drinking society called the CRABS (Clare Rugby and Boating Society), which required recruits to drink twelve pints of lager in under two hours. Clare ladies, not to be outpissed, formed a rival group called the Lobsters (no acronym, just crustacean fealty).

To me this intemperance seemed wholly out of character. The British, after all, are supposed to be refined. Their language is thought to be mannered, their manners are said to be dignified, and their dignity is supposedly manifest in their stiff upper lips. "The English have all been trained in one severe school of manners," wrote Ralph Waldo Emerson. "They are never betrayed into any curiosity of unbecoming emotion." As I soon discovered, however, behind this prim Victorian mask lives a thoroughly modern world of sin. If anything, the British approach to drinking and sex—on display in its rawest form at Cambridge—reminded me of the Japanese habit of dividing people's lives into two separate realms: public and private spheres.

In Britain, as in Japan, the public face is arid and pure, almost haughtily above such juvenile desires. This is the face of the highest icons of the royal family; this is page one of the *Financial Times*. The private face, on the other hand, is lush and lascivious, never outgrowing the adolescent urges even if temporarily storing them away under a three-piece suit. This is the image of politicians cavorting with low-grade prostitutes; this is page three of *The Sun*, where a busty, buxom, half-naked bombshell flashes her breasts to readers every day while fondling the handle of a tennis racket or the curve of a banana.

This schism between public persona and private self is widespread in Britain, but nowhere is the split more apparent than at the country's elite universities. Indeed, with their volatile mix of youth, wealth, and overeducated hormones, Oxford and Cambridge are probably the two most concentrated centers for decadence anywhere in the country. On the surface the university appears unflappable and dispassionate, but underneath the students find creative ways to skirt the authorities. "I think it is no exaggeration to say that, in my last year, I and most of my friends were drunk three or four times a week," wrote Oxford alumnus Evelyn Waugh. "It took very little to inebriate at that age and high spirits made us behave more flamboyantly than our state of intoxication really warranted."

To be sure, most students do take their academics seriously. Yet because they are tested only at the end of every year (and sometimes only at the end of two), students are under little pressure to study every night. Also, because of limited social opportunities, they are under a great deal of pressure to drink. In fact, if one considers the number of students involved or the amount of time, money, or calories spent, drinking is probably a far more popular sport than rowing. It is also a far more decadent and desperate game at Cambridge than I ever witnessed in America. Since many Oxbridge students have come from straitlaced boarding schools or tight-lipped families, university is the first time in their lives when they can throw prudence to the wind and indulge in deadly sin.

By the time Susanna and Peter returned to the rooms, the party had advanced most of the way through the chili and rice but was still one step shy of the coffee and mints. Most of the DJs had been long since discarded and barely a tie was still bowed like a shoelace. With plates scarcer than showers, the crews ate chili from bowls, platters, plastic bags, and even, in my case, an overturned Frisbee with a dog bite in the side. With utensils even scarcer than plates, the lads and ladies drank the "vodka jelly" out of stained coffee mugs and used their callused hands to pick off chunks of the mandarin orange rum-side-up cake.

"Everybody . . . hello. I mean, good evening. May I have your attention, please?"

Susanna stood atop one of the tables, staggered slightly from the effects of the wine, and flicked her hair back with sly seduction. "It's time for the first dance of the night. In Boat Club tradition, I would like to ask Peter to deliver a toast."

Peter grabbed one of the few unopened bottles of wine and rose to embrace Susanna atop the table. His shirt tail was untucked around his waist and the sleeves rolled halfway up his forearms. His bright gold First Boat tie dangled like a neglected shoelace around his muscular neck.

"Ladies and gentlemen," he intoned, "please be upstanding."

The crews rose to their feet. Peter took a moment to lift the cork halfway out of the bottle, leaving it slightly engorged in the lip.

"To the Queen," he said with his arms outstretched and his voice quaking with inebriation. "To Lady Clare . . ."

He retrieved a knife from the waistband of his trousers and flashed the blade to the crowd. The crews responded with hoots and howls. Susanna stepped off the table and hid her eyes in her hands.

"What's he doing?" I whispered.

"It's an old aristocratic ritual," said Halcyon, who had stepped to my side. "The host must always open a bottle of champagne with a sword."

"But that isn't champagne," I said. "And that is hardly a sword."

"Boys will be boys," she said.

"To the Clare Boat Club!"

With a dramatic slicing gesture that easily could have decapitated a lamb, Peter not only defenestrated the cork but decimated the glass neck as well, sending the bottle somersaulting toward the carpet and the wine fountaining through the air onto the outstretched arms of his white dress shirt. Susanna gasped. The room tenant cursed. But the rest of the crew burst into applause as Peter responded to the gurgitated wine by summarily ripping off his now blueberry shirt and tossing it into the air like a rock-and-roll star.

"Gentlemen!" he cried. "Find your partners."

What followed was stage two of the Cambridge sock hop. Shoes flew everywhere and DJs were kicked even farther aside as the boys and girls paired off with one other, pretty much corresponding to seat. Halcyon grabbed me by the arm and gestured for the male cox of the ladies' boat to seek out his Number Five instead. Someone turned up the music, a synthetic electric bop, and the crews began to dance.

For the next several songs the dancing was oddly coordinated, with Peter on the table dancing with Susanna—his hands around her waist and hers around his neck—and all the lads gathered dutifully below, watching their coach with a studious eye. Welcome to Sharking 101, the only course in which these novice students dared not procrastinate. If Peter slid his hand up the curve of Susanna's back, the boys all rushed to follow; when he stepped away and bucked his waist, soon half the room was gyrating like roosters. At one point he further roused the roost by flexing his hands, rubbing his body, and sliding his hands up Susanna's legs.

"Hands, body, slide!" he called.

"Hands! Body! Slide!" the lads echoed.

Feeling old, Halcyon and I began retreating from the dance floor. We had just arrived at the door when suddenly we heard a shout from the back of the room. We turned toward the central table underneath the window just in time to see Susanna's arm moving at full-pressure speed, slapping against Peter's face.

"No!" she shouted. "I said *enough!*"

Peter reeled from the weight of the blow and went tumbling off the table and onto the broken glass on the floor. Susanna, meanwhile, leapt from the table toward the tiny attic window, which was closed to keep in the sound. She thrust open the window, lurched her neck out, and vomited down the roofing tile, like a gargoyle come to life.

Just at that moment the Clare Chapel chimed, a loud knock bellowed through the wall and Terry burst through the door. "*What* is going on?!" he shouted to the shocked faces strewn about the floor. "*What* have you horrible people done? *Shut* that window, *turn off* that music, and *get* your sorry asses back to your rooms. Wait till the *tutor* hears about this!"

Halcyon and I moved toward the window to help Susanna back inside the room. As we turned to get some water from the sink, she lunged toward Peter on the floor, dropped her head into his lap, and as he rubbed his cut-up hands across her bright red cheeks, they both began to weep.

"You were good in there."

Walking home from the party that night, on slate pathways slicked down from the rain and alongside pine trees pruned by the college to look like overgrown bonsai, Halcyon eased close to my side and put her arm through mine.

"So were you," I responded. "I think we were the only ones sober enough to react."

"You like her, don't you?"

"Susanna?"

"I could tell," she said. "You're strange, do you know that? On one hand, you're friendly. You flirt with all the girls you meet, give them hugs and a kiss good night. But then you go home and close your door. I think you're an introvert."

Halcyon was the first person I met at Clare. Indeed, in those early, unsure days she was a fellow spy: foreign, friendly, and eager to run joint reconnaisance missions on the alien world of Cambridge. But as I grew more accustomed to the place and less dependent on her, she grew more attached to me and less inclined to hold back.

I laughed off her remark as we passed through Mem Court. For several minutes we walked in silence, until we started up our entryway stairs, when Halcyon again turned to me and said, "Why don't you like me?"

"What are you talking about?" I said. "I do like you. You're the first person I see when I wake up in the morning, and the last person I see at night."

"But you don't really like me," she said. "You never touch me." She stopped at the top of the stairs.

"But I do much more than that," I said, cringing at my knee-jerk sensitive male tone. "I tell you what's on my mind."

"It's not the same," she said. "I'm a woman. Sometimes I want to be touched."

Somewhere in the course of those early months, Halcyon had become much less of my coconspirator at Cambridge and much more of a kind of male fantasy gone horribly wrong. Here was a woman—attractive, enticing, and all but undressing before my eyes—who was goading me for not coming on to her when the outcome of the come-on was all but certified. I thought of myself as a girl-shy teenager: how could I possibly turn down this offer? I remembered myself as an upstanding adult: how could I possibly take advantage of her when my designs were so short–term and base?

I managed to utter a feeble apology as the two of us split at the hall. Back in my room I turned on the light, slipped off my DJ, and began untying my bow, which through the cocktails, chili, and jelly had remained true to the soul of a shoe. In a moment there was a knock on my door.

"It's me," said Halcyon with a nervous giggle. "I need your help."

I opened the door. Halcyon was standing in her sheer Chinese evening dress, leaning against the frame of the door. One of her feet was curled around the gentle slope of the other leg.

"I'm afraid I'm stuck," she said, staring straight into my eyes. "Can you help me out of my dress?"

I took a breath and stared at the floor. I thought of Simon. "I'm only human," he had said. "I enjoy having sex." I thought of Ian. "If you say you're only human," he had preached, "and give into your urges, you can never find true love."

"I'll help you," I said, "but let's go to your room."

We walked the several steps into her rooms and Halcyon shut the door. I undid the four clasps at the shoulders of her dress and watched it fall to the floor. For a moment, she stood in the center of the unlit room and stared at the moon through the open pane. Pausing at the cusp of a friendship that was about to change forever, I reached my hand toward the cool touch of the doorknob and stepped out into the dark.

VI

LEARNING

The Pledge of
Allegiance

O Cambridge, home of Culture's pure delights,
  My fostering Mother, what a desecration!
Yet England chose you (out of several sites)
  To be a bulwark and to save the nation.

—Sir Owen Seaman
"Cambridge in Khaki," 1914

"Good morning, ladies and gentlemen, fellow students of the
world. It is a pleasure to be speaking to you in these rich
and august surroundings. Very much of a pleasure, indeed. . . ."

The tattered leaves of Newton's apple trees were swirling in a
mid-autumn storm and sticking like mud on the thick lead windows
of the School of Pythagoras. Outside, boats on the river were brav-
ing the gale for a last week of practice before the regatta; bicycles
crossing the bridges toward class were skidding on the film of chestnut foliage that covered almost every walk; and stone buildings with
names like Milton, Darwin, and Erasmus were leaking faster than
the bathtubs of Clare in a kind of compensatory shower. Inside,

where guests dared not mention the holes in the roof for fear of offending the ghosts of Genius Past, students were shaking off their dripping black brollies, which I still called umbrellas, and draping their trench coats and college-striped scarves over the fold-out white plastic chairs. It was a Thursday morning in Michaelmas Term and time for the weekly seminar sponsored by the Centre of International Studies. The week's topic: The Crisis at Hand.

"What I have to say to you this morning may seem to have very little to do with the Crisis," said J. G. Lund, director of information for the European Community and visiting lecturer at Cambridge, "but I think it's important to view this event in a wider context and paint a fairly broad canvas. What we are facing is not merely an immediate concern but a threat to our very survival—at least in the medium term."

After love, which is clearly the most prized, most discussed, and most "mucked up" part of university life, and drinking, which serves as a wobbly undercurrent to undergraduate living, various other activities slot into the A-list of prioritized endeavors on a university campus, including athletics, politics, pizza, movies, and the logical outcome of most of these: sleeping late. On this list academics would probably rate a respectable last. To be sure, this scale changes depending on the proximity of the next examination or the length of the next term paper, but for much of the time on most university campuses, and most of the year at Cambridge, academics is the activity of last resort.

For graduate students, this equation is meant to be slightly altered. Ian, for his part, plunged himself wholeheartedly into his SPS papers: "The Politics of Love in Homeric Tragedy," "The Tragic Implications of My Personal Life." I, on the other hand, was studying the distinctly nonpersonal subjects of NGOs, nongovernmental organizations; IGOs, intergovernmental organizations; and UFOs, organizations whose purpose in life is unfathomable. In the meantime, as I listened to heightened British concerns about the European Community and thought about my thesis, I hit on the idea of comparing the Occupation of Japan with the parallel one in Germany. When I looked in the books Dr. Long had given me, however, I found no references to Europe. I decided I must be onto something, but wondered if he would approve.

Meanwhile, the daily drone of lectures continued. The members of my course had long since decided to forgo most of our lectures, except the all-day seminars held once a week. These meetings were the only time we saw one another and even then, in established Cambridge monologic tradition, we rarely spoke. The myth in Cambridge is that students participate equally in their one-on-one tuition; the reality is that only one side usually gets to speak. Exceptions to this formula are so rare that when a student does speak up in class and breaks down the invisible barrier, the incident becomes, in an academic sort of way, exciting.

"My approach to this topic is to touch on the issues of medium-term relevance to the current Crisis, and by that I mean effects that last longer than twenty-five years and perhaps as long as two hundred." Mr. Lund was sitting behind a table on a tiny stage with a bright yellow spotlight shining directly on the crown of his balding head, casting shadows on his eyebrows worthy of Groucho Marx and distorting his nose so that it appeared like that of Charles de Gaulle. "I intend to start with a lengthy preamble that will offer a quick review of the events of our time and then end with a discussion of our fast and fleeting planetary occupation."

Because of its reputation for academic excellence, Cambridge tends to bring out the worst in its guest lecturers. Mr. Lund's preamble was, as promised, lengthy, taking fully three quarters of his one-hour time. He talked about the passing of the Pax Britannica, the arrival of a unified Europe, and the need for people to abandon their national identities. He mentioned global warming, rapid population growth, as well as some of the problems of pesticides, herbicides, deforestation, and dwindling water supplies. In short, he discussed every conceivable threat to world peace except what his topic demanded.

"As you can see," he said near the end, "I have adopted a some-what global perspective. But I intend to make a point much closer to home. British policy, your policy, over the last several hundred years was based entirely on self-interest. The interests of the states came first; the interest of the earth, last. Today the ethics of imperi-alism can no longer be defended. We live in *ensemble* now, and future leaders such as yourselves must learn to overcome your prej-udices. To take the famous words of John Donne, a poet with whom I'm sure you're all familiar, 'No man is an island. . . .' "

"Sir," a voice called out from the back of the hall. It was a student from Durham, in the north of England, and a recent graduate of Cambridge. "Sir, this is all very interesting, but what does it have to do with the current Crisis?"

A few snickers skidded across the floor.

"In the current Crisis," he answered, "we have two states—one has attacked the other. The whole world has rallied to defend the invaded. We have gone to the brink of war. But we have to ask ourselves, *'Pourquoi la guerre?'* Is war necessary, my friend? Is it wise?"

"Sometimes," the student said, "it is. War is what made this country great. We defeated Napoleon, we withstood the kaiser, we turned back Hitler. Under those circumstances, war would seem to pay, now wouldn't it?"

"No, sir," Mr. Lund pronounced. "It may be what built your country. But it will also be what tears it down. We must step back from the brink and learn to fit into nature, the global envelope as a whole. The nation is dead in Europe, my friend, and Britain is just the last to go."

The student stood still for a moment before speaking. "If we let it go, we have let down ourselves," he said. "What is British history, if not our sovereignty?"

"Young man," Mr. Lund said. "Death is the price you pay for sin. I can only answer your question by returning to my old friend John Donne and say, 'Don't ask for whom the bell tolls.' Do you know what comes next? I bet you do. Why don't you tell us."

For a moment the class sat gripped by the scene: a student challenging the authority of a lecturer; a lecturer insulting the intelligence of a student. Finally, after a painful pause, the lecturer claimed
the last word.

" 'It tolls for thee.' "

One of the most striking features of life at Cambridge is how overwhelmingly content the students seem to be. Unlike their peers
around the world, Cambridge students—both graduate and undergraduate—hold few demonstrations, march in few picket lines, and
attend almost no public rallies. As I wandered through Cambridge,
I found myself longing at times for the sight of a hand-painted
banner hanging from a window, a graffiti slogan spray-painted on a
wall, or even a student daring to walk on the grass, unaccompanied.
I longed for something—anything—that would demonstrate a
sense of vitality and independent thought. Students at Cambridge
not only walk on the sidewalks, but they wash behind their ears, eat
their vegetables, and even, like grown-ups, defend their leaders in
public.

This sense of filial loyalty lies at the heart of the Cambridge tradition and, therefore, is not left to chance. Traditionally, Oxbridge
colleges have fulfilled part of their founding covenants by providing
graduates who would go forth from their halls to serve the state as
clergy in the Church, officers in the military, or diplomats in the
foreign service. Half the viceroys of India came from these two
schools, as did most of the prime ministers in the last two hundred
years. (One Cambridge great, Lord Cornwallis of Clare, is remembered for leading the British forces to defeat at the hands of the
Colonists in Yorktown, Virginia. Perhaps if he had studied international relations instead of Greek tragedy, I would have been able to
pay Commonwealth fees instead of the threefold foreigner rates to
eat beneath his portrait in the Clare College Hall.)

In short, when Britain was great, Oxbridge was great, and the
two worlds enjoyed a symbiotic success, with Cambridge and Ox-

ford like giant royal oaks that drew life from the realm and gave it back in turn through stability, shelter, and a steady supply of ripe, young fruit. For students the notion of duty long included military service. When Napoleon threatened the British Isles in 1803, nearly a quarter of the eight hundred students at Cambridge volunteered for the infantry corps. A century later students again flocked to fight for the Good and the Just in what they believed would be a Great War. In 1916 over three quarters of the three thousand registered students volunteered for military service, and those who remained were asked to assist the cadets who were training on campus. Sadly, most of the men who left for the Continent never returned to class. The war to end all wars may have been a military victory, but the loss of a generation of men and several generations of hope was nearly enough to fell the university and the youthful spirit it symbolized.

Students in particular felt the blow. Gone were the days of mindless abandon and extravagant wealth; gone were the times when young men flocked unquestioningly to the beck of the Crown. Oxbridge undergraduates once again fought for their country during World War Two, but not before the Oxford Union in 1933 passed a resolution saying it would never fight for King or Country, and not before Cambridge fought a similar battle that divided the faculty ranks. Far from the heroes of the past, the Cambridge students who made the greatest name for themselves in the mid twentieth century were Messrs. Philby, Burgess, Maclean, and Blunt, who sold their souls to the Soviet Empire and have come to be known to most of the world as the Cambridge Spies.

Fifty years later, the cynicism that bred the spies seems to have faded. Most students today seem remarkably patriotic and openly desirous of their place in the Establishment. Simon, like many, voted Conservative and disapproved of European unity. Ian, like nearly as many, planned to practice law and dreamed of becoming a member of Parliament. Even the head of the Cambridge Socialist Party wore a DJ to Union debates. Cambridge reinforces this sense of tradition and goes out of its way to cultivate it. For the university, the key to achieving its goal is the presence of over two dozen colleges that can monitor students' lives. Each college is set up along strict hierarchical lines, somewhere between a tight family and a loose prison. At the top is the master, a largely ceremonial title bestowed upon an aging don (or some other dignitary). Beneath the master is a group of senior officers, including the dean, the bursar, and the head tutor. Below them is the platoon of sixty fellows, who in effect hold ownership of the college and set its rules of conduct.

The colleges take their parenting duties extremely seriously. Beyond the myriad rules governing parties, music, and spend-the-night guests, colleges have a variety of other patriarchal tendencies. While waiting in the Clare Office one day, for example, I happened onto a guidebook for future students of the college. The booklet, written in a tone reminiscent of a free-market Mary Poppins, contained advice on how prospective students should spend the months before they come up to Clare. It included tips on traveling (*If you are going abroad, you should plan the trip carefully and make the necessary preparations in good time*), looking for work (*Earning as much money as possible is a perfectly legitimate aim: money greatly enhances the quality of life*), and even padding one's C.V. (*Typing is a skill that will be useful for the rest of your life. Many jobs have secretarial support, but sometimes you will have to do your secretary's work as well. So acquire these skills now*).

It was almost unimaginable to me that an American university would send such a booklet to its students (*Maybe you should learn to tie your shoes; Don't forget to look both ways*). But in Cambridge, where college fellows are considered *in loco parentis*, such activities are normal. Indeed, I came to believe that what I was witnessing in Cambridge was comparable to what I had seen in Japan, where schools regulate students' dress, the length of their hair, even the tread on their shoes. As late as the 1960s, for example, teams of Cambridge dons, known as bulldogs, used to patrol the streets at night penalizing students for not wearing the proper gown, or even the proper legwear (in days past, students were required to wear hose with their gowns instead of full-length trousers).

Of course, some students do rebel. One woman at Clare was famous for never wearing underwear; her boyfriend never wore shoes (whether he wore underclothes was not as readily apparent). But conformity still rules most endeavors at Cambridge—even down to spelling. Several weeks after our dinner at Ian's, I went to visit Cyprian, who was busy correcting proofs of his Ph.D. thesis that the Cambridge University Press was about to publish. One matter, however, was delaying publication: the name of the greatest Roman poet. Cyprian wanted to spell his name *Vergil;* the Press insisted on *Virgil.*

"It's ridiculous," he said. "Academic totalitarianism. The *e* was changed to an *i* in the Middle Ages to echo the Virgin Mary, the mother of Christ, the source of Western culture."

"And what's wrong with that?"

"It's dishonest," he said. "Vergil didn't believe in Christ. He hadn't even been born. The name should be spelt with an *e.*"

"So why can't you?"

"The chairman of my faculty says the name has an *i,*" he said, "so for anyone who wants to get published, it does. He's such a Sagittarius."

As with secondary schools in Japan, Oxford and Cambridge act as surrogates—both for students' families and for the state. Students may resent the intrusion, but they know that those who comply with the rules and mind their *p*'s and *q*'s will be rewarded with a place in the Establishment. After all, two thirds of upper-level civil servants still come from Oxbridge, as do a similar percentage of top-level bankers and barristers. In many ways, Oxbridge is like a giant finishing school and the code of conduct the colleges enforce is, in effect, a pledge of allegiance for the ruling class. Ironically, the leading enforcers of this code are not the masters and fellows of the colleges, nor the professors and lecturers of the university, but the people who have much closer contact with the students and much greater influence over their lives: the porters of the colleges, the unspoken parents-at-large.

"Bruce, how do you do it? You're a ladies' man."

Terry handed me a written message that Thursday afternoon as I stepped into the Porters' Lodge. The Lodge, a crowded foxhole at the foot of the giant archway that leads into Memorial Court, featured two walls lined with mail slots, called pigeonholes, one wall plastered with outdated announcements, and one wall filled with duplicate keys for the daily gaggle of students who locked themselves out of their rooms. The responsibilities of the porters are somewhat vague but seem to resemble the duties of a ruling junta in a Third World dictatorship. They issue visas to visitors, deport illegal aliens, control all the incoming and outgoing mail, and maintain paramount authority over the one telephone in the college where all the students and most of the professors receive their incoming calls. In addition, they also possess the only keys to the gates of the college, which they lock every night at 2 A.M. with penitentiary finitude.

"I'm afraid I'm far from a ladies' man," I said. "If anything, I have the opposite problem. I'm in a slightly awkward position with a woman on my hall."

"Ah," he said. "Young Halcyon."

I looked at him, dumbfounded. "How do you know?"

"I told you," he said, "it's my business to know what goes on in this college." He moved from behind his swivel chair and handed me a message. "Anyway, maybe this will help you. A young lady from King's telephoned today and invited you to her birthday party."

I looked at the memo. "This is no help. She doesn't even like me. I'm more worried about the situation closer to home. I've tried to be indirect with her, Terry. I don't want to ruin our friendship. But she doesn't seem to get the message."

"I've seen this kind of thing before around here," he said. "But whatever happens, just remember this: always be a gentleman—be honest and direct—and you'll never have anything to be ashamed of. That's what we try to teach you at Clare."

"Is that the college motto?"

"Why, it's the British motto," he said. "The Dunkirk spirit. Never sacrifice your principles. Never drop your chin. In the end, it'll all work out. We learned that during the Second War."

"I guess what they say is true," I said. "You Brits don't easily forget."

He tugged smugly at his lapels. When he had finished, I asked him if he liked the job of turning teenagers into ladies and gentlemen.

"Are you asking me a serious question?" he said.

"I'm trying."

He took out his pocket watch and checked the time. "I'm going to Old Court exactly at eight to have my tea with Richard," he said. "But let me try to answer your question."

He sat down on his swivel chair and began telling me the story of how he became a porter at Clare. Originally enlisted into the Royal Air Force, Terry quit his post in the early 1950s and went to work for the Royal Mail. Several years into his job, however, he was knocked unconscious one afternoon by a football, "what you Americans call a soccer ball"; and six months later, after recurring bouts of vertigo, he was asked to leave. Frustrated, he took up retail, went back to school, and became a manager in a friend's sporting goods' store. Again, however, his luck ran out and the store went bust. "At the ripe old age of thirty-two," he recalled. "I was finished . . . washed up." A friend asked him to join Clare. All his family had been around the university—his great-grandfather and grandfather had been porters; his mother had been a bedder—so he decided to give it a try.

"I find the job is quite challenging," he said. "There's a side of me that I like—the friendly side—and I use that as much as I can. But sometime I have to use that other side. I don't like giving people a wiggle in the ear, but I do it if I have to. Take the other night at that party in the attic. Every year the kids in the novice boats think they have to lose it all in one night. They've heard the stories about drunkenness in the previous year and think they have to top them. Somebody invariably gets hurt. Last year we had a boy running around the Bridge and barking like a dog. We had to take him to hospital."

"So you never lose control, do you?"

"If we didn't have certain rules around here, it would turn into a jungle. In the past, people used to go into the army. That taught them discipline. But now they have to get it in school. Every year about a hundred and twenty freshers drop through that gate, plus another dozen graduate students. Out of that hundred and twenty, about five or so usually think that being friendly and outgoing is a sign of weakness. They have to break the rules to show off. So I try to show them what it means to be members of this college. *Freedom* is one of the scariest words, Bruce. Many of these students don't know what it means. We have to keep them in line and let them know that they have a certain responsibility to uphold the tradition of the college."

I looked around the office—the portable stove, the walkie-talkie, the black-and-white television with the sound turned down. "So do you like it?"

"Well, I enjoy the architecture, the life-style, and of course I enjoy being deputy head porter of Clare College." He nodded his head in deference to the title and straightened up in his chair, as he might have done to the first deputy head porter he ever met and, no doubt, as I was supposed to be doing to him. "But I think what I enjoy most is the kids. . . .

"The students come in and talk to me when they have a problem. I remember a young girl from Edinburgh who was around here when they were building the library in the middle of Memorial Court, you know the one that Prince Philip came to dedicate. She was pretty to look at. Not attractive, you might say, but not unattractive. Well, the boys who were working on the library were whistling at her one day, so I put them straight with a chat. Several weeks later a young boy from Trinity was pestering her. One night I was on patrol when I heard him being a bit too familiar for my tastes. They were having a row in the middle of the court and, well, I put him out of the college. Several days later she wrote me a letter thanking me for my assistance. What I had done anyone would do. A little kindness goes a long way—"

The telephone rang abruptly. Terry straightened his glasses and moved to the edge of his seat.

"Now go on," he said. "Get out of here. That's Richard giving me a call. Nothing waits for tea, my friend. Nothing waits for tea."

VII

SHARKING

How to Pick Up a Rhodes Scholar

Half-past one,
The street-lamp sputtered,
The street-lamp muttered,
The street-lamp said, "Regard that woman
Who hesitates toward you in the light of the door . . ."

—T. S. Eliot
"Rhapsody on a Windy Night," 1917

Simon knocked on my door at ten minutes to noon, rapping against the *Guardian* headline I had taped beneath my name: MIND OF A SCHOLAR, BODY OF A LIBERTINE.

"Wake up, Mr. Feiler," he shouted in his high-mocking tone of public school English. "Get your libertine body out of bed."

I pulled the covers from around my head and crawled to the end of the bed.

"Turn the knob," I grunted. "It takes three hands."

"Good morning," he chirped as he bounded through the door. "I just came to bring back your gown."

"How was the dinner?" I asked, falling back on my pillow and straining through chalky eyes.

"Halcyon and I sat across from Dr. Jones. I don't think he liked me very much. I was told I could be 'sent down' for wearing an M.A. gown." He hung my gown on the hook behind the door and flopped down in my chair. "Then I went home and indulged in some stimulation."

"With Halcyon?"

"Not with Halcyon, fool. Her heart is set on you. With my neighbor, Kiet Khiem Koh. I call her Triple K. She came into my room around midnight and caught me in bed with no clothes on. She sat down on the end of the bed and started talking, and it was only a matter of time before— Why, Bruce," he said when he had settled in and caught a good look at me, "did you consume vast quantities of alcohol last night?"

"Don't bother me," I said. "Finish your story."

"I don't need to," he said. "You know the end. Now tell me, how were your parties?"

"I only made it to one."

"What time did you get home?"

"Quarter to seven."

"Good God," he said, "you're worse than me. Did you have a stimulating conversation?"

"You could say that."

"Was it debauched?"

"Worse," I said.

"What do you mean? What could be worse than debauchery?"

"Genuine attraction."

It was eight-thirty on the previous night when I emerged from the bath and stood dripping wet on my orange floor mat wondering what to wear. At the Crew Meal I had kept my tie laced all night and felt donnishly overdressed. The following week I had worn sweats to a party in Cauis and felt sophomorically underdressed. Cambridge parties, I realized, bring out the extremes—a student population that all week conforms to a standard fare of dark pants, called trousers, and baggy sweaters, called jumpers, rushes to the edges of its cupboards on weekends to make dramatic statements. I, on the other hand, had few extreme clothes and was forced to choose middle-of-the road gray striped trousers and a maroon button-down shirt. Mind of a libertine, wardrobe of a scholar.

After dressing down I grabbed my requisite bottle of red wine and walked out of Mem Court past the University Library—a one-block mud-brick monstrosity topped by a twelve-story tower that some member of the Royal Family is reputed to have labeled "the largest erection in Britain"—and headed toward the Grasshopper Lodge, which houses students from King's.

PARTY UPSTAIRS, said an envelope attached to the door. PLEASE RING 14, 15, OR 18.

I rang 14. Nothing happened.

I rang 15. Nothing happened.

Then a woman using the building's pay telephone opened the door and let me in. The party, she said, was in room 18.

"Oh, Bruce, thank you for coming," gushed the hostess, Melinda, as I arrived at the door and tendered my wine. "Come in and have a drink. Let me introduce you to my friend Serge."

I knew no one at the party other than Melinda, who had invited me to her birthday bash despite having decided during our previous meeting that my knowledge of philosophy was sufficiently tertiary to disqualify me from stimulating conversation. Despite my murky intellectual status and the usual difficulty of mingling in Britain, however, I managed to meet three people in the course of the evening.

The first was Serge.

"I'm a socialist," he said. "I don't believe in parties."

Serge was wearing a mustard blazer and a green silk tie.

"Cambridge must be difficult for you," I said. "How do you

manage to be a socialist with all these public school boys running around in their *Brideshead* clothes?"

"They're an anachronism," he said, "just like the Royals. And besides, they're always drunk."

The second was J.B.

"I'm a Buddhist," he said. "I don't believe in God."

J.B. was dressed in ripped black jeans and a leather jacket.

"I guess that means you never go to Chapel."

"I go every week. It's a great place to meditate. I just sit in a comfortable spot, cross my legs, and concentrate on my breathing."

"Sounds like going to lectures."

"Except you come out relaxed."

The third was her.

"I'm Rachel," she said. "I don't believe we've met."

During my time as a single man in Japan, I was given clear, albeit tongue-in-cheek, advice on how to pick up a Japanese girl. Befitting the formulaic culture of Japan, the rules were very explicit, from the pickup line ("Would you like to drink some tea?") to the check-in desk (an illuminated bank of photographs at a rent-by-the-hour "love hotel"). In Britain the native culture is hardly less formulaic, but the rules for a single student at Cambridge are considerably more complex. To begin with, unlike the ski slopes and department stores where I was told to go scoping in Japan, there are almost no locations outside of college for single students to meet. Except for the library, with its bookish limitations, and the pub, with its inebriatic illusions, few places in town receive anything resembling a cross section of students. As a result, the first rule of sharking in the fishbowl of Cambridge is to nibble at every bait.

"I'm Bruce," I said. "I believe you're right."

I stuck out my hand, which she took in hers with a commanding grip that rippled up her uncovered arm to the arc of her upturned smile. Her hair rained black in well-combed streaks, her neck was as tall as the library tower, her shoulders were covered with a black leotard that scalloped at her breastline toward her leather-belted pants and the pointed boots on her feet. With dark green eyes and ivory skin, she had all the regal aura of Princess Diana, except for a notably pronounced English nose that was more reminiscent of Prince Charles. She was not my type; she was probably not my sign. I couldn't let go of her hand.

"Would you like a drink?" she said.

"Sure. I mean—I have one. Well, yes." I smiled, putting down my half-empty glass and picking up a full-empty one from the table. "What do you have to offer?"

"Just wine."

"That's fine."

"Why don't I take your glass."

She took my glass and filled it with standard PBAB vintage—Bulgarian table wine—as I plucked a piece of pecan cake from a pan and leaned against the fake fireplace to steady my hand. Rachel, she told me, was not at Cambridge but at Oxford. She was not from Britain but from Canada. She was a Rhodes Scholar.

"I'm reading English," she said. "It's extremely exciting. Language here is so clear."

"But the English are so understated," I said. "American English is much more direct."

"Americans," she said, "are much more direct. The English are more precise."

Among students, tourists, even professors, there is one indisputable manner in which Cambridge promotes love: it is an incredibly, at times overwhelmingly, romantic place. For some, the charm is in the setting. Cambridge, wrote Henry James, boasts "the loveliest confusion of Gothic windows and ancient trees, of grassy banks and mossy balustrades . . . of single-arched bridges spanning the little stream, which is small and shallow and looks as if it had been turned on for ornamental purposes." For others the appeal is in the students. "So many happy youths," wrote Wordsworth. "So many divers samples from the growth of life's sweet season." But for many the spell is in the stunning number of poets who lived and wrote in Cambridge. For as long as the university has existed, its legacy has been passed down in verse from one generation to the next: Milton swam in Spenser's river. Wordsworth sat under Milton's tree. Tennyson walked over Wordsworth's bridge.

Women, of course, were long kept away from this sacred core. Virginia Stephen, daughter of eminent don Sir Leslie Stephen and future wife of Leonard Woolf, complained that she was forced to eat plain soup and prunes at a nearby "women's college," while her male friends enjoyed partridges, pudding, and, most importantly, stimulating conversation around the tables at King's. "I have to delve from books painfully all alone," she wrote to a friend, "what you get every evening sitting over your fire and smoking your pipe with friends." Over time, she, more than anyone, helped eliminate this state of affairs with a memorable portrait of Cambridge men in *Jacob's Room* and a powerful manifesto for Cambridge women in *A Room of One's Own.*

As a result, women at Cambridge these days have not only joined the conversations but also joined the hunt. In Japan, the process of *nanpa,* or picking up dates, is mostly a one-way affair, with the men making most of the moves. In Britain, however, especially at its elite universities, the game of sharking is much more of a two-way street. Thus, if rule number one is to nibble at every bite, then rule number two when sharking in Cambridge is to strike a pose of mutual respect.

As Rachel and I slipped into conversation, I slowly leaned my elbow on the hearth to my left. Without seeming to notice, I watched as she pressed her shoulder slowly against the same fake fireplace. After several more minutes, when it became apparent she did not plan to flee, I extended my hand in Sistine Chapel fashion along the top of the mantelpiece in an outrageous gesture that anyone watching would have taken for a move to touch her arm. Finally, after Melinda announced that everyone was going dancing in the King's cellars and Rachel responded that she was staying at

Melinda's to continue her conversation with me, I took the final plunge into deep-sea sharking by lifting my left arm à la John Travolta in *Saturday Night Fever,* leaning it against the wall, and cocking my body in a mock disco pose by crossing my left leg over my right. Rachel reacted by taking one step forward into the empty room and tilting her head into the flagrant void left by my upturned arm.

The telephone rang.

"Should we answer it?" I said, secretly cursing my fortune and thinking to myself, "I can't believe King's has phones."

"Sure," she replied. "I'll answer it."

To my chagrin, she walked to the other side of the room to pick up the receiver, and to my horror, she knew the person on the other end of the line. It was a he. He was calling from Oxford. They joked about a previous conversation. She invited him to her place for dinner the following night. She stood on her feet and arched her back. Her voice took on the rising tone of someone being tickled.

My heart sank. I sat down on the floor. I looked for something to occupy my mind and settled on a poster of a Sumo wrestler and tried to practice my Japanese.

"That was a friend from Oxford," Rachel said after she returned to the room and plopped down on the floor directly in front of me. "He called to wish Melinda happy birthday."

I stayed silent and waited for a hint.

"He's actually something of a playboy," she said. "He likes to have a lot of girlfriends and avoid commitment. Recently, someone fell in love with him, but he lost interest. I told him he should try having a serious relationship, and he called to tell me he was trying."

"That was fast," I said. "When did you tell him that?"

"Yesterday."

Although the news from Oxford was not that bad, the call still had a shrinking effect, like an incident of *sharkus interruptus*. After several more minutes of rather tepid conversation, Rachel stood up, announced she was going to bed, and began to clean the room. I helped carry some paper plates into the gyp, then ducked into the

W.C. for some reevaluation. Here I was, the last person at a party where I hadn't known a soul, engrossed in a conversation that had moved from get-to-know-you to know-you-and-like-you-too, and the person whom I was actively sharking and who moments earlier seemed to be sharking me too had declared she was ready for bed and begun to tidy the room of someone who wasn't even there. Not my idea of debauchery. I decided to throw in the towel.

"I think I might go over to the Perestroika Bar after all," I said when I returned to the gyp.

"What's the Perestroika Bar?"

"It's what everyone else calls the King's cellars. Inside is a dungeon of grey concrete block, with tie-dyed paintings on the wall and big black letters that say P-E-R-E-S-T-R-O-I-K-A. Communism may be dead, but King's students are still trying to reform it."

She paused for a moment, then said, "What's it like?"

"It's radical chic. All the women wear leather jackets and most of the men wear punk black shoes with those one-inch rubber soles. It's the only place I've been in Cambridge where the number of motorcycle helmets was higher than the number of pin-striped shirts."

"Sounds exciting," she said, throwing her own towel into the kitchen sink. "I think I'll go."

Hope sharks eternal.

"Now remember," I said as we arrived at the door, "you have to admire King's chapel before we go underground. You'll enjoy the cellars more if you know they're just beneath 'the climax of Western civilization.' "

Call me Ishmael. Call me hooked. But as Rachel and I walked the fifteen minutes to King's in search of Melinda's party, our relationship shifted into a kind of one-to-one tuition of the most seductive variety. If, as Captain Ahab once said, whaling was his Harvard and Yale, then surely it's possible for students in Britain to say that sharking can be their Oxford and Cambridge. As it was, my shark was shaping up to be an extended pop test in deciphering a text. As Rachel and I secretly surveyed each other, I tried to search for clues in her behavior as to her general interest in the subject of snogging. Unfortunately, during most of the walk she kept her hands deep in her pockets and focused her eyes directly ahead. She also dragged her feet. Every now and then, however, as she paused to consider whether to bite on a piece of raw bait I had tossed her way ("How long will you be in town?" "Would you like to meet my bedder?"), Rachel would tilt her head ever-so-slightly in my direction, a move that so filled me with desire that I would lurch my suddenly erect neck toward hers in the hopes that our heads might rub up against each other and that, from the static, a spark might fly.

It didn't happen. And when we finally arrived at King's and paid our respects to the Chapel, we turned, still not touching, toward the cellars. The door was locked. We knocked on a window; no one answered. We tried a side door, it led to the library. We tried another, it led to the kitchen.

"They must have gone fishin'," I finally remarked.

"But where?" she said.

"The Cam?"

"Don't be silly. We have to find them. They couldn't have got far. Cambridge, after all, is much smaller than Oxford."

"I'll take that as a challenge."

We started back toward Grasshopper Lodge, and in the rush we picked up the chase. Whereas before, both of us had acted cautiously—circling, testing, and measuring each other only from afar, now we were both more aware of the game. Indeed, we started goading each other like nervous eight-year-olds in the door of an attic eager to prove we weren't afraid to proceed but secretly terrified. With each step in the dark we drew closer together, but if, by accident, we happened to touch, we would both recoil in nervous laughter, while I, at least, would try to think of a way to make it happen again.

After checking the river and beneath the bridge, we arrived at the giant iron gate of King's, which—though still before two—was locked, trapping us in. Like any upstanding student not about to risk losing a potential shark to a college regulation, we scaled it. Actually, we skirted it, swinging around the side of the gate and landing, still apart, in a ditch. We brushed ourselves off and kept moving. The night was dark and growing wet. Up above, the mist had grown so dense we could no longer spot the library tower. Down below, we barely missed a pair of lovers entwined in an *X* underneath an orange streetlamp. No cars were out; no bicycles either. The only moving object we saw was a white pickup truck with an illuminated pink telephone receiver on its cabin that said FLYING PIZZA CORPS.

Back at Grasshopper, no one answered buzzers 14, 15, or 18. But then, as before, the same woman appeared. The party, she said, had been closed down at King's and was moved to the flat of a friend in a place called Owlstone Garden.

"Which is where?" I asked,

"Do you go here?" she said.

"No," Rachel answered. "We're from Oxford."

"In that case, go down this road, cross the street, and head past the park. After a while . . ." She paused to scratch her head. "I've never gone from this direction, so I'm not sure I can tell you how to get there. But anyway, go up this road, past the garden, then take a left."

"Do we need to look both ways?" I said.

Rachel hid her face. The woman shut the door. Our shark, like a catfish, had won a new life.

While Cambridge is an undeniably romantic place, which naturally serves to promote love, it is also, at times, an overwhelmingly dreary place, which naturally conspires to hinder it. Some people are turned off by the scenery. "Hail, horrors, hail!" wrote Thomas Gray. "Ye ever gloomy bowers, ye gothic fanes, ye antiquated towers." Others are dismayed by the people. "A mockery of the world," complained William Cowper. "[Mere] gamesters, jockeys, spendthrifts, and brothellers impure." If handled poorly, the occasional misery that comes with the place (like most places in England) can overwhelm even the most romantically inclined. But if handled wisely, the gloom and doom of Cambridge—the bad food and worse weather—can be put to good use. The secret, as ever, is wit. In Japan the seminal rule in making a good impression is not to talk too much. But in Britain, especially in Cambridge, the opposite is true: foreplay is in the tongue. Thus, rule number three when negotiating with a shark (or a sharkee) is to keep talking at all times.

"Can you answer a question for me?" I said to Rachel after we had moved away from the Grasshopper and were back in unknown waters again. "How is it that the British could have colonized some of the greatest culinary countries of the world—India, China, Malaysia—lived there for generations, and not returned home with a single spice?" Rachel acted insulted. "Why, it's because they have so much respect for their food that they don't want to spice it," she protested. "By boiling a potato for three days its 'true' nature is allowed to shine through."

"Well," I agreed, "that could explain a lot. Maybe the fog in Britain comes from overboiling potatoes."

Rachel laughed out loud, stumbling on the curb and lunging in my direction, thus allowing me in the levity of the moment to steady her arm, set her upright, and quickly withdraw my hand. The pace seemed to quicken. Swelling up, I moved closer.

"Take this word *overboil*," I said. "Perfectly decent word, but I didn't use it three times in my life before I came to Cambridge. Now I use it three days a week."

"I know what you mean," she said. "Did you know that the word 'bland' was invented to describe English food?"

I stopped in my tracks and started to say "Really?" when Rachel stopped, too, and told me it was a joke. To my chagrin, she had outwitted me; to my delight, she was now playing along.

Several moments later we arrived at an intersection and stopped to review how far we had come. Like two hares with no tortoise tendencies, we had raced through the early stages—the first glance, the first touch, even the first caress of the arm. But now we were entering fresh territory, and Rachel still seemed somewhat hesitant.

We rehearsed our directions. "Walk to first crossing, then past the park, and turn left at the next major road." Assuming this to be the first crossing, we continued, winding our way through a block of flats, past a pub closed down for the night, and arriving several moments later on a clear stretch of grass.

"This must be the park," Rachel said. Renewed, we set off down the path, groping and giggling with occasional teenage giddiness, until the trees over our heads began to close with a growing menace, the muddy patches under our feet expanded to the size of small lochs, and the dainty patch of garden green seemed to extend for miles beyond our path in an unending stretch of hillocks and valleys that slithered right up to the fog. With the wind howling across the plain and my mind quickly losing its way in the surging hormonal mist, I felt a bit like Heathcliff wandering the moors around Wuthering Heights.

"We may have taken a wrong turn," I suggested. "I think we're in Wales."

"Wales?" she said, lifting her voice. "That sounds foreboding."

In the darkness the mood had shifted. The sky had grown more agitated. The wind mussed up our hair. It seemed as though a biblical storm were brewing on the horizon. Rachel dashed from my side into the open field and stared out over the heath. Desperately seeking an excuse to take her in my arms, bring up the violins, and put my shark to a test, I spotted a hut to the side of the field, and in it saw a chance.

"I think I'm going to get out of the storm," I called, shamelessly exaggerating the mist we were in. "Maybe we should rest for a while."

Until this point, as a novice shark, I had dutifully followed the rules—sampled the bait, struck my pose, cracked a wit or two—yet sooner or later I had to breach the ultimate frontier.

"I like being out in the open," she replied. "It keeps me on my toes."

Snaked. Far from a captain of the seas, I felt at this point more like a hack taxidermist: my shark, in short, had been stuffed.

When I was in college, a friend and I used to have a theory about what time of the night things happened on dates. Our formula went roughly as follows: before twelve o'clock both sides are cautious and nothing ever happens. Between midnight and two a small window of opportunity prevails. But later, between two and four, both sides are so tired that neither has the energy for ignition. Then, after four, both parties become so desperate to stop talking they usually end up in each other's arms. For me the last option seemed the only choice. Having failed as Ishmael, Heathcliff, and Romeo, I was left in the end playing Oliver Twist, hoping against hope for a little bit more.

At close to three o'clock in the morning, we finally emerged at the far side of the field into a crowded neighborhood of prefab houses that seemed more than several centuries removed from the medieval grandeur of Cambridge. Defeated, downcast, and thoroughly drenched, we decided to abandon our quest for Melinda's party and try and find our way back toward town. With all the pubs closed at eleven, however, and all the "convenience" stores closed at seven (the British imported the 7-Eleven from America, but somehow switched the numbers in transit and ended up with only 11-Sevens), we had no one to ask for directions.

"Wait!" Rachel cried after several wrong turns and more than several dead ends. "I hear something."

"What?" I said.

"Her."

"Who?"

"Melinda."

"Be serious."

"I am."

"But where?"

"Up there."

Rachel followed the lure of laughter, wandering up our road, down an alley, into a garden, and to the base of a wall, where two floors up a light shone from a window where a party was under way.

"Hello!" we cried, but no one answered.

"Help!" we tried, but no one came.

Finally, we tossed stones at the window until a shadow appeared in the light.

"It's them!" someone shouted.

"It's us," we agreed.

Relieved, revived, yet somehow reluctant, Rachel and I made our way toward the door and waited for it to open. And in the hour of that final moment, with nothing left to lose, I lifted my arm to touch Rachel's back and felt my finger, long since numbed by the cold, slide through the chill of her tightly wound scarf and brush the flint of her naked neck. At that instant the night must have struck four, for the door flew open with a brilliant spark, flashing night light into our owlish eyes and capturing Rachel as she glanced at my face and kissed it from afar.

"And . . ."

Ian was sitting on the edge of my bed, having come in from fencing practice as I was telling the story to Simon.

"And nothing," I said. "We went inside, had peppermint tea and chocolate cake, and when the sun came up, I came home."

"No shag?" Ian said.

"No shag," I confirmed.

"No snog?" Simon asked.

"No snog," I conceded. "But I did get her telephone number."

"That's not a shark," Simon protested. "It's more like a gold-fish."

"No, wait," Ian said, pounding his fist into his hand. He had thrown off his jumper when he arrived in the room and was sitting on my bed, guzzling my milk and eating his way toward the last crumb of a box of Cadbury Fingers. "This is good. It must be good.

Why else would he get all teary-eyed over a conversation about potatoes? I knew you had it in you, Bruce. That's it, you must be in love." He reached to embrace me.

"Wait," I said when I had wiped his crumbs off my face. "I don't know if it's love. I don't know if it's a shark. In fact, I don't even know how to tell the story because I don't know the ending."

"You're so *old,*" Simon said with more derision than respect. "You think too much. If this is what it's like to get an M.Phil., I think I'll politely decline." He stood up and announced he was going to lunch. Ian got up to follow, remembering as he did that he had brought along my morning post.

"Oh no," I uttered reflexively, as I flipped through the meager pile. "There's a letter."

"Who from?" Simon asked.

"Don't be naff," snapped Ian.

"Dear Bruce," I read aloud from my seat on my bed. She mentioned she was tired, still a little bleary-eyed, and apologized for any English expressions that were not completely precise. And then she dropped in those man-eating words "about last night . . ."

She had enjoyed meeting me, she said. Our conversation was stimulating. But perhaps, she realized, she should have thought to tell me she was involved with another man . . .

In despair I fell back on my pillow, hearing only the echo of a silent splash. My story finally had its ending: Perhaps there was a chance we might be able to keep in touch.

VIII

RACING

Head over Heels

I met a solid rowing friend, and asked about the Race.
"How fared it with your mind," I said, "when stroke
   increased the pace?"
But Five made answer solemnly, "I heard them fire a
   gun,
"No other mortal thing I heard until the Race was
   done."

               —R.C. Lehman
               "Trinity Boat Song," 1901

The river on race day was a road of dreams, roused by an unlikely shower of sun that spiced the bleak December sky like
a splash of orange pekoe in a steady diet of Earl Grey. The road of
dreams was filled with ghosts—skulls and swans and owls out of
sight, as well as the vision of novice-shell crabs that danced like
devils in the mind's eye of every virgin crew. The ghosts of races
past were alive and bright: red on the oars of the St. John's boys,
purple on the backs of all the King's men, and pink on the necks of
the Girton girls cheering from the bank. It was a rainbow of color
when we arrived at the start, but the crew of gold was at the wrong
end.

"Hey, Clare, bloody hell! Where the bollocks have you been?"

A crew-cut student with a megaphone and a giant clipboard was barking instructions from the bank.

"Sorry," Halcyon cried with a hint of desperation. "We've lost our coach. We don't know where to go."

"If you don't hurry up, I'll tell you where to go." He flipped his green scarf around his neck. *"Now hurry down to the bicycle bridge and spin your boat around. Your number's almost up."*

At almost eleven o'clock in the morning three dozen novice boats were gathered in the narrowest part of the Cam for the start of the annual Fairbairns Race, the first of a series of competitions that marked Rowing Week of Michaelmas Term. The Fairbairns was designed as an endurance test for novice rowers, with boats taking off one after the other and rowing the complete length of the practice stretch in a timed race that usually takes the winners about fifteen minutes. It would be followed several days later by the Clare Regatta, a head-to-head elimination tournament to crown a novice champion. The most famous competition of all, the bumps, in which boats line up in a single file several lengths apart and try to catch the crew ahead while eluding the one behind, would not take place until Lent and Easter terms. For the Fairbairns, starting times for each boat were determined by the finishing times of the same boat in the previous year. The Clare Gentlemen's Second Novice Boat was starting ninth out of sixty-four.

"Buckle down, lads," said Max the Stroke. "This is our day."

"I have a question," said Charlie Chaplin from the bow. "What do we do if we catch a crab?"

"Don't think about it," said Goofy the Redhead. "If you don't think about it, it won't happen."

"But it might," he insisted.

"Peter would have told us if he were worried," said Max.

"But Peter's not here."

"Okay, Clare, take the chain. Madame, raise your hand when you're ready."

"Now, boys," Halcyon scolded. "Settle down. You know what to do."

"Be stylish," Max urged. "And mean!"

Pushing off from the bank with our starboard oars, we wobbled bow-and-stroke toward the middle of the Cam. Halcyon grabbed the garden chain that was stretched across the river at the starting line and positioned the boat pointing toward the first curve where the river banked to the left.

"All eight," said Halcyon in her formal tone. "At front stops."

We eased forward on our slides, bringing our knees to touch our chins, stretching forward our arms, and arching our backs with near Gothic symmetry. In Clare tradition each of us was wearing skimpy black shorts, a black T-shirt, and a slinky gold tank top, or singlet.

"Ready, boys," she called again. "Square your blades."

With the snap of sixteen wrists we dropped our blades beneath the surface and waited for the grip of the water to press against our arms.

"Balance the boat. Now count off."

"Bow. Two. Three. Four. *Five*. Six. Seven. Stroke."

Halcyon released the chain and pointed her hand toward the sky.

"Ten. Nine. Eight. Seven . . ."

The voice of the starter seemed to dim with every passing tone.

"Six. Five. Four . . ."

While the breath of the water seemed to rise and engulf the megaphone.

"Three. Two. One . . ."

Until the last gasp when both became one with the throbbing of my heart.

"Start."

It is a curious feature of Cambridge life that time is kept by the river. Students come and go, buildings rise and fall, but the river never changes. It remains today in the age of prose, as it was in the era of poetry, the ultimate test of time. And on the last day of that Michaelmas Term it taught a lesson to eight young men that you can't beat the river by pulling alone but must tie your individual ambition to the rhythm of the crew.

We pulled away from the starting line with a burst of speed, building with the second pull, leveling out with the third, but on the fourth stroke of the first test of the year, the seventh rower in the Second Boat of the House of Lady de Clare stuck his blade into the water and couldn't pull it out again, thus lumping his crew into a crab stew and thrusting his boat with its dangling limbs up onto the bank where it could hardly avoid the illicit temptation of walking on the grass. The Clare Gentlemen's Second Novice Boat began the day in ninth place but would return the following year as Number Sixty-four. The river ebbs, the river flows, but the river never forgets.

And when I returned to my rooms that day, I understood how the river gives life to reputations that last much longer than any exam. On my door was the familiar sign:

MIND OF A SCHOLAR,

BODY OF A LIBERTINE

But just below it was taped a swipe from the indelible wit of Simon Farrady:

LAUGHINGSTOCK OF THE CAM!

The next day she called.

I took the message from my pigeonhole and pretended only to walk to the nearest telephone. Her line was busy. I tried again. It was still busy. I counted halfway to a hundred, then called back. She wasn't there. I left a message. She called back. I got the message. I went to the phone. I tried again. She answered. We talked. I ran out of change. Then the next morning when practice was over, I took a bus to the coach, took a coach to the tube, and took a tube to the center of London where I met Rachel beneath Marble Arch at half past three.

We started walking.

Regent Street was awkward in the holiday lights. Picadilly Circus was clumsy with so many people around. The ducks in the water at St. James's Park were drifting without conviction and changing their course in midstream. We were overly courteous and increasingly expectant. We looked at each other in department store windows while pretending to look at the goods on display. We wandered and shopped and avoided discussion until we realized we had to stop moving and finally have something to eat.

She ordered chicken noodle soup.

We sat at a café across the street from Big Ben, where Rachel unfurled her purple scarf and laid it along with her matching beret over the chair in front of the window that overlooked the Thames. My sandwich was damp. She offered me a taste of her boiling broth, but with her fingers quivering just inches from my lips, she stopped herself, pulled her arm back, and clutched her lips in a wistful sigh. My stomach clenched in fear. She smiled at me across the table and began to tell her story.

She thought he was the love of her life.

Rachel had come to Oxford in pursuit of her past. Her parents, both lawyers, had met in England a generation earlier and eloped one weekend in the Lake District, without so much as sending a telegram to their families at home. Rachel had idolized her father since she was a child. All through high school and later university, she had worked as he did all day in school then studied as he did in the evenings at home, pushing, pulling, whatever it took, to recreate his passion for words and to succeed—through sheer dedication—in stealing his eye from his books. Rachel came to Britain to continue her quest—to read Shakespeare, Spenser, Milton, Keats, and other poets of the realm. She came to become a scholar. Then, in her first week at Oxford, she met a man. He was a historian,

passionate, intense, and the first person she had ever met who reminded her of her father. They began seeing each other and for a
year lived in a state of perpetual clinginess that English students call
being "married." They talked and traveled and punted and swam;
they did not, however, elope. Then, during the summer, things
began to fall apart. He graduated and moved to London. She got
sick and he stayed away. But worst of all, at the start of the year, he
met her father, who told his daughter that he did not approve.

Her soup had gotten cold.

Rachel was trapped in this confusion when she decided to visit
an old friend in Cambridge who was throwing herself a party. She
didn't go to meet anybody. If anything, she was hoping to avoid
other people by circulating around the room and serving the other
guests. But then she started talking and forgot her vow. Later she
went walking and got lost on the way. And by the time she realized
that there was more in the air than just fog, she was enjoying herself
so much she didn't know what to do. She still didn't know.

We got up to go.

Night had come when we stepped outside and the air was thick
with dabs of light that hovered around every lamp. We walked
down the stairs to the side of the Thames and strolled along the
Victoria Embankment. The absence of others made the night come
alive. The gulls bobbed for food at the edge of the river, the trains
shook the beams of Blackfriars Bridge. Rachel climbed atop the
iron sphinxes on the promenade like a character she was following
in *Mrs. Dalloway,* her favorite novel by Virginia Woolf. We started
up the steps of Waterloo Bridge and stopped in the middle of the
span, glancing right at the stretch of popcorn lights that surrounded
the cathedral of St. Paul, then left toward the peanut-brittle walls of
Westminster Palace and the lunar face of Big Ben, night-light of the
British Isles. We stared at the water for so long that it seemed for a
moment we were lost on our way and had once again arrived in
Wales.

"Excuse me."

A slightly stooped man in a dark brown coat tapped me on my shoulder and doffed his weathered top hat. "I hope you're both enjoying yourselves this evening. My name is Henry. I'm a bum. I wonder if I could trouble you for a quid tonight. I want to buy a drink."

I stared at him, stunned.

"I know this sounds quite odd," he continued. "Most bums would ask for money to buy food. But I can't lie to you, mate. I don't need food, I need a pint. So, there, what do you say?"

At that particular moment I could think of absolutely nothing to say.

"Very well," he said, as if not expecting a response. "Thank you very much. I hope you have a nice evening. Cheerio!"

He doffed his hat politely again and disappeared into the night. We stared at his shadow for a second, then looked at each other and laughed. After all my failed literary pretensions, the moment had all the unlikely charm of a Barbara Cartland romance. With the moon overshadowed by fluorescent streetlamps and any hint of perfume overwhelmed by sludge from the Thames, I ran my finger across Rachel's smile, and, standing in the road, above the river, we kissed on top of the bridge.

The entire college came out for the Clare Regatta. Simon, who was counting the nights until his return to his Japanese girlfriend by swapping all-body massages with his neighbor from Indonesia, joined the crowd at the Pike & Eel pub along the starting line and emerged at various times to run alongside Clare boats as they made their way toward the finish line, which was conveniently located across the river from the Plow—another pub. Ian pressed ahead with his courting of Louise and brought her to the afternoon regatta along with a basket of miniature soaps and jellies that he thought would make an appropriate end-of-term gift but that seemed in its overwhelming daintiness more like a consolation prize in a Ladies' Bingo Tournament. Cyprian, for his part, managed to talk Sophie, his French *amour*, into tromping around in the muddy grass as he tried to explain in pidgin Italian the basic rules of the game: *mano, corpo, scivolare*.

The boys in the boat were fairly relaxed. After our poor performance in the Fairbairns most of the crew had been deeply upset, cursing our coach for oversleeping, drowning their sorrows for underachieving, and snapping at one another like adolescent turtles. But after several more practices most of the rancor had been washed away and by the day of the regatta had been replaced with a new upbeat perspective. In violation of our strict but stylish dress code, Oliver, Number Six, wore bright green socks with Christmas trees on the sides. In mockery of the prerace guidelines, the crew performed a warm-up drill to the children's song, "Head, Shoulders, Knees, and Toes." And in defiance of all rules of decorum and etiquette, Max the Stroke led the boys in a rendition of our informal call-and-response cheer:

> Lift your heads and hold them high
> *(Lift your heads and hold them high)*
> Clare Second Men are comin' by
> *(Clare Second Men are comin' by)*
> I don't know but I've been told
> *(I don't know but I've been told)*
> Clare Second Men have poles of gold
> *(Clare Second Men have poles of gold)*

By the time we eased up to the starting line for our first race against Trinity Second Men, our confidence level had reached an all-season high.

"Gentlemen, are you ready?"

We slid our bodies forward and cocked our oars back. Halcyon reiterated the strategy: We would start slowly—with short, steady strokes—then escalate as the race progressed. She would count each stroke aloud.

"Ready all . . ."

We dropped our blades, she raised her hand, we waited for the start.

"Row!"

The first stroke of a race is at quarter pressure, the second grows to a half, and not until the third swing in the set do the blades arrive at their full-length stride, driving through the water with increasing speed—stroke four, five, six, seven—until splashing free at the count of ten in a burst of adrenaline. For the next several strokes the blades rise and fall in silent ebb with the river, until the uneasy pace of the boat settles down and the cox raises an alarm.

"Next . . . stroke, Power . . . Ten!"

In a surge of emotion all the rowers scream as one, then tug with sudden strength for ten "power" strokes. Beginning with a primal pull that starts in the balls of the feet, rolls up through the thighs, and climbs the ladder of the vaulted back to the boomerang of the arms, these ten strokes are the loudest yet, as the voices of the coaches and fans on the bank are lost beneath the din of the oars—slicing into the river and pushing against the onrush of time. For a moment, at the end of the Power Ten, the bank reemerges with its colorful cheer, but then, as before, comes a warning knell:

"Next stroke, Power Twenty."

At the beginning of the set, the thrill is intense and the boat begins to soar. But halfway through, the pain begins to raise its voice—louder than the fans shouting from the shore, stronger than the blades carving out the wake. Slowly, inevitably, like growing old, the thighs begin to quiver, the palms begin to burn, and the mind starts to rely entirely on reflex, leaving the body in a headless race like a chicken that continues to run after its head has been cut off.

"Five more, you're almost there."

The final five strokes are the easiest of all, like the last few steps up a mountainside. The blade seems to row right through the body, with the handle yanking the body forward on the slide and pushing it back with the man-made tide in the reverse of the cause and effect in place at the starting line. The ultimate stroke is a grunting jerk as we lift our eyes from the necks of the person in front and look out at the river in a hopeful scan. For a moment we search in desperation until settling in unison on the exhilarating sight of a boat in desperate eight-legged paddle several lengths behind.

"You did it!" Halcyon cried. "We won!"

We were not stylish that morning in December, we were hardly mean, but poised briefly at the head of the river and well ahead of our time, we were, for a moment, young.

The face-off came at one minute to midnight. The Clare Gentlemen's Second Novice Boat had gone on to win one more race in the afternoon, before losing in the round of sixteen to the First Boat from Caius. Our performance was good enough to restore a modicum of glory to the Clare Boat House and to make us the fastest Second Boat on the river, a feat of some distinction in the boatie world since most Second Boats are made of wood while First Boats are fiberglass. The Clare First Boat, meanwhile, leap-frogged all expectations and went on to win first place in the regatta for the first time in eleven years. Still, the biggest rivalry was within the college itself and the First and Second boats had yet to compete in head-to-head competition.

"Gentlemen, are you ready? Fill your mugs."

The hundred or so members of the Clare Boat Club were crowded in their DJs and evening gowns in the semidarkened cavern of the Clare Buttery. Earlier in the evening, after the regatta, the various teams and coaches of Clare had gathered in the ornate College Hall for the annual Boat Club Dinner. In addition to downing a three-course meal, we listened to platitudinous speeches from our supervising tutor ("All of you competed today. Some of you won; some of you lost. That is not only the nature of competition, it is also the nature of life"); we watched as several members of the club drank deathly sconces (a penalty drink for various offenders, like Peter the Coach, that consisted of milk, ouzo, raw egg, malt vinegar, and bitters whipped in a blender and served in a glass); and we passed around our embossed menus for everyone else to sign (from Leslie, "Love those corridor romances"; from Max, "Nice bow tie"; from Alice, "What happened to the tradition of beating the First Men's Boat?"). After dinner the club retired downstairs to answer the lingering question with the year's most important boat race.

"When you're ready, stand in line. Then count off from Bow."

A "boat race" is a classic team sport that surely is older than competitive rowing, and may even be as historic as the original Olympic games. In its current incarnation at Cambridge two crews stand face-to-face holding pint glasses of lukewarm British ale (a British pint, larger than its American cousin, is similar in size to a tennis ball can), which they drink in rapid succession from stern to bow in a race that defies not only all laws of intoxication but also most conventions of common sense.

"Bow. Two. Three. Four. *Five*. Six. Seven. Stroke."

"Are you ready?" called the starter as the club pressed tightly round. "Drink!"

The burst of cheers from the surrounding fans was as strong as on the river that day. At first came the coxes, two diminutive ladies who were exempted from downing pints of beer and given shots of brandy instead, and they were followed by the rows of novice lads. Max, going first, showed his experience and pushed off with great verve, being careful not to spill a drop on his shirt and to finish as per instruction by turning his glass upside down on his head to reveal no drool inside. Number Seven, our soft-shell crab, experienced some difficulties, pausing several times to take a breath; Number Six nearly incurred a penalty by dribbling down his neck. The cumulative effect of our disappointing stern was that by the time the race arrived at me our team was behind by nearly half a pint, a positively insurmountable lead for a supposedly over-the-hill American weaned on cold, watery beer. Drawing on the reserve of an empty stomach (I had drunk merely half as much that night as any other competitor in the race) and a vast array of international experience (I had, after all, already been through college once), I swallowed my pride in true service to my country and crew, closed my eyes, opened my gullet, and poured the bottomless pint of ale directly into my soul.

When I looked up several seconds later, I saw beer in the glass of Number Five across from me and felt a surge of patriotic glory, not only for the Second Novice Crabs but also for that turncoat country that crowned Budweiser king. Number Four finished his pint smoothly; Goofy, at Three, had no trouble at all; Number Two experienced a slight delay when Number Seven distractingly lurched over in place and began to refill his glass from the bottom up. But before the judges had a chance to make a ruling on this regurgifraction, Charlie Chaplin began to drink the final pint in a lip-to-lip race with his opposite number to determine the novice champs. The teammates gathered around their Bows. The club members climbed atop the chairs. Finally, at ten minutes after midnight, six weeks after the start of the season, on the last day of Michaelmas Term, the smallest of the rowers in the largest club in college tossed his glass into the air and for the fourth year in a row the Gentlemen's Second Novice Boat defeated the Gentlemen's First Novice Boat in the *official* Clare College Boat Race.

She came in without knocking.

I had taken off my DJ and my unstained shirt and was standing bare-chested in my side-striped pants holding a toothbrush under the tap. Outside, the threat of winter was pressing hard on the temples of the window. Inside, only my bedside lamp was burning, giving the room the lopsided feel of a half-formed recollection. Consumed by my own reflections, I reeled at the shock of cool fingertips dripping down my spine.

It was Halcyon, standing in her Chinese robe.

"Why didn't you tell me?" she said.

"Why didn't I tell you what?"

"You know what I'm talking about. You didn't tell me, but I found out anyway. I know all about her."

"About whom?"

"Susanna."

"Susanna?" I said, relieved. "There's nothing to know about her."

"Don't lie to me!" Halcyon shouted. "I saw. I saw the umbrella outside your room the other night. That wasn't your umbrella. It was hers. And to think that you would do it right here on our hall."

Since the Crew Meal my relationship with Halcyon had rapidly deteriorated. Gone was the sense of shared exploration. Gone was the feeling of joint espionage. In their place was a new mood of tension. For my part, I went out of my way to avoid being too friendly, sneaking by her door when I came home at night, dashing by her room when I went to the bath. Halcyon, meanwhile, became even more friendly, bringing me gifts, baking me cookies, and sliding messages under my door just moments after I had gone tiptoeing past her room. With doors opening and closing, people coming and going, the atmosphere seemed like a British sex farce, except we weren't British, we hadn't had sex, and neither of us could act. At one point, as the farce began slipping toward drama, Halcyon even went to see Ian to get some direction from him. No subtle thespian himself, Ian managed to throw oil on a burning house by giving her a copy of Ovid's *Art of Love* and drawing her attention to one line: "Love is a kind of warfare; every lover is a warrior."

"That wasn't Susanna's umbrella," I said to her. "It was Ian's. I was in his room late that night and it started to rain."

"Do you know what it's like?" she said. "Do you know what you do to me, walking in and out of your room, running up and down the stairs?"

"Halcyon," I said. "You have to believe me. I'm not trying to hurt you. It's just . . ." What followed was one of those horrible impromptu speeches, the equivalent of a "Dear John" chain letter, which everyone hates when they receive, but which no one can resist passing on. Several months later, after I had inelegantly passed on that letter myself, Simon told me a story that Halcyon had told him. The previous year, following an incident in which her fiancé in Hong Kong broke off their engagement, Halcyon became extremely distraught. To recover she retreated to an aunt's home in Birmingham where she stayed for a year before coming to Cambridge. When I heard that story, I felt I finally understood what had happened between us; that night I still did not.

She started to cry. She leaned her head against my chest and relaxed her fists into open palms. Then just as suddenly as before, she stood up and took a step back.

"Where are you going?" she demanded.

"When?" I asked.

"Over break."

"I don't know."

"I don't believe you."

"Okay," I said. "Spain."

"With whom?"

"Don't be ridiculous."

"With whom?"

"Why does it matter?"

"Is there somebody else?"

I stood on the floor in my bare feet. Halcyon stood just inches away. I realized at that moment that I had been horribly wrong about college life. When I left the "real world" and returned to school, I looked at the university as an endless river of friends and encounters I would row, row, row myself through, gently as a stream. The beauty of Cambridge only heightened this expectation. "It's so perfect," I heard a tourist exclaim from the Clare Bridge. "The river, the grass, the trees, and the sky . . ." But once on that river, I found I couldn't always maintain control. I could pull my weight and feel my way, but I couldn't control the people around me so that we all pulled together, in the same way. I couldn't control the river within us that flows in different directions. The real myth of Cambridge, I realized at that moment, is that life is but a dream.

"Yes," I said. "There's somebody else."

She took a step back.

"I knew it," she whispered. "I knew it all along. I can't stand this. I have to get out of here."

"Get out of here?" I said. "What are you saying?"

"Don't stop me," she said. "I know what to do. If you can go away without me, then I can go away without you."

She lifted her chin and pulled open my door.

"When you come back from your trip," she said, "I won't be here to get in your way."

"You're not in my way," I said.

"Not anymore."

Halcyon walked across the hall and into her darkened room. I watched for a moment without saying a word and then lay back onto my bed, letting the wind cling to my body and leaving my door open onto the hall.

LENT TERM

IX

DATING

The Language of Love

Someone is always looking into the river near Waterloo Bridge; a couple will stand there talking for half an
hour on a fine afternoon; . . . sometimes the river is
opulent purple, sometimes mud-coloured, sometimes
sparkling blue like the sea.

—Virginia Woolf
The Voyage Out, 1915

The road was a glacier, snowed by the sky. The glacier was
slippery, swamped by the sludge. From the Thames to the
fens, all along the M-11, cars were splayed in an awkward sprawl
like fruit flies caught in a stream of glue. Shivering, I stood in the eye
of the maelstrom at Knightsbridge, craning at occupied black taxi-
cabs and looking forward to thawing out on the afternoon train
from Liverpool Street Station. I had come to London by myself the
weekend before term to meet a friend, see a show, and enjoy a last
tasty dinner before the abstinence of spice that would return with
the advent of Lent. All around me the city was tense. Terrorists
from the North had set off a bomb, closing down the Underground

for an anxious rush hour. The prime minister had stepped out of
No. 10, calling the act a cowardly deed and adding that the Crisis in
the East would not be cleared up without a fight. The climate was
moving from bad to worse, and the worse it got the colder it
seemed.

"Where're you going?" said the driver of my black snowmobile
as I waded through the knee-high drift and plunged into his cab.

"Liverpool Street Station."

"Have you been there before?"

"I was there yesterday."

"Sorry," he said, turning back to look at me, "I thought for a
moment you were a Yank."

"Actually," I said, "I am a Yank, except I was born in the South."

He peered into his rearview mirror with an admiring snicker.

"Nicely done," he remarked.

"Do you think so?" I said. "I'm trying to learn British wit."

As the taxi eased through the maze of tiny streets, the driver, a
young man with a stud earring, began asking me about England,
about America, and even about what he should buy his wife for her
birthday. In return, I asked him about London.

"I have this theory that Waterloo Bridge is the most romantic
place in London," I said. "What do you think?"

"Well," he said. "There're also bridges at Battersea and Chelsea.
On the Albert Bridge they have a sign that was written way back for
the troops. It says, PLEASE BREAK STEP WHEN CROSSING BRIDGE. Recently, however, someone crossed out STEP and wrote the word
WIND."

"That doesn't sound very romantic," I said.

"What's all this stuff about romance? Are you writing a poem or
something? If you ask me, a bridge is just one easy way of getting
from here to there without getting wet."

"I think they can be very romantic," I said. "Perhaps you should
take your wife."

"I don't think she'd go for it," he said. "She prefers the beach."

"Maybe you should bring her up to where I live."

"Where's that?" he asked.

"Cambridge."

"Aha," he said. "That explains it. You lot are meant to be poetic up there. Down where I come from, we're much more humble. If you ask me, the most romantic places in London are not the bridges but the roads. We've got top-notch motorways in England, pal, always flat and smooth. They may not have many poems written about them, but they're real nice on the tyres."

Arriving at the station, I paid the driver my fare and sent greetings to his wife. Heading through the snow-drenched corridors, I sloshed down the stairs, stepped onto the platform, and slipped through the doors of the 5:58 to Cambridge. I took off my coat, settled into my place, and had just begun to stretch my feet toward the open seat in front when the voice of the conductor burst into the air with a startling familiarity:

"Good evening, ladies and gentlemen, welcome aboard. I regret to inform you that due to weather conditions beyond our control I must ask you all to alight. . . ."

Ours was indeed a poetic romance.

In the weeks since our first kiss on Waterloo Bridge, Rachel and I had begun the exhilarating, yet awkward process of peeling off our protective skins and offering them to each other. In an endless stream of storybook encounters, we walked through ever-green parks in London as she told me about her first boyfriend, who sent her notes in Latin class. We watched the guards at Buckingham Palace as I told her about my first kiss in eighth grade while on a date to the circus. We walked and talked, retelling stories oft told before and forever reliving our trip to "Wales" until we transformed it into myth.

Yet rarely did we walk at home. Oxford and Cambridge may be linked by tradition, but they are hardly connected by public trans-portation. Since all roads in England lead literally to London, the only effective way to travel the sixty miles between Oxford and Cambridge is to take a train to London, switch stations by Tube, and take another out again. The trip takes three hours. Barring that, the only alternative is to board a coach that crisscrosses many M-motorways on a series of smaller A-level roads that are neither flat nor smooth. That trip takes four hours. Fed up with this romantic cul-de-sac, we flew to Spain at the end of Michaelmas Term and celebrated the New Year with a champagne brunch of Seville oranges, prune yogurt, and elephant-ear danish all served in bed on a stolen road sign. It was, in a word, romantic, poetic, illicit, ecstatic. It was also extremely traumatic.

Despite the magnitude of love to most university students, romance and scholarship would seem to require conflicting faculties. The first—romance—demands fealty to the heart, while the second—scholarship—loyalty to the mind. The problem is that students learn how to train their minds but are left on their own with matters of the heart. I, for example, had spent much more of my life in school than in love and, as a result, was much better at doing homework than conducting romance. Not everyone I knew had the same problem. Simon, for his part, reacted to the freedom of college life by indulging in a myriad of sexual fantasies he imagined as romance. Ian, on the other hand, responded to the wealth of women on campus by "falling in love" several times a day and following nameless Valentines around town and dreaming of starry-eyed romances that would never see the light of day.

As far as I could tell, my feelings on the subject seemed to fall somewhere between my two public school friends, who despite their opposite approaches were equally obsessed with the same primal quest. I was too romantic to be satisfied with an endless stream of sexual adventures and too analytical to believe that love could happen twice a day in the glint of an eye or the curl of a hair that triggered feelings closer to lust than spiritual admiration. My beliefs, when uttered out loud, seemed strident at best, self-serving at worst, and riddled with enough inconsistencies to be morally indefensible. In my defense, they had led me through the laboratory of love with most of my values intact. Yet they also had left me alone, with no brothel fines to my name. Thus, when I met Rachel near the end of first term and felt in one evening the twin blows of admiration and desire, I shut my mind down to academic skepticism and gave myself up to the promise of romance.

We wrote letters.

Short of port, the love letter seems to be the ultimate English aphrodisiac: why muck up in person what you can say better, and with more muse, in the mail? The post is notorious in Britain, often reflecting in the range of passion it incites both the pride and shame of the nation. On one side nothing in the country, with the exception of the weather, is the butt of more jokes. On the night I met Rachel, for example, I told her about my experience sending a letter to the United States by a special, "express" service. After two months my letter had yet to arrive. "Don't be silly," she said. "Don't you know that 'express' service only means they lose your letter faster?"

On the other side, the mail in Britain is a marvel of efficiency, on a par with what I witnessed in Japan. Post is delivered twice a day during the week and once on Saturday mornings. Letters posted late Tuesday in London, Oxford, or even Edinburgh, regularly arrive in Cambridge by Wednesday afternoon. This system enabled Rachel and me to maintain an almost daily correspondence that was better than that I shared with many of my friends in Cambridge, who, though they lived less than one mile away, had no telephones in their rooms, no free time, and no inclination to walk through the rain, climb up the stairs, and drop by my rooms for an unannounced chat, only to find me away. (The university's internal mail network, like its internal telephone service, takes three times as long as the national system.) Finally, to someone who had dreamed about those passages in the great Russian novels where lovers could correspond

furtively through the daily post and arrange a secret rendezvous on
an hour's notice, the postcards that came from Oxford every day
only heightened my sense of romantic escape.

The cards, like my fantasies, were mostly plagiarized.

As foreign students, Rachel and I were both allowed to remain in
our bed-sitting rooms after the British undergraduates went down
in December until the time they would come up in January. In
between our fleeting meetings I stayed home and read turgid text-
books on international law, while Rachel holed herself up in Oxford and read, underlined, reread, and notated the collected works
of Virginia Woolf. Her daily notes to me were taken directly from
English evenings past that still at century's end had the ability to
enliven the walls of my rooms.

From *The Voyage Out:*

Did love begin that way, with the wish to go on talking?

And the next day, from the same place:

She wished to kiss him. But all the time she went on spinning out words.

And the day after, the same:

During the two or three weeks which had passed since their
walk, half a dozen notes from him had accumulated in her
drawer. She would read them, and spend the whole morning in a daze of happiness.

The cards had paintings from Michelangelo, Leonardo, Tou-
louse-Lautrec, and one from Monet of a river in the morning,
which prompted Rachel to write on the top, "Monet in Cambridge? Oxford? On Waterloo Bridge? Funny how landscapes in
the fog all tend to look vaguely reminiscent of one another!"

From *The Waves:*

When we sit close together, we melt into each other with phrases. We are edged with mist. We make an insubstantial territory.

From *Jacob's Room:*

True, the words were inaudible. It was the intimacy, a sort of spiritual suppleness, when mind prints upon mind indelibly.

And occasionally from the inspiration of these cards, I might uncover an echo of Rachel in a passage from *The Waves:*

Now let me try, before we rise, to fix the moment in one effort of supreme endeavor. This shall endure. From discord, from hatred my shattered mind is pieced together by some sudden perception. I take the trees, the clouds, to be witnesses of my complete integration. Here on this ring of grass we have sat together, bound by the tremendous power of some inner compulsion . . . [All of this] hints at some other order, and better, which makes a reason everlasting. This I see for a second, and shall try to fix in words, to forge in a ring of steel: It is you I need; for it is you who inspires poetry.

Ours was indeed a poetic romance, it was words, and pictures, and, as she signed her name at the bottom of the cards, "Love, Love, Love."

Simon, for his part, was more prosaic.
"Come in, old man, I'm in trouble. Serious trouble."
I arrived at his door at close to midnight on Sunday night, after waiting for several hours in a crowded Liverpool Street Station and riding even longer on the only line out of London that British Rail

had managed to clear. Simon had come from Tokyo the previous
day before the snow had hit. His blue jeans, baggy sweaters, and
green striped boxer shorts were already strewn about his room.
Several new snapshots of his mother and father were pinned on the
bulletin board the college hung from our ceilings to ensure we did
not tape posters on the walls. A half-empty bottle of Bell's whisky,
an overflowing ashtray, and an open jar of crusty lemon curd (the
citron equivalent of peanut butter) lay open on the squat table,
where my wet Top-Siders and Simon's suede brogues settled themselves, tête-à-tête.

"Well," I said, "start at the top. Are we expecting a visitor?"

"The short answer is, no."

"What's the long answer?"

On his first day back in Tokyo, Simon met Emi. They went to a
bar in Roppongi, had a few drinks, and he advised her that he
thought a February visit would not be such a good idea. She should
think about her future, he said. Cambridge was no place for a young
girl who did not have a job or a place in school. She listened very
carefully, he said, and then she started crying. Simon felt horribly
guilty. "After a few more beers," he said, "we went back to my
parents' flat and had what could only be described as a 'bad fuck.' "

"What happened?"

"I wish I knew, but it was the first time I couldn't . . . you know.
I was really worried. Maybe I'm becoming old like you."

With the relationship on the rocks, they went out two more
times after that, and then on his final night in Tokyo she spent the
night in his room and he redeemed himself. In the morning his
father knocked on his door and found that it was locked. "Simon,"
he said, "what's going on in there? We're going to be late." Moving
quickly, he snuck Emi out the door, bid her goodbye, then headed
off to the airport with his father, who once again advised his son to
have multitudinous affairs.

"So what are you going to do?" I said.

"A friend of mine told me that you spend your second term at

Cambridge shedding the friends you made during the first. I don't have a philosophy about these things. I came back to Kiet Khiem and basically told it like it wasn't. We went out last night with a couple of other people in college and were laying around my room late at night playing spin the bottle. Triple K was lying between my legs, with her head on my crotch, and this girl I didn't know, Lucy, was sticking her hand down my trousers—just far enough to get a response from me, but not far enough to get a reaction from Triple K."

"So what did you do?"

"I just lay back and smoked a cigarette." He imitated his smug exhale. "I'm like a scientist, you see. I have an open mind. At Marlborough I always had to write on the top of the page 'Be open-minded.' I'll never find the truth, I figure, unless I experiment."

Knock, knock, knock.

"It must be Edna," I said. "Maybe she's working the night shift."

"Come in," sang Simon in his sing-songy voice.

After a moment of anticipation the door flung open, a boot emerged, and Rachel jumped suddenly into the room, beaming with a grin from ear to ear and twisting her hands behind her back. She leaned to the left, pulled her arm to the right, and launched a snowball directly at my face, in clear violation of Article 3, Section 1 of the Geneva Conventions of War.

Within minutes the three of us were chasing one another toward the center of town with several dozen other students from Clare, scooping up snow, packing it tight, and tossing jawbreakers randomly into the air. Intent on surprising me, Rachel had driven with a friend from Oxford earlier in the day and stumbled into the biggest snowstorm in a decade. The normally striped college lawns were coated with a solid layer of vanilla icing. The fingery limbs of the chestnut trees were glistening in a Popsicle glaze. The snow, like a giant feather tickler from the sky, had transformed the entire tight-lipped, buttoned-up university into a veritable candy store, where all of life was a gumdrop delight and all the children had not a care in the world.

Once in town, the converging horde of students divided into college platoons for a massive snowball fight. Jesus attacked Corpus Christi along King's Parade. St. Catherine's bombed Clare from the Senate House Passage. And a group of students called the Magdalene Marauders armed themselves with buckets of snow and tried to storm the locked gate of Trinity until a porter requested that they kindly desist, a request the Marauders responded to by stepping back, lowering their arms, and kindly vaulting their ammunition directly at his turned overcoat. Turning away myself, I finally avenged her unprovoked attack by landing a barely rounded snowball on the back of Rachel's neck. When I went to pull it out of her purple scarf and perhaps rub it in a little, I stepped around to smile at her face and first noticed that she was crying.

A jolt of fear surged down my spine.

"I can't do it," she said, her eyes shot with blood. "I can't go on. It's all gone horribly wrong."

Back in my room, cradling a cup of English breakfast tea before the glowing bulbs of my fake fireplace, Rachel told me what she could not write.

Earlier in the day, arriving to find me away, Rachel had gone to Grasshopper Lodge to seek out Melinda. The two friends, who had not seen each other since the night we met, took a walk around King's, where Rachel told Melinda she had split with her boyfriend and where Melinda told Rachel she did not approve.

"She said you weren't very clever," Rachel said. "She said you weren't an original thinker."

At first I thought this must be a joke, a humorous reference to my admissions interview for Clare: What would Melinda think of my thesis proposal? How about my B+ in French?

"It's okay," I said to Rachel, who had started to cry. "Melinda doesn't know me. She's never really talked with me. It's not like she's seen my transcript."

I leaned forward, hoping for a smile.

"But I don't know you either," Rachel said. "And you don't really know me. What happens when you find out . . . ?"

It was sometime around that moment when I realized how horrible it can be to have your dreams come true. After lifting my fantasies from the pages of Dickens, Austen, even Emily Brontë, I had now stepped feet first into the script of my own Victorian melodrama: boy meets girl, boy gets girl, then girl's best friend casts aspersions on the intellectual fitness of the boy. As I lay on the floor, digesting this story, Rachel sniffed a large breath of tea and slowly let her story escape.

Her previous boyfriend, Jamie, had been a law student at Oxford. He was brilliant, she said, even inspiring: his mind was a field for their recreation. He was also demanding. He wanted her to look a certain way; he wanted her always at his side. She agreed. For months she did exactly as he wished. Later she learned that during that time he had been seeing another woman. She wanted to lash out, to strike him back. But she didn't. She couldn't. She needed him back. All through the summer and into fall they maintained their chilled connection. Then one night she came to Cambridge. Then we went to Wales.

"I hope I am not dizzying you too much," she said, reaching up from the depths of her mug and reaching out to me again. Her face was pale, her hair twisted in streaks, her eyes narrow and dark. "I feel shaky and solid all at once," she said. "I need your embrace . . ."

For a long time we lay arm in arm on the floor, looking a bit like two baby shrimp reaching for our feet. Although we were still raw to the touch, our story line seemed back on track. Rachel's story, instead of pushing me away, had drawn me into its realm. Indeed, after all my protests about the tensions between universities and love, I began to feel the experience was oddly parallel to an academic quest—feeling a spark, acting on instinct, and searching dusty corridors of the past, trying to assemble a coherent narrative that might illuminate the future.

Later, after the snow had stopped and the chill had started to ebb, I tried to relieve the tension by offering a parable of my own. When I was young, I told Rachel, I used to juggle. Before my first show someone said to me that every juggler is allowed to drop a ball three times before he has to quit. The same rule, I suggested, applies to men. "You just dropped me for the first time: you only have two left."

Instead of being perked up by this line, Rachel, to my horror, was more perplexed. My hopes, like my parable, collapsed to the floor. At the end of the night both of us were still up in the air.

X

SPARRING

Mind over Manners

§§

JEREMY: Sir, I have the seeds of rhetoric and
oratory in my head. I have been at Cambridge.
TATTLE: Ay, 'tis well enough for a servant to
be bred at a University; but the education is
a little too pedantic for a gentleman.

—William Congreve
Love for Love, 1695

*T*erry, predictably, was philosophical about the weather.

"It's just like the Battle of Waterloo," he said as I stepped into the Porters' Lodge the following morning, with Rachel close behind.

"And how is it like the Battle of Waterloo?" I asked, ever the obedient foil.

"Well," he said. "Do you know how we beat Napoleon? We used cunning and ingenuity. We fought with bravery and courage. The British had the greatest soldiers in the world and the stupidest generals."

There was a pause as Terry leaned back in his chair and reflected on that crowning moment in British military history and I reflected on his novel theory of British meteorology.

"But how is that like the weather?" I asked.

"Adversity," he declared. "The British are expert at triumphing over adversity. If we can overcome our generals then we can overcome this. Don't worry, it will all be over in a couple of days."

The British, I had discovered after nearly two seasons, like to measure weather in time. If British Rail is delayed for merely two hours, the weather must be clear; if trains are held up for over four hours, a storm is under way. A one-hour slowdown along the M–25 in January, for example, means spring is on the way, while a two-hour holdup means the country is in for six more weeks of winter. A "couple of days" in this lexicon meant we were in for a rough term.

"Terry," I said when the prognosis was complete. "I have someone for you to meet."

"Then I'll stand up," he said.

"This is Rachel."

"Ah, Rachel," he said. "You have called here many times." He took her hand and kissed it gently. "Are you at college in Cambridge?"

"No, sir, I'm at Oxford."

He took a step back. "Now hold it, young lady. No blasphemy in here." He held his pose for a moment, then looked both ways in the miniature lodge to ensure no one was listening. "Actually," he said, stepping back toward the counter, "I'll tell you a secret—I like Oxford better than Cambridge."

We feigned horror at his remarks.

"At least the architecture, that is. Of course, we have the Cam running through the colleges. And we have a little more, well, order."

"Order?" Rachel said. "What does that mean?"

"Well, let me tell you, young lady. I was once offered a job in

Oxford. A professor I know was visiting here and asked me if I would like to become head porter at St. Peter's College."

"You mean to tell me they have head-hunting for porters?" I asked.

"Well," he said, brushing back his sideburns. "I suppose one could say I was poached. . . . Anyway, this gentleman invited me to come and stay for several days at St. Peter's. So I went; but I knew from the first moment I stepped into that lodge that I didn't like it. The architecture was nice, but the atmosphere . . ." He paused to take a drag from his meerschaum pipe and run his hand down the curve of his protuberant vest. "Whilst I naturally like an atmosphere that is relaxed, this was what you Americans might call laid back. I walked in that day and the porter on duty had his tie loosened around his neck and his sleeves turned up to his elbows. I just wanted to brass him up."

"You wanted to what?" Rachel said.

"To smarten him up. You can't expect students to learn any dignity if the porters are all slouching around like loblollies. Some people in this country think that all the universities are meant to teach you is *maths,* or English, or classics. I say bollocks. You can learn that at the polytechnics. We're here to teach you much more than that. We're here to teach you manners."

"So what's her sign?"

"How do I know?"

"When's her birthday?"

"New Year's Day."

"That makes her a Capricorn."

"Which means what?"

"Black."

"Black what?"

"Black clothes. Black personality. Good at business. Good with money."

Cyprian and I were walking across Clare Bridge to dinner at Ian's. As usual, he slouched a little as he walked, and constantly straightened his foggy spectacles. Part of his squirrelish ponytail was caught in the strap of the yellow tote bag he carried over his arm.

"Well," I asked. "Do we match?"

"It depends on what time of day you were born."

"But I have no idea."

"Let me try this out: if you hear a logical argument do you respond immediately, or do you have to feel whether the argument is true?"

"I don't know," I said. "Let me think."

"There," he said. "You answered it. You're a Mercury."

"But Mercury isn't a sign, is it?"

"No," he said with all the patience of a remedial teacher explaining two plus two for the fourth time, "Mercury is a planet, but it's part of your chart, and it's the order of all the planets and all the stars in the sky that make up your sign. Sometimes it's the lesser elements that determine how compatible you are with someone else."

"This stuff cracks me up," I said. "I hope you realize that I'm only learning it for you."

"You should be learning it for yourself," he said. "You aren't going to learn it in class."

"I bet I can say something you disagree with."

Cyprian was sitting on Ian's baby blue comforter less than an hour later, plucking sticky rice with chopsticks from a Buttery bowl in his lap. I was standing nearby at the desk-buffet spooning out tofu squares with a red bean sauce.

"Okay, try me."

"Literary criticism is art."

"You're right," I said. "I disagree with that."

"Hey, Ian," came a call from the other side of the room. "Do you have a fork?"

Thaddeus Bull was sitting on the far side of the attic room staring helplessly at his stick-twisted fingers. A friend of Ian's and a fellow at Pembroke, Thaddeus was having difficulty handling his meal, not to mention the conversation.

"Look under my bed," Ian called from the kitchen.

Thaddeus stuck his hand underneath a pile of empty seltzer bottles and some crumpled dart scorecards that documented my victories over Ian, and retrieved a set of stolen utensils embossed with the red and gold Clare crest. He stepped to the sink to clean the knife and fork and, after admiring his face in the blade, returned to his seat.

"I don't agree with that either," he said. "Literary criticism is higher than art. It doesn't have to sell."

I sat down on the floor. "So anything that sells is corrupt?" I said. "Any idea that can be applied outside the university is somehow reduced?"

"Excuse me," Thaddeus said, wagging his knife in the air. "Please don't misrepresent me. All I'm saying—and I'll try to be very clear about this—is that our responsibility in the humanities is to interpret what others have said, not to say it, or do it, ourselves."

He retracted his knife and returned it to his plate.

"Then why is it that people do not think creativity takes place in a university?" Cyprian said. His voice was slow, almost melodic, as if he were offering the opening prayer over a family dinner he knew would end in disagreement. "Why don't great novelists stay in school? Why don't great musicians come from the great universities?"

"Because a university is not the place for art," Thaddeus snapped. His manner was curt, almost definitive, like a ten-year-old picking a playground brawl. "It's the place for scholarship. We teach students how to be critical, not how to create. Just take the footnote. The idea behind the footnote is that no idea is created from whole cloth. It comes from someplace else."

"But I can be creative," Cyprian said. "I think what I do is original, not all of it comes from somebody else. Should I footnote my father for conceiving me? Should I footnote my mother for having me under the Scorpion sky?"

Thaddeus considered his reply. "Only if you think your best ideas come from outer space."

Cambridge, like most universities, is set up like a chess board, with a clear hierarchical grid. Among fellows, there are professors, lecturers, readers, and dons (in Cambridge the term *professor* is used only for a few senior teachers; while *don,* which comes from the Latin *dominus,* or "lord," is a more general term). Among graduate students, there are Ph.D.'s, M.Phil.'s, and M.Litt.'s; and lined up beneath them are the vast platoon of B.A.'s, who think they rule the place since they live on the front lines but who are regarded by all the others as pawns.

On the surface the three tiers seem secure in their place. At Clare, for instance, the Junior Common Room—for undergraduates—is located one floor below ground, and is decorated with fluorescent lights, vinyl benches, and easy–clean-up bathroom tile. The Middle Common Room, for graduates, is on the ground floor, and is trimmed with track lighting, fluffy sofas, and polished hardwood floors. The Senior Common Room, for fellows, is on the second floor (which the British, perhaps fearing heights, call the first) and is adorned with antique brass lamps, red leather chairs, and tattered Oriental rugs. Within these supposedly secure worlds, however, the rivalries can be quite intense. This is especially true among fellows, and even more so among junior fellows, whose tenuous position on the board means they often squabble among themselves to defend their space.

"Are you a fellow?" Thaddeus asked Cyprian when they first met.

"A research fellow," Cyprian said.

"How much?"

"Fourteen a year, plus dinner in Hall every night."

"Nicely done," said Thaddeus. "And you teach?"

"Ten hours a week."

"Well," he scoffed. "That explains it. I'm excused from supervisions."

Thaddeus Bull was a pint-sized Ph.D. with an overinflated C.V. He wore his black hair short, his dark clothes tight, and his manhood dangling above his upper lip in the form of a French pencil-thin mustache. A research fellow with no teaching responsibilities, Thaddeus lived in pampered rooms at Pembroke and labored on a book about a modern French poet, Edmond Jabès, who was as far removed from the mainstream of European literature as Lucan, Cyprian's subject, was from that of Latin poetry. Individually, these two young dons were as close to the rarefied core of British academia as one could be: they had passed the tests and survived the inquests that determine admission into that most sacred club. But once together, they allowed their manners to slip and their minds to fall into a curious intellectual duel.

"Oh, you like Camus," Cyprian said at one point in the evening. "He's my favourite author. What do you think of the murderer in *L'Étranger*?"

"He was a racist," Thaddeus barked. "He thought being an Arab was more important than being an individual."

"But the law said it was acceptable to shoot an Arab," Cyprian responded. "Haven't you read what Northrop Frye said about the role of nativism in postwar existential writing?"

"Did you say Frye?" snorted Thaddeus. "How passé. Frye is extratextual. Now Roland Barthes, he says we must examine the subtext of the words themselves to place the actions of the hero in context. How can you bring the law into a discussion of literature?"

"Because literature is a living art," Cyprian said. "If you'd ever taught a class of first-year students, you would know."

To and fro the two dons went, tossing around their pointed references and bandying about their pet theorems. One, Cyprian, was passive to the point of being aggressive; the other, Thaddeus, was aggressive to the point of nearly passing out. Just as Terry believed that students came up to Cambridge to learn to be ladies and gentlemen, Cyprian and Thaddeus each had ideas about the purpose of higher education. When the food was served and Ian returned, it quickly became apparent that their ideas were incompatible—with each other, and with mine.

"I think Cambridge has a bad name," Cyprian said. "People have one of two ideas about us. First, there is this image that all we do here is dress in white suits, sip port, and have garden parties. This group thinks universities are all about learning manners."

"That's what Terry thinks," I said. "He's got a point."

"Second, there are those who believe that all we do is sit around in leather chairs and shuffle shards of facts around with no discernible purpose whatsoever."

"That's what I think," said Ian.

"I'm offended by this notion of superfluence," Cyprian said. "Education is much more than just 'Bean Counting for Intellectuals.' I want my students to contribute to the world—to be artists in their own right."

"So you want them to be novelists," said Ian.

Cyprian rested his chopsticks on his lip and thought for a moment. "In a way," he said, "yes. I think what I do is art. Art is all relative anyway, and I'm creating something that is as beautiful as anything I read."

"But wait a minute," Thaddeus said. "You don't footnote art. I may be more than a bean counter, but I see myself as a critic. It's my role to be removed from the world, to examine a text and interpret its meaning. Scholars should be readers, not writers."

"But universities have to create more than scholars," Cyprian suggested, never shifting in his chair, never raising his voice. "They have to be extratextual. There's a list of skills on the wall in my faculty listing all the things students can take from classics into the work force. We must teach them to think for themselves, to take what they learn from here and apply it in new and creative ways."

"I don't want those skills," Thaddeus scoffed. "If everything has to be applied, the mind becomes corrupted. Scholarship doesn't have to change the world. It just has to understand it."

"Then who will change it?" I interjected, as they turned to look at me. "Look at the Crisis we're in today. The world may go to war this week and you don't seem to care. For some people ideas are more than criticism. They are more than art. Shouldn't ideas have a role to play outside of this place, outside of our heads?"

Thaddeus thought for a moment, and then said, "No. A university should be a place for thinking, not acting. It's the last remaining empire. . . ." He let this last phrase role off his tongue, then set his spoon down to consider it. "It's an empire of the mind."

Cyprian smiled at the artful move.

Ian nodded his head with admiration.

I sat back and tried to check the blow. "But empires don't last forever," I said.

That only set up his rhetorical mate. "This one will," he said. "And I should know. After all, I have a 'Doctor' before my name."

For an American, living in Britain is often like living in a time warp. A variety of elements contribute to this feeling. Telephones have numbers that range from five to seven digits and receivers that weigh from three to five pounds. Rooms have light bulbs that are sixty watts too low and electrical outlets that have varying configurations of holes so household appliances are always sold with no plugs attached. Even the air is congested with a postnasal drip that impedes the passage of time. But nothing contributes more to this sense of delay than the national obsession with conversations, which proceed slowly and surely around the country every day with a passion for language, a zest for altercation, and the occasional whiff of old-fashioned snobbery.

Given the national fixation with interpersonal communication (the great British hobby, for example, is accent spotting: foreigners, they say, can never learn how), it comes as no surprise that the famed

institutions of higher learning in England have long been dedicated
to cultivating conversation. Since their inception, Oxbridge colleges have made the art of breeding a central priority—learning to
dine in Hall, learning to debate at the Union (where I, very much
in need of breeding, was already preparing to take my turn). Victorian dons, for instance, believed their role was to help students
assume their place in "our happy Establishment of Church and
State." "The University's job is to teach you the language of being
a gentleman," Terry might have said. "The rest—the mere grammar—you can learn on your own." Students, meanwhile, indulged
in the luxury of their exclusive training by mingling conversation
with camaraderie. "As Cambridge filled up with friends it acquired
a magical quality," wrote E. M. Forster at the end of the nineteenth
century. "People and books reinforced one another, intelligence
joined hands with affection, speculation became a passion, and discussion was made profound by love."

Over time, this love of conversation at Oxbridge was transformed from an idle pastime of the upper classes into a broader ideal
of higher education. Nowhere was this philosophy more apparent
than in the meetings of the Apostles, an elite Cambridge debating
society founded in 1820 to ponder such questions as "Is there any
rule of ethical action except general expediency?" or "Have the
poems of Shelley an immoral tendency?" The group, officially
called the Cambridge Conversazione Society, eventually included
such luminaries as Alfred, Lord Tennyson, Alfred North White-
head, Bertrand Russell, G. E. Moore, Lytton Strachey, Leonard
Woolf, Maynard Keynes, Rupert Brooke, and—at least once, a
foreigner—Ludwig Wittgenstein. "It was a principle in discussion
that there were to be no *taboos,* no limitations, nothing considered
shocking, no barriers to absolute freedom of speculation," Russell
wrote in his autobiography. "We discussed all manner of things, no
doubt with a certain immaturity, but with a detachment and interest
scarcely possible in later life." This spirit captured the essence of the
English university: a perfect conversation, a pure critique of ideas, a

virginal analysis of the natural world untainted by practical concerns. As Thaddeus might have put it, the role of a university education is to learn the language of analysis—the *lingua franca* of the Empire of the Mind.

But the language of discourse changed dramatically over time. In the Middle Ages all students at Cambridge were required to study a single curriculum, comprising grammar, logic, rhetoric, music, arithmetic, and geometry. They were also asked to demonstrate proficiency in Latin, Greek, and Hebrew. In the 1850s, in response to pressure from Queen Victoria's husband, Prince Albert, the university began offering its first degrees in the natural sciences. Within a century, Cambridge scientists had split the atom, discovered DNA, and won over twenty-five Nobel prizes. But as the fields of knowledge expanded exponentially in those times, Cambridge resisted the moves in other countries to broaden its course requirements. Instead of bringing such applied subjects as chemistry, physics, and engineering into the classical curriculum, Cambridge isolated them as second-class faculties. "The true enthusiast rejects and scorns the application of any test of practical ability," wrote don Leslie Stephen. "Knowledge, he thinks, is knowledge; the more remote it is from all contact with concrete things the better."

By requiring students to narrow their course of study, Cambridge (and Oxford as well) undermined their students' broad-minded education. The "conversation," in short, began to break down. Gone was the universal curriculum; gone was common knowledge. What developed in Oxbridge during the twentieth century was a new hierarchy of learning with the top being reserved for abstract, philosophical subjects (such as classics, or French existential poetry) and the bottom being assigned to practical, applied subjects (such as engineering, or international relations). Real men read Caesar's *Gaelic Wars* in the original and discussed its use of the subjunctive; neophytes read it in spotty translation and then, of all things, tried to apply it. The stigma against mingling with the present is so great in the Land of the Past that at least one person I knew in my course would lie to any woman he met by telling her that he was studying history, while I—Egads, he reads the newspaper!—was doing I.R.

In essence, Cambridge in the twentieth century became a place to seek refuge in the past. "The pursuit of learning, like every other great activity, is unavoidably conservative," wrote Michael Oakeshott, a prominent philosopher who is still memorialized in Cambridge by a dining society that bears his name, in 1950. "It is not a race in which the competitors jockey for the best place, it is not even an argument or a symposium; it is a conversation." A conversation, he said, has no predetermined course, "we do not ask what it is 'for,' and we do not judge its excellence by its conclusion—it has no conclusion, but is always put aside for another day." Above all, a university offered students what Oakeshott called "the gift of an interval"—an interim in the tyrannical course of time to taste the mystery of conversation without the necessity of at once seeking a solution.

That interim in time still thrives in Cambridge: it is what gives the town its timeless charm; it is also what gives the university its unaltered, time-warped pace. While in some ways I admired the isolation that kept Cambridge students true to their heritage, I couldn't help wondering how equipped they would be to leave their guarded courtyards. Also, in a time of international crisis, I wondered how concerned they were with nonacademic problems at all. The messages, on this front, were quite clear: universities exist for cultivating the individual mind, not the public good, insisted the former philosopher-prince of King's College, Noël Annan. "The need to mix classes, nationalities, and races together is secondary," he wrote. "The agonies and gaieties of student life are secondary. Even the awakening of a sense of beauty, or the pursuit of goodness itself—all these are secondary to the cultivation, training, and exercise of the intellect."

On the surface, I should have been the ideal participant in the "conversation" at Cambridge. I had left school several years earlier but had come back looking for more "stimulation." I had traveled extensively but had still returned to the academy for more "intellectual" training. Yet when I arrived at Cambridge I found myself uneasy in the university environment, where insight is rarely measured by breadth of experience but by breadth of bookshelf instead. Had I read Plato in the original? Did I agree with Northrop Frye? Was I extratextual or intravenous-symbiotic? At one point in my evening at Ian's, for example, Thaddeus asked me what languages I spoke. "Japanese," I said, to which he replied, "What else?"

In the upper reaches of academe one is always one language, one theory, or one book too short. Outside the academy I rarely discussed books in the course of a day so as not to seem too pedantic; inside the academy I rarely discussed books so as not to seem insufficiently read. Above all, as I wandered around Cambridge, I longed for a conversation in which the university and the universal could speak with each other, without regard to specialty, nationality, or, even worse, degree, such as who has the word "Doctor" before his initials and who has more initials after his name.

"So what did you think of our little feud here tonight?"

Ian and I were carrying dishes into his gyp later that evening. He had taken off his camel-hair jacket and was wearing only a droopy black jumper with the logo of a British fencing society emblazoned on the chest. As he walked with dirty glasses in his hands, he would suddenly lunge forward every now and then and pretend to stab an invisible enemy.

"I think you're all full of crap," he said, parrying in my direction, pretending to riposte, and thrusting some leftover beer onto my sweater. "The problem with this place is not that we don't have enough art, it's that we have too much. We've all lost our balls. We've forgotten that underneath all the mind games and the gentle manners we're all still animals." He set down his glasses and grabbed his crotch for emphasis. "Aristotle said that all our thoughts, even our souls, begin in the deepest part of our bodies."

"I suspect that most dons would rather discuss existential philosophy than animal instincts," I said, turning back toward the room.

"Isn't that the problem with the academy?" he said as he followed, happy at last to offer his undisclosed theory of education. "We're all trapped in this bubble, removed from the rest of humanity."

"Don't look at me," I said, even though he hadn't. "I agree with you."

"We're just learning how to masturbate—intellectual masturbation. I learn how to argue, you learn how to argue, but neither of us learns anything from the other. That's the problem with what Thaddeus was saying: here we only learn how to talk; we don't learn how to touch." He sat on the edge of his bed, ran his fingers through his hair. "In the end, we just go back to our rooms and wank off with our books. . . ." He picked up a copy of Thomas Hobbes from his bed and threw it on the floor.

"Is something bothering you?" I asked.

"No," he snapped. "Well, yes." He lay down on his bed and pulled the covers up to his chin. I sat down in the one chair in the room that didn't have a broken leg. "What happened to my passion?" he said. "I wanted to be great. I wanted to be famous, and brilliant, and beautiful, too. I'm already beautiful, I know."

"Allow me to disagree—"

"But I've lost the rest. I used to have ideals. I believed in Plato and the higher good. I believed in virtue. 'Virtue,' Socrates said, 'is aspiring to fine things and being able to achieve them.' But I can't believe that anymore. My girlfriend of two-and-a-half years leaves me for no reason. Louise Rogers won't even respond to my letters. This place, with its books, is corrupting my mind. It's telling me I have to be gentle, and soft, and kind. It's telling me I have to be rational and ignore my body."

He rolled to one side and propped his head on his elbow.

"Take this war thing. I've been listening to the radio recently— all the talk about midnight deadlines and lines in the sand. It's really brought out the male instinct in me. It's made me want to stand up and fight. Do you know what I mean?"

He stuck out his hand to prevent me from answering.

"It's the same with women. When I see a beautiful woman, I want to be an animal—a tiger—and jump all over her. It's my Persian side, my father in me. But I can't. I'm supposed to be sensitive and considerate—all this crap about English manners. My mother wanted me to go St. Paul's so I would learn the Book of Common Prayer. 'Good Lord, deliver us from the deceits of the flesh and the devil. . . .' They don't get it. Mankind is basic instinct, and all the books in the world can't get rid of that. Thaddeus is like Plato with his idea that we have to separate the thinkers from the doers. It's very Cambridge. Aristotle knew that you can't take the body out of the mind any more than you can take a man out of his world. . . ."

When he finished his soliloquy, Ian curled himself into an embryonic ball underneath his comforter. I stretched my legs onto his bed. For a moment we sat in silence, two bodies in fact cut off from the world, and then simultaneously we both sat up and looked at the radio: "What's the time?"

Ian reached out from beneath his duvet and flipped the switch of his beat-up box with the broken rabbit ears. We didn't hear any words, at first, we didn't hear the call, but the whistles, the blasts, the cries from the earth, and even the static from the live microphone were unmistakable. Shutting my eyes instinctively as if somehow that would help me see, I felt my muscles—from my groin to my head—stiffen in anticipation of the inevitable blow. The Crisis, at last, had turned to War. The bubble, I thought, had burst.

XI

TALKING

The Fruits of War

Come away, O human child!
To the waters and the wild
With a faery, hand in hand,
For the world's more full of
    weeping than you can understand.

—William Butler Yeats
"The Stolen Child," 1886

The chaplain's voice was quiet. His eyes serene. His words flowed into the fire-baked room in a caramel whisper that palliated the mind and relaxed the body as cough syrup coats an aching throat hoarse from too much abrasion.

"Good evening, my friends. Thank you for joining us here tonight. I hope you all will take this opportunity to open your souls and speak from your hearts. This is an experiment in conversation."

Nick Sagovsky, the chaplain of Clare, was seated cross-legged on the edge of a chair rubbing his palms in a circle. His black shirt was ironed against his slight frame, his pale skin clung to his high cheekbones. A bowl of fruit—orange, violet, dots of pale green—sat open in the center of his room atop an old sailor's chest.

"I don't expect that we will come to any earth-shattering conclusions in this meeting. I don't think we will solve any problems. But I have been struggling with how to understand my conflicting feelings over the last few days, and I wanted to share these struggles with you."

He clapped his hands together silently.

"That was a personal note," he said. "Now I thought we could go around the circle and each of you could say why you came to this meeting. I didn't want experts to come and tell us how far a missile can travel or how fast a Tornado can fly. I wanted to hear you speak. I am wearing my collar tonight, but in truth I am wearing a different hat."

Nick sat back slowly in his chair, leaving a pause in the center of the room like a hole in a pond where a pebble had been dropped.

After several moments a woman to my right—at three o'clock in our circle—began to speak. "I came because I'm overwhelmed," she said. Her name was Amanda, she had reams of frizzy red hair. "I have been watching the news on television, but somehow I don't feel anything. I don't know what I'm meant to feel. It's partly because I don't know anyone who's there. Partly because it takes place so many miles away. But I find it all very distant. My country is at war, and I don't understand why."

Jane, a thin, brown-haired woman in a long brown skirt, spoke next. She was seated in an upright chair to my left—at nine o'clock to my seat at six.

"I must admit something," she said. "I never cared much for the news. I read a newspaper every now and then. I listen to the radio in my car. But I am going to be married this summer, and my fiancé is in the reserves. Now I can't ignore this problem anymore. It could be him over there, so now I have to care." She took a deep breath. "What I discovered was that there are some people in my commu-

nity who are affected deeply by these events, and I want to know
how to comfort them."

"That's a very generous remark, Jane. And one that is very important." Nick leaned forward in his seat. He opened his arms as if
parting a book. "I have noticed a split in our community between
those who don't seem to notice the war and those who listen to the
news all the time. I wonder if this rift is irreparable?"

"I am one of the junkies," said a thin boy with spectacles and
tennis shoes who was seated across from me—at eleven. His name
was Dean. "Since last summer this crisis is all that I have thought
about. The reason is that one of my best friends has been living in
that area and he spent four months in hiding. If the people who were
sheltering him had got caught, they would surely have been shot.
This is not an abstraction. This is real. And people are making jokes
about it. It hurts to think that people don't want to fight this war.
I want my friend alive."

"It hurts me, too," said a woman named Leslie in a green flannel
shirt and bright yellow socks who was seated between Amanda and
me at four o'clock. "I was in London for a peace march yesterday.
I don't think our country should be at war, and I resent the war
being fought in my name. All of this patriotic fervor—the posters on
the street, the flags in people's car windows. I think we have lost our
minds and are just following others into war for the sake of our own
misconceptions. I came here tonight because I'm upset, because I
don't feel I can stop anything. To me there is not enough of a split."

"But now our forces are in battle," said Ben, a handsome public
school boy with a crew cut who was seated at two o'clock. "So now
we should support them. During my year off I was a member of the
Royal Marines. Of course, I never saw any combat, but I expect
someday to be among them. I think it is important to back our
country. I don't really know what to think about this conflict and I
came here to talk about that. But I do know that we must show
support."

The hole in the pond grew larger.

"I agree with Nick," I said, finally joining the discussion. "There is a split in our community. And that split makes me frustrated." I felt the group turn and stare at me, startled by my accent. "I am American, so by sheer force of numbers there are people I know involved. But I am concerned that only those of us who know people directly involved think the war is important, while everyone else doesn't care. This level of apathy really bothers me. I want to proselytize. I want to grab people by the shoulders and tell them that this matters to them whether they know it or not."

"But why does it matter?" Amanda asked. "Why should I listen to the radio? What can I do?"

"You can do a lot," insisted Leslie. "We have the power to stop this. Think of Vietnam. If we protest, our voices can make a difference."

"Don't think about Vietnam," countered Ben. "Think of World War Two. That's a better example. Before the war I was opposed to the idea of conflict. But now that it has begun, I feel we must show solidarity with our troops. It is impossible to fight a war with everyone second-guessing every decision."

"I have a real problem with this question of support," said Nick, for the first time revealing his feelings. "How can I offer my support when I have questions about the cause? I feel very deeply about the casualties. My wife is a doctor, so I know the hospital is preparing hundreds of beds for the wounded. But I know that all the troops, on both sides, have parents, and I feel deeply for them, too."

"You don't think about the enemy in battle," said Jane. "The troops are just doing their jobs. If my fiancé were involved, I would want him to shoot the enemy before they shoot him."

"Yes, I agree," said Amanda. "But all of this talk about us versus them makes me very confused. Why do we have to hate the enemy? I remember all the Argie-bashing during the Falklands War. I just have a lot of doubt. I just want to know, well, who do I pray for?"

The question lingered in the pool, rippling through the academic roundtable with the quiet force of doubt. For a moment the circle was muted and the people thrown into indecision. The athletic contests in college were hard-fought and fierce, but ultimately they were friendly. The personal battles for love were heartfelt and strong, but finally they were for pleasure. Even the life-or-death struggles for exams proved in the end to be less than apocalyptic. But the reality of war, like few other events on a university campus, had the power to pierce through the cocoon of isolation and force students to engage their world. At that hour I couldn't help wondering, could Cambridge be penetrated?

"We must pray for peace," said Leslie, breaking the silence. "We must take back our government from the military leaders and run it ourselves."

"I don't think that's accurate," added Ben. "Once the war has begun, we must let our elected officials lead."

Dean squirmed in his seat. "But some countries have said that if they are attacked they will use enough force to end the conflict."

Ben sat upright. "Are you implying that one side might use nuclear weapons?"

Dean stared back at him. "Yes."

"Well, that might be a good idea," Ben said. "At least it would save casualties."

"Not their casualties," Dean countered. "Only ours. Then what have we accomplished?"

"You have taught him a lesson," Ben asserted. "You have stood up for what you believe."

Jane, the bride-to-be, raised her finger. "Perhaps if I might be permitted," she said. "I would like to use a homely metaphor—a family. It seems to me that this situation is like when you are a parent and your child is bad. Even though you love him, you have to punish him so he won't do it in the future. Although it may hurt a little, it's the only way."

"But I don't love dictators," said Amanda.

"Yet surely we love his people," said Nick.

"What about our people?" Leslie said. "We are not parents to the world. When I hear that kind of talk, I notice a paternalistic attitude. We can't just discipline the rest of the world as if they were a pack of wild dogs."

"So what do we do?" Ben said. "Do we just let them roam?"

"The world is not that simple," added Dean. "War is not black and white. We can't expect to tame the mad dogs out there, because we're just the same as they are."

Round and round the sailor's chest we went—point, counterpoint, press ahead, plant our feet—in a never-ending litany of private concerns.

"What about my fiancé?"

"What about my friend?"

"What about our troops?"

"What about our enemy?"

The conversation was going nowhere. Each of us had learned to express ourselves. We had taken advantage of the interval offered by the university. But despite our well-honed language skills, we had lost the ability to listen. As Thaddeus had hoped, we were all being critics. As I had feared, we were all cut off from one another. We could take apart ideas, but couldn't build a bridge. We could recreate the war, but couldn't create peace.

"Wait!" I said after several more minutes of the mind-numbing rhetoric. "We're fighting the war among ourselves. What happened to the idea of thinking beyond our personal lives—our own identities—to reach out to one another?" I went on to talk about preaching and posturing. My voice was rising higher. My face was turning red. "We're in a university," I said. "If we can't come to an understanding, who can?" My words came out like a speech of sorts, a ranting plea for reconciliation. When I finished, my voice whirled around the pool for a moment, then Nick leaned forward toward the chest and rubbed his hands together as he had at the start.

"I said at the beginning that we wouldn't come to any conclusions tonight. We wouldn't solve any problems." He smiled and looked around the circle, dissipating the tensions with his charm.

My manifesto had failed. "But I thought we could open some lines of communication. We have all mentioned some people that we know are involved in this war, so I would like to take a minute and reflect on what we have said."

As the group took a moment to pray, I stared at the fruit in the center of the table. In the silence I thought not of the people I knew in the war but of the ones I had just met in the room. We were seven corners of a circle, children of the academy, who couldn't agree on a simple idea but had agreed to disagree, who had come separately into the group but had not come together, and who would leave the room soothed by the voice of our gentle father but with little wisdom to bear. In the end, the circle reminded me of that bowl of fruit in its center—individuals united by a common family but separated from joining together by thick, distinctive skins. The university— the "conversation"—had brought us together, but our different voices—our different languages—had kept us apart.

"Thank you very much for coming," Nick said. "May there be peace on earth."

XII

PARTYING

NARGs from the Underground

§§

> Mathematics may be defined as the subject in which we never know what we are talking about, nor whether what we are saying is true.
>
> —Bertrand Russell
> *Recent Work on Mathematics,* 1901

"Hey, Bruce, come inside."

Terry called out to me from the Porters' Lodge as I walked into Memorial Court on a dark, dank Friday afternoon. The second term, as Simon predicted, had developed differently from the first. For starters, I opted not to row and concentrated instead on picking up squash, poking around Clare, and preparing for my upcoming exams. Yet when war broke out these priorities shifted. In the midst of real-life international relations, our morning lectures on eighteenth-century weaponry or the causes of Peruvian inflation seemed even more remote than usual. Mr. Langley, our course director, dismissed requests from the class that he assemble the diplomats, generals, and journalists in our program for a roundtable discussion. "We are academicians," he said, "not therapists. We don't care about your feelings."

Dr. Long, my supervisor, also didn't care about my feelings, though he did, at least, remember my name when I went to see him in early February. "Jolly well," he said when I proposed my scheme to compare the Allied occupations of Japan and Germany. "It's not been done. It might be difficult. Bring me an outline at the start of next term." The biggest change of all, however, was that I spent much less time in V Entryway, after Halcyon returned two weeks into Lent and indicated that she did not intend to speak with me again.

"What is it?" I said to Terry as I stepped into the Lodge.

"You have a message," he said. "It's from a chap called Bernard. He's having a party tonight in Trinity. He said please bring a bottle and some food—what do you say?—midgets, morsels, mouthfuls..."

"Munchies."

"Yes, that's it. Please bring a bottle and some munchies. So tell me, what's a munchy?"

"Well, munchies are different from food," I said. "Food means turkey or baked potatoes; munchies are cookies or potato chips. Or—how do you say?—biscuits and crisps."

"I get it. Munchies are party food."

"That's right," I said. "You're a fast learner."

"This is good. I'm teaching you how to be an English gentle-man—"

"And I'm teaching you how to be an American teenager."

"No, you're teaching me how to talk with American tourists. I have occasion to talk to all sorts of people, you know. I've said hello to Prince Philip, Prince Charles, and the youngest one, too, Edward. I said hello to him a couple of times when he was at Cambridge. But I don't want to be a snob. I like to talk to you *Colonists* as well."

He laughed uproariously at his own joke, caressing his mustache and patting his bald pate as he did.

"Which reminds me," he continued, "where did you say Barney was from?"

"California."

"Ah, California, I should have guessed. I suppose that means he wears sneakers a lot."

The party was humming when I arrived—a dull, whining, staticky hum like a shortwave radio caught between two stations. Three men wearing polarized glasses and flannel shirts were standing in the corner of the basement room fiddling with a six-piece sound system, which responded to their proddings and provocations with the excruciating cry of a UFO in surgery. The undergound room was unlit, except for a glimmer from an orange streetlight that careened through the horizontal ventilation windows and reflected off the whitewashed walls. Water dripped from the windows in several places and gathered in puddles on the floor.

I hadn't wanted to come to this party. My exams were several weeks away; Rachel was stuck in Oxford; my dinner of mashed meat and refried potatoes was fossilizing in my stomach. Yet the invitation had intrigued me. I had run into Bernard several times the previous month and he had mentioned he was having a birthday party and that I should come and meet his friends.

"Hey, Bruce-man," Bernard said as he bounded over to bid me welcome. "Howya doin'? Let me introduce you to my pals."

Bernard was a Type A Californian. He wore his hair long, his shirt loose, and his pants impossibly tight. He came to his twenty-fourth birthday party dressed in bleached white jeans creased to his crotch, a pink Hawaiian shirt opened to his baby-bare navel, and—indeed—sneakers: red. A Ph.D. student in artificial intelligence and a master chess player, Bernard was trying to write a computer program that could defeat a prodigy like himself in chess. If he suc-

ceeded, he would pass and lose his pride; if he failed, he would flunk
but feel much better.

"Computers will never beat good humans," he said. "We have to
tell them what to do."

Bernard, like many childhood computer hackers, had a brain that
matured when he was nine but a body that never quite caught up.
As a result, he was always eager, often bouncy, and—like a Labrador
retriever—invariably ready with the wrong emotion at the right
time. He was, in short, a puppy savant. I first met Bernard at a formal
dinner at Trinity in the fall, and at that time he told me he was
organizing a special group to discuss the correlation between diplomacy and game theory.

"It's all a matter of the correct syllogism," he said with the excite-
ment most people reserve for discussing ice cream or sports results.
"If I say, 'Socrates is a man; all men are mortal; therefore Socrates
is mortal,' I make sense, right?"

"Yes."

"But if I say, 'Socrates is a goose; all geese are immortal; therefore
Socrates is immortal,' I also make sense, right?"

"I suppose so. But what does this have to do with diplomacy?"

"Well, reality depends on which knowledge base you choose.
Socrates is not a goose. A goose is not immortal. So Socrates is not
immortal. If diplomacy is based on a false assumption, then the result
is war."

Inside the cellar Bernard led me to the center of the room and a
clump of men standing silently in a square.

"I want you to meet Kenneth," he said, gesturing to a man with
curly dark hair and a thick dark beard. "He's from Trinity. He can
beat me in chess."

There was a pause.

"Hello," I said.

"Hello."

There was another pause.

"Where are you from?" I asked.

He squinted his eyes and stared blankly at me.

"What do you mean?" he said.

"I mean where did you grow up?"

"You mean where do my parents live?"

"This is not a difficult question."

"I was born in Liverpool."

"Well," Bernard said, as if interrupting, "now I will say something about each of you for the others to hear. This is Bruce. He wrote a book about Japan."

"Oh," declared Kenneth. "That's strange."

"Kenneth also wrote a book," Bernard said.

There was a pause.

"What's your book about?" I asked.

He opened his mouth with the gust of a downhill skier who had just taken off and could not be easily stopped. "Computer logistics in a post-Cartesian world—"

"Oh," I interrupted. "That's fascinating."

"This is Sean," Bernard said, pressing on unawares. "He's my neighbor. He beats me in Othello."

"Nice to meet you, Sean." I stuck out my hand; he wiped his on his jeans and drooped it into mine.

"Do you play?" he asked.

"Do I play what?" I answered.

"Othello."

"No, but I played Hamlet in high school."

He stared at me blankly. Clearly, my American wit was still too wet.

"Sorry," I said, "I'm afraid I haven't played Othello since high school."

"Oh," he sighed. "Too bad."

"Sean has published ten articles," Bernard said.

"Actually, it's only one article," Kenneth added. "He just keeps rewriting it."

"So, what do you do?" I asked Sean.

"I write computer programs that translate Swedish into English and play bridge."

"So you transfer Swedish into English in order to play bridge?"

"No, not exactly. I play bridge in either language."

He grinned. Kenneth chuckled. Bernard clapped his hands in delight. I excused myself and went to fetch a drink.

When I first came to Cambridge, I expected to find a student body that was a unified class. It would be a charming, chatty group, I thought, with members sharing a common background, an uncommon accent, and, naturally, a communal uniform. What I found was quite the opposite. Inside the otherwise exclusive world that comprises a Cambridge class lives a seething, unspoken set of standards that confines a Cambridge student to an "arm" within the student body, and a "class" within the class.

I first learned about this tacit social ladder from Cyprian. We were sitting down to a plate of chips and beans early in Lent Term when he outlined the system for me. (In the British culinary patois, fries are chips, chips are crisps, and beans, even baked, are just called beans.) The two most prominent undergraduate classes at Cambridge, Cyprian explained, are the NARGs and the Yahs.

"It's like a civil war," he said. "The two sides battle each other for control of the college. They eat in different parts of Hall, drink in different parts of the pub, and generally scorn the company of the other side."

A Yah, so-named because he speaks with a patrician *yah* instead of the more plebeian *yes,* is the Cambridge man of myth. He, and now she, is often dressed in corduroy slacks, linen shirts, and 110 percent silk cravats. He owns two colors, or colours, of all-cotton, all-weather Barbour jackets and has three pairs of all-leather, all-weather brogue shoes, preferably the kind with the doily design on top like the ones my grandfather used to wear everywhere, from the bank to the beach.

"I don't own a pair of white shoes," Cyprian said. "I don't even own white socks."

"What do you do when you play football?" I asked.

"I always wear black."

Class, however, is thicker than feet; it's also a question of soul. According to Cambridge standards, a Yah is someone who probably comes from the South of the country, probably went to a boarding school (or to a state-run school that is over five hundred years old), and probably studies the humanities. History is good; English is better; classics, last refuge of scholars, is best. Over the years, Yahs have been called everything from Hooray Henries to Sloane Rangers, from swells to snobs. Today, with declining social standards, they go mostly unregistered and must secretly aspire to a whispered entry in the unofficial Yah Who's Who.

NARGs, on the other hand, have no Who's Who; they don't even have a what's what. "The Yahs always end up with 'She loves me,' " Cyprian said, "while the NARGs get stuck with 'She loves me not.' " The term NARG itself is an acronym for Not a Real Gentleman, but in the Cambridge lexicon it can be used as a noun, as in "There's a NARG in my soup," an adjective, as in "That shirt is very NARGy," and even an adverb, as in "She dances NARGily to Barry Manilow." A NARG wears denim jeans instead of corduroy trousers, flannel shirts instead of linen blouses, and thin black leather ties instead of silk cravats. He, and even she, owns a navy blue anorak parka that hangs NARGily from the shoulders, and two pairs of NARGy plimsoll tennis shoes—one grey, one black—that constitute the single condition of membership in the unofficial NARG Club Mod.

"You can always tell a NARG by his glasses," Cyprian said, pointing at someone across the Hall. "See how they have those wire rims. Always the latest alloys."

Like the Yahs, the NARGs are known for their accent and their interests as much as for their clothes. NARGs tend to come from the North of the country, speak with a clipped tongue instead of a mellifluous mutter, and study science. NatSci (natural science) is common; CompSci (computer science) is worse; and engineering is downright vulgar, because one runs the risk of getting dirt beneath one's fingernails. Since Cambridge students study only one subject for all three years, these labels take on even more permanence than they otherwise might. As a result, a Cambridge class is classified by a separation of words and numbers: I write therefore I Yah; I count therefore I NARG.

Bernard's birthday party was a classic example of an underground NARG fest. There was not a brogue in the place, not an ascot or waistcoat anywhere in the joint. After white and black, blue denim was the color of choice. On one side of the room a group of students huddled around the music system, which had now been repaired and was screeching with the latest sounds of American bubblegum pop. One person would select the tape. The next person would take the tape to the kitchen with her Walkman and find the correct song. Another person would place the correctly cued tape into the right deck. And a final person would select the right deck at the appropriate time. Occasionally, we would get a spurt of Gloria Estefan in the middle of George Michael, but on the whole the organization was impressive.

On the other side of the room, meanwhile, the two dozen or so guests were gathered around a foldout table littered with warm bottles of beer, store-bought biscuits, and garlic-and-onion potato crisps. When I arrived at the table, a bag of these crisps was just making its way around, preceded only by the breath of its bearer. I declined the bag and took a plastic cup to the kitchen to wash out the breath of the previous user before filling it with some warm ginger beer. Barely refreshed, I made my way across the room and sat down on a stack of three Sunday school chairs in front of an underground window that looked out on three feet of dirt.

Around the room several people had moved from the food corner to the dance corner (NARGs tend to take corners with them wherever they go). I noticed two people, both less than five feet, who were busily embracing in the corner beside the stereo. They weren't wiggling or writhing or particularly advancing; they just stood face-to-face, enjoined at the lips, with their arms interlinked like jigsawed pieces. I was looking at them, puzzled, when Bernard sat down on a stack of chairs to my right.

"Did you pay those people to stand in the corner and make out?" I asked.

"No," he said, "it was their idea."

"But they don't come up for air."

"It's their first time."

"Tonight?"

"Yeah, man. Isn't it awesome? Earlier I asked that guy if it was better to have the lights high and the music low, or the lights low and the music high. He said we should keep the lights low so people have a chance to get off. I guess he was planning ahead."

"Getting off" is the British euphemism for what Americans variously call getting on, getting down, or getting at it. In a world where language rules, it seems somehow emblematic of a larger cultural divide that Brits are forever rushing to "get off" while Americans are ever clamoring to "get on." But the true British handicap is much larger than words. It took me a while to catch on, but I eventually realized that the real reason the British are so skittish about sex is that they don't know how to play baseball. As a result, British adolescents (not to mention college prudes) don't have terms to mark their sexual progress, such as first base, second base, third base, and—the ultimate teenage fantasy—a homerun in the backseat. In contrast, the English national sport—cricket—is notoriously slow. Games take five days instead of three hours, and still they often don't produce winners. Also, cricket lovers don't make pitches, they bowl; and they don't hit towering home runs, they hit gliders that roll merrily along the grass and occasionally across a tidy white line.

As Bernard and I admired the lovers' stamina, if not their drive, a guest sat down next to us on the stacked orange chairs, and Bernard perked up, ready to try out his intro bit again.

"This is Bruce," he said to his friend, who was dressed like most of the others in tight-fitting jeans and a black T-shirt. "He was the one I was telling you about." Turning to me, he continued. "This is Daren. We traveled together in the South of France."

"Did you play any games?" I asked, thinking of our earlier encounters.

"Yes," Bernard answered. "Go."

If Bernard were just a puppy, he would have stopped at Monopoly. But as a full-grown savant, he also played chess, bridge, Othello, mah-jongg, and go—an ancient Japanese game involving black and white stones on a simple grid board. Bernard, moreover, took his games seriously. He was the treasurer of the Cambridge University Go Society and the vice president of the Bridge Club.

"That reminds me," Bernard said to Daren. "The Chess Club didn't come tonight, did it? I guess that means I wasn't elected president."

"You ran for president of the Chess Club," I said, "and you were opposed?"

"By three people," he said. "We have about forty members, and I had to make a speech. It was very competitive. But I left to come to my party so I didn't get a chance to vote."

"Bernard, Bernard!" A NatSci genus female scampered over to our group and squatted on the floor at Bernard's feet. "No one will dance with me. Won't you come?" She was wearing black jeans, a baggy denim shirt, and purple high-top sneakers. She pulled Bernard to the middle of the floor, squeezed her legs together, and shook her head like a pom-pom. Bernard, meanwhile, leapt around the floor, waved his arms like a cheerleader, and jumped up to touch the ceiling.

I turned back to Daren, who now had sweat running down his

neck from a previous round of dancing and who was shaking the front of his shirt, letting fresh air in and stale air out.

"What are you reading?" I asked.

"Maths," he said.

"For what degree?"

"Ph.D."

"What year?"

"Second."

I was beginning to feel a bit like a tax assessor trudging through a list of questions.

"What college are you in?"

"Trinity."

"I hear that's famous for maths."

"I live in the rooms where Newton lived."

"I guess that means yes, huh?"

Trinity is the oldest and crustiest of Cambridge colleges and the scones and cream of the Cambridge myth. The home of Bacon, Darwin, Russell, and Wittgenstein, Trinity has long been the *locus philosophicus* of the university and is still the home of the newest generation of mathematical prodigies. Newton's apple fell inside Trinity, and for many it remains the, well, *pi* in the sky. But genius, as I was ascertaining, does not necessarily make for good conversation. Scientists at Cambridge, because of their exclusive training, rarely have the skills to conduct a simple exchange. Daren, like Kenneth and Sean before him, reminded me of many of the undergraduates I knew in Clare who were for one reason or another incapable of conversation. I felt like grabbing his shoulders and shouting: "*We are having a conversation!* The technique is very simple. I ask you a question. You answer. You ask me a question." I knew Japanese junior high school students who were more conversant after two months of studying English than students at Cambridge who had spoken the language all their lives. NARGs, I reluctantly concluded, don't have conversations; they grow them—in petri dishes.

Finally, starved for discourse, I asked a question that had been bothering me for some time. "Can you tell me why maths are called maths in Britain but just math in America?"

"I don't know," he said. "Maybe it's because you leave off the *s*."

He stood up to leave.

"Hey," he said, "do you want to have a push-up contest? I bet I can do more."

"No, thank you," I said. "I think I'll dance."

As I moved to the center of the room, Daren flung himself to the floor and began counting push-ups. This gauntlet proved to be too much for Bernard, who soon joined his friend on the floor and challenged him to a race. Within seconds the entire party had gathered in a clump to cheer for one of the boys on the ground, as if they were cocks in an alley.

"Push it, Daren!" someone shouted. "God save the Queen!"

"Power Ten, Bernard," called another. "Born in the USA!"

Daren was the first to reach twenty-five (perhaps the Red Coats should have worn black), at which point he flipped onto his back and began spinning around in a Cambridge slam dance that seemed to embody Newton's fourth law of physics: any student when filled with alcohol will act like a juvenile delinquent until an external force acts to suspend him.

As I stood by myself, with Daren and Bernard on the floor and the vestal virgins still in the corner in their hammerlock embrace, I thought for a moment that we combined to make a strange syzygy. The guests at this party seemed to be part of an elaborate underground world, a subterranean galaxy complete with its own constellations of spinning dancers, dancing lovers, and loving puppies. Many of these people had probably not been above ground for days, maybe weeks. Some of them had beards that had never been shaved, as well as red and black plaid shirts they first put on when they went to school at age thirteen and had not since taken off. They lived underground, worked in labs without windows, and most, I suspected, had come to this basement room for Bernard's birthday party without even thinking about walking on the grass. There were probably secret tunnels connecting all of these labs in different colleges that required passwords, or maybe pass numbers, to enter. These were men made by machine, nourished by code, and inspired by the glow of the terminal screen that offered them access to a heaven higher than earth.

I, on the other hand, rarely dipped into this realm. I could recite Newton's laws, write a letter on computer, and do simple long division, but I met none of the conditions of numerical supremacy. When I played chess, I never managed to think more than three moves in advance. When I saw Daren spinning on the floor, I did not think in vectors and curves but in simple sentences. When I got dressed in the morning, it never occurred to me to wear white jeans.

I began to wonder why I felt so out of place in this environment. It wasn't a matter of nationality, for Bernard fit in perfectly well. It wasn't a matter of chronological age, since many of these students were older than I. It was, as Cyprian warned me, more a matter of class. Not the class that comes from money, not the working class or leisure class or any other class that comes from an individual's relationship to the means of production. It was the class that comes from the classroom. This was a group of people who lived, worked, studied, ate, drank, danced, dressed, courted, kept and—eventually—lost their virginity with one other. No one forced them to do it; they were all self-selected; and most of all they were free to leave at any time. But they didn't. They were part of each other, and I was not. It was I who had to leave.

"Goodnight, Bernard," I called after gathering my coat, emptying my glass, and catching a last glimpse of the lovers, still answering the question "Who's on first?" "Happy Birthday," I said.

"Oh, Bruce," he said, looking up with hurt puppy eyes from the arms of his genus female. "You're leaving?"

"Sorry," I said, mustering an excuse. "I didn't get much sleep last night."

"Hey, thanks for coming anyway. Let's do dinner this week."

"Sure."

"I'll get in touch." Most people in this situation would promise to drop off a note or leave word in my pigeonhole, but Bernard, true to form, had another idea: "I'll E-mail you," he said.

"Don't bother," I said. "I never use the system."

"You never use the system!?" he cried. "No wonder you haven't been responding to my messages. How am I supposed to contact you?"

"You can give me a call at the Porters' Lodge," I said.

"Will they take a message?"

"Sure," I said. "Just ask for Terry. He'd love to speak Californian with you."

"Cool, man. I'll do it. That Terry's a hip dude."

XIII

RAGGING

Incline and Fall

No wonder that Oxford and Cambridge—profound,
In learning and science so greatly abound;
When all carry thither a little each day,
And hardly a soul carries any away.

—Anonymous,
"Epigram," 1801

"Students today are no longer romantic. They are afraid of heights."

Christine Martin sat forward in her chair and pushed her spectacles down the ridge of her nose to show Rachel and me her well-read eyes and the depths they had seen in forty years of selling used books at No. 6 Turl Street.

"But this place is full of social climbers," I said. "They're crawling their way higher and higher every day."

"Love is different from class," she said. "If you're going to reach the highest peak, you must accept the risk of a fall."

"Even for those at the top?" Rachel asked.

"Even those at Oxford, my dear. You people have the most to lose."

Oxford in winter, like Oxford anytime, is a city of considerable elevation. With few tufts of green on the lawns and the trees and few spots of color in the gardens and the parks, the grey walls that line the town's haggard streets give the city a stark dignity like a gathering of aging gravestones tucked behind an old stone church. If Cambridge is famous for its river and roads, and the bridges that splice the two, Oxford is famous for its buildings and towers, and the spires that rise above them all. To be sure, Oxford has its rivers, the Isis and the Cherwell; it also has its roads, both Broad and High; but the town is known around the world for the simple shapes that crown its halls: the blue cupola with the black weather vane on top of the Sheldonian Theatre; the elongated tower like a wizard's cap atop the Church of St. Mary the Virgin; and the bulbous dome attached like a lens to the top of Radcliffe Camera. It's also known for its students, who come to Oxford when they are young to learn the lessons that defy age.

I, for my part, came to Oxford in mid-February and soon felt the pressures of time. Rachel had been hoping for several months to introduce me to Oxford. On my first night we went to a dinner party with her friends from the English faculty, where the topic of conversation was the rise of ambition among undergraduates. The second night we visited her faculty adviser, a young don who was editing the journals of Virginia Woolf and trying to encourage Rachel to abandon her dreams of becoming a lawyer and write a D.Phil. dissertation. (Cambridge, like most places, gives Ph.D.'s; Oxford, like no place, gives D.Phil.'s. instead.) On the morning of the third day, as we woke up to rain, Rachel again broke down in tears.

"I'm so confused," she suddenly cried. "I don't know what to do with myself. I don't know what to do with you. . . ."

Rachel had the charming, at times frustrating, habit of living every moment as if it were three. Perhaps she picked it up from

Virginia Woolf, or perhaps from the water in Oxford, but a remarkable number of our conversations followed a similar pattern: remembering the past, how silly we were then; fretting about the
future, how serious we would be; and all the while ignoring the
present, how could we make the right decisions? Universities are
thought to be cut off from life—separated from the pressures of
"real" time. But time does tick for university students, often in
suprisingly powerful ways. The reason is simple: anytime you take
a group of precocious young people, cut them off from the outside
world, and give them unlimited time to think, they invariably spend
most of their free time thinking about themselves.

Later, after Rachel had calmed down and I had picked up the
second dropped ball, we took a walk around the rare-book shops of
Oxford looking for a copy of *To the Lighthouse,* Virginia Woolf's
ode to the passing of time, which I had promised to buy her as a
Valentine. No shop had a copy of the book, but one dealer, Mrs.
Christine Martin, did have some thoughts on the topic of students—what they should learn while they're in school and what
they should not forget.

"Do you know the story of Atalanta?" she asked us after sharing
with us her theory on the fear of heights.

"Is that the one about the race?" I asked, thumbing through
volume six of Winston Churchill's official history of the Second
World War.

"It's actually about love," she corrected me. "Atalanta was a
beautiful maiden who feared marriage and lived in the woods. But
her many suitors would not leave her alone, so Atalanta—the
daughter of the king—announced that she would become the bride
of any man who could defeat her in a foot race. Any man who lost
to her, however, would have to be put to death."

Rachel peered around the corner from a particularly dusty strip of
Thomas Hardy novels. "I think I remember this story from when I
was a child," she said. "Something about apples."

"That's right," our guide continued. "Many men tried to defeat her, but all of them faltered. Until one young man, Hippomenes, went to pray before Venus and ask for her assistance. Venus gave the boy three golden apples. When the race began, Atalanta was faster, but just as she seemed to pull away, Hippomenes tossed down the first of his golden apples. Atalanta didn't pick it up, but she did hesitate for a moment, thereby allowing the boy to jump into the lead.''

Mrs. Martin arrived back at her rolltop desk and sat down with a slight spring in her legs. Her alcove was a nest of yellowed papers, splintered bindings, and mottled-leather covers in an otherwise tidy orchard of shelves. A four-prong fan hung limply from the ceiling, fussing up dust from the cracks in the floor and blending in fumes from the kerosene stove. The shop smelled like a mixture of Dickens's *Bleak House* and Blake's "The Chimney Sweeper."

Atalanta quickly reclaimed the lead, she said, so the boy was forced to drop the second of his apples. Again Atalanta paused, but continued to run. Finally, as they neared the last turn, Atalanta regained the lead and seemed on the verge of winning the race when the young boy tossed the last of his golden apples at the foot of the finishing line. "Atalanta hesitated for a moment," she said. "But this time she could not resist the temptation and reached to retrieve the apple. Hippomenes won the race."

Rachel applauded her performance and ambled over to the desk with a big smile on her face.

"Not so soon," she said. "You haven't heard the end of the story. Venus was so upset that she did not receive gratitude from the couple that she turned them into a pair of lions and harnessed them to a chariot for the rest of their lives."

"That's not very romantic," I said. "I thought you said this story was about love."

"It is, young man. You shouldn't think love is about two people who simply fall for each other and live happily ever after. Love is more than ambition, it's more than desire. It's a struggle, and the only way to triumph is to come face-to-face with your own mortality."

"Your mortality?" Rachel said.

"Your death," she repeated. "Without pain, or the threat of pain, your joy is always diminished. Think of the war. The men and women who come back from battle have a heightened sense of death, so they have a heightened sense of life. The students when they come up to university have no fear of dying. They are on top of the world."

Rachel was rapt by the woman's authority. The two of them stared at each other as if in a trance. I felt as if I were being locked out of a private conversation.

"And what happens to them?" Rachel asked.

"The same thing that happens to you," the woman said. "They learn it. Somehow in the course of their time here, they learn what it means to die. By the time they leave, they have often experienced pain for the very first time. It's the greatest thing you learn in school, and the hardest to teach. It's called growing up, my dear, and it's not in any book."

Rachel thanked the woman, accepted her card, and came hurrying down the stairs after me, already halfway out the door.

"Books?! Bollocks. Who needs them? I learned most of what I know from the front seat of a bus."

Harriet Catterall was sitting at an antique cherry table on Kensington Place eating roast beef and Yorkshire pudding from the back of her fork.

"The front seat?" I said. "That's surprising. I would have guessed you'd prefer the back."

She looked at me with a grin. "The front's got a better view."

The longer I stayed in England, the more I discovered that almost everybody I met had a different opinion of the purpose of higher education. From learning to be a gentleman to learning to read my horoscope, from practicing literary criticism to winning the race for love, the goal of higher education seemed to shift depending on the seat one occupied, or the seat one hoped to acquire. Not long after my trip to Oxford, I was invited to a luncheon party in London at the posh Victorian home of a friend of a friend, where the touchy topic of Oxbridge education came boiling to the surface.

"Just look at me," said Harriet, a thirtyish woman who was plump in the cheeks and the waist. "I went to one of the best public schools in this country and it didn't do me a damn bit of good. All they taught me was how to pour tea."

"But Harriet," interrupted her boyfriend, Mark, "you're different."

"Damn right I am."

"So you can't use yourself as an example."

"The hell I can't!" she demurred. "I didn't learn a bloody thing in school because my teachers all had polo mallets up their bums. I didn't know what I wanted to be when I was sixteen. In this country you have to decide then, so I went to America and learned everything I need to know on the streets. Screw all this university business. Now I got me a job that makes twice as much money as you."

Mark Riley did not return her fire, but stared down the handle of her knife. Unlike Harriet, who had returned from her unconventional jaunt in America and opened her own independent catering firm with recipes she learned from abroad, he had proceeded orderly through state-sponsored schools, moved on to the University of London after failing the entrance exam to Oxford, and later passed the qualifying test to become an actuary.

"I want my child to be successful," he said in a dispassionate air that masked his intensity. "To do that he has to work hard. Very hard. If the only way to gain power in this country is to go to Oxbridge, then my child will have to excel in school."

"Well, you can forget having a child with me," Harriet snapped. "I don't want my child to go to Oxbridge. They're too isolated and don't know anything about the streets."

At this word her neighbor Charles, who had been quietly mind-
ing his peas and stews, perked up and leaned into the brawl.

"I think you would be making a grave mistake not to send your
child to Oxford," he said. "It's the greatest education in the world."

Charles Stanton was a graduate of Eton College, which we call
a high school, and St. John's College, Oxford, which we call a
university. He was a tall, dapper man in his late twenties, with
flowing blond hair, a thin, sly smile, and a bank of misaligned British
teeth, purple from too much wine. When he first arrived at the
party, two hours late from a pub, I asked him what he did.

"I'm an actor," he said.

"Are you working?" I asked.

"Well," he responded. "Think of me as Robin Hood: I steal
from my parents to make myself poor."

He went to pour a drink.

"The purpose of higher education is to remove a man from the
streets," Charles said, gesturing to Harriet with a dip of his nose.
"That's the great contribution of the English. America just doesn't
compare. I remember when I was in school, I once played in a golf
tournament in the Bahamas. My opponent was an American. I was
fourteen; he was eighteen. But I was much more sophisticated than
he was. He didn't even know any Latin."

"Who gives a damn about Latin," countered Harriet.

"I do," Charles responded. "And you should, too. The people
who are successful in this country are the ones who can talk about
the cherubs on the ceiling or the painting on the wall. In America
they teach their young how to fight, how to make war, how to beat
up each other. In England—especially at Oxford—we teach our
students how to behave."

Harried scoffed at his prepared speech, but Mark nearly applauded. "Bravo!" he cried, uplifting his glass to clink with King
Charles. "In America students learn to make war. In England we
learn to make tea."

.   .   .

"Ladies and gentlemen, may I have your attention. . . ."

A sweatshirted student stood on top of the snooker table in the Junior Common Room of Clare and tapped a cue ball against a pint glass.

"Please move away from the centre of the room," he said. "The race is about to start."

In Cambridge, February is the cruelest month. The food that during Michaelmas Term seemed humorously flavorless begins somewhere in the middle of Lent to turn unbearably bland. The sun that even at the height of summer merely provides occasional lighting sees fit by the middle of winter to retire before afternoon tea and not return until the following morning, well past coffee hour. The cold that threatened all through the fall settles into College rooms by Valentine's Day like an influx of rodents that refuses the daily exterminating balm of two coats of sweaters and a pot of hot tea. At Yale students confronted the onset of winter by creating an institution called the February Club, which sponsored a party every night of the month for frosty scholars to come in from the cold. At Cambridge students took a similar tack by cobbling together a series of relay races, charity bashes, and thematic cocktail parties into an annual event known as Rag Week.

Rag Week, similar in frenetic tone to Greek Week at American universities, is nominally about raising money for charity. The idea of linking rags, or pranks, with charity began after the First World War with the widespread celebration of Poppy Day on the Saturday nearest to Armistice Day. Over time the ritual was shifted from Michaelmas to Lent and expanded to include a massage marathon, a hitchhike to Paris, and a grand prix race around the streets of Cambridge using rolling beds as cars and pushing students as fuel. The highlight of Rag Week at Clare occurred on the last Saturday of the month with the annual Pie & Pints Relay Race. The rules of the race were quite simple. Each paying contestant must drink a total of five pints of beer and in between each round he must run to the far side of the room and eat, in succession, an orange, a bag of crisps, a pork pie, and a Cadbury's Creme Egg.

"If you knock over a pint, you are disqualified," the judge announced. "If you don't eat all of the food, you are disqualified. You are, however, allowed to discard the orange rind."

A cheer went up from the hundred or so students gathered beneath the whitewashed vaulted ceilings of the Clare crypt lounge.

"Where should we stand?" I asked Simon, who was already craning his neck for a view of the starting line.

"Near the drinking?" he suggested.

"How about near the food," said Lucy, Simon's newest girlfriend, who had all but moved into V Entryway after Simon gave up Kiet Khiem for Lent. "There's likely to be more action there."

"Are you ready?" The starter called. "Three, two, one, *go!*"

The four contestants rushed from the snooker table, where the food was displayed, toward the "table-footie" (foozball) table at the end of the room, where the beer was perched. The referee ran along beside them lugging an oversized white bucket.

"What's the purpose of the bucket?" I asked Simon as the first round of beer sailed down.

"It's a vomitorium," he said.

"Does that mean we should stand back?"

"Not necessarily," answered Lucy, a feisty, first-year lawyer from Clare. "Just watch out for flying debris."

The first person to arrive back at the snooker table was Henry, a first-year engineer and close pal of Simon's. He scurried up to the table, took a large bite of orange peel, and spat it onto the ground. Moving with the force of a forward swan dive, he plunged into the core of the nonnavel orange and devoured its contents with three gargantuan sucking motions. After he finished, he deposited the flayed peel on the ground, bowed to the cheers of the audience, and hurried back to his remaining four pints.

Two other athletes—Paul, a spiky-haired third-year and Jeff, a ringer from another college—quickly followed. They were trailed by the last contestant, Mark, a prominent, army-coated lefty from Clare who was currently making news on campus by serving as the first liberal president of the Union Society in over a generation and by boasting the weirdest haircut in town with half his scalp shaved from the bottom up and the rest of his hair left to hang down in a samurailike ponytail.

Mark was less flashy than the other competitors, yet more strategic. Conserving energy, he hovered near the back of the pack as first Paul and then Jeff dropped out somewhere between the orange and the bag of crinkle-cut, sea-salted, cheese-and-onion-flavored potato crisps. By the time he arrived at the third hurdle, a hockey-puck-sized pub pork pie with a raw chili pepper inserted enemalike up its bum, he was within striking distance of the leader. He downed the pie in several bites, spit out the pepper, and staggered slowly across the Buttery tile, saving his energy for the inevitable confrontation with young Henry the First-Year.

As one of the few events in the year that drew participation from all the colleges, Rag Week revealed a lot about how students view their relationship with the outside world, and about how they feel they should spend their time while inside the university. Almost everyone in college participated in one event or another. But, befitting the Elysian qualities of Cambridge, most joined out of a feeling that might best be described as *intelligentsia oblige*. Few of the students involved knew which charities their money was going to support, and even fewer put themselves out to assist these organizations in any way other than drinking on their behalf. Unlike at Yale, for example, where social work was so trendy during my time there that it became almost obligatory, I met no one in Cambridge in the course of a year who did volunteer work. Those on the outside may idealize Oxbridge and the manners its students supposedly learn, but those on the inside spend little time wasting those manners on anyone else. Indeed, with its glorification of drinking, emphasis on public humiliation, and general celebration of bad taste, the Pie &

Pints Relay Race was the perfect allegory of the underside of the
Cambridge myth. Here were students chasing students across the
floor in the crypt of an antique church, clambering higher and
higher into drunken oblivion, lifting themselves into an orbit of
superficial prominence, while all the time sacrificing their insides on
the altar of hubris.

After close to half an hour the race came down to two finalists
who hobbled up to the snooker table to face the final barrier between them and pubwide adulation—a six-ounce milk-chocolate
egg inside of which was a white liquid center and a candied bright
orange yolk. These candy treats, known as Cadbury's Creme Eggs,
are the closest thing the British have to a national snack. I had eaten
my first one in Ian's rooms only the week before and had to let some
of the white candy syrup dribble out into an ashtray before I could
get it down. I could not imagine eating one in front of a hundred
screaming classmates with an orange, a bag of crisps, a pork pie, and
four pints of beer already inside my stomach.

The finalists reached the table at almost the same time. Henry the
First-Year picked up his egg and began to peel off the outer foil as
if it were a shell. Mark the President, proved more experienced. He
grabbed the chocolate egg, slammed it into the table, and began to
eat it from the inside out. This fit of inspiration garnered him precious seconds as the two wobbled toward their final pints just in
front of the upright piano. The crowd, like polite guests at the final
hole of a golf tournament, followed the two toward the table-footie
table.

"Come on, Henry! Do it for the first-years."

"Hurry up, Mark. He's catching you!"

The boys did their best to drink with haste, but inevitably more
beer dribbled down their necks than flowed down their gullets. First
Mark, and then Henry, put down the pint glass. But both were still
half full. Mark pounded his chest and began anew; Henry slapped
his head and reached for his pint. His stomach, however, reached
out first, and with a synchronized finish worthy of *Chariots of Fire,*

the audience cheered, the cameras flashed, as Henry the First dou-
bled over in pain and Mark the President tossed his empty glass into
the air.

The race was over. The river was run. But instead of a victory
celebration, the two finalists clasped each other around the waist
and headed off—like Hippomenes and Atalanta—directly to the
loo. In the end, as Christine Martin foretold, the gods would have
the last word: the heroes would take a fall.

XIV

FLIRTING

A Yah Who's Who

You round a corner, enter a room, pick up a telephone—and there are *that* voice, *those* mannerisms,
those clothes, that *style,* THOSE PEOPLE. It all comes
back. It never went away. It's all going on now, *still.*

—Ann Barr and Peter York
The Official Sloane Ranger Handbook, 1983

My invitation was the last to arrive. For weeks the trendiest
members of the college had been chitchatting about the
venue. For days the toniest CRABS and Lobsters had been wish-
washing about what to wear. For all these days and weeks, however,
I hadn't been chitting or chatting at all, because I—a low breed—
was so out of the loop I wasn't even aware that I wasn't in the know.
Then one day I was eating in Buttery when Nigel—the top breed—
was forced to sit down next to me. Halfway through our well-
starched meal, a first-year upstart came rushing to his side and
wondered aloud what time the party would start. Nigel glanced at
me, turned his face toward the floor, and mumbled something inau-

dible that sent his friend scurrying toward the door. That afternoon an envelope appeared in my pigeonhole.

> Nigel Parkhill, Pegram McIntosh, *et tu,* too,
> will be celebrating Shrove Tuesday
> with drinks,
> in the Thirkill Room, Clare College,
> from 7:30 P.M.
> Dress: Fabulissimus   PBABSpWW

I knew that PBABSpWW—the eight most important letters to any aspiring *bon vivant*—meant "Please bring a bottle of sparkling white wine," but I didn't know the meaning of "Fabulissimus," so I asked.

"It means smart," said Ian, the trendiest person I knew and also the most blunt. "Except it's in Latin, which probably means wear only natural fibres."

"Very funny," I said. "But that doesn't help. Are we supposed to wear DJs or togas?"

"We?" he said. "Am I going with you?"

"Yes," I said. "You can be my escort."

"In that case," he said. "The only way to be sure is to have a look for yourself."

"You mean stick my head in the door?"

"I mean take a peek through the window."

"I can't believe I came all the way to Cambridge to learn fashion espionage."

"What did you expect?" he smirked. "The only things we're famous for are cocktail parties and spies."

Ian had a reputation in Clare for always wearing the right thing and often saying the wrong. On the outside he was a gentleman-scholar—a slightly cavalier Yah—forever strutting around college in his baggy tweed jacket, tight black trousers, and embroidered leather boots, while carrying in his back pocket a well-fingered copy of Nietzsche with the cover strategically facing out. But on the inside he was a childish terror—moody, feisty, and often uncontrollably blustery, not unlike the weather. Proudly unpredictable, he would alternate without warning between mild-mannered socialite and hotblooded lout. I watched him charm women with brooding renditions of Rainer Maria Rilke's love poetry; I watched him offend others by asking them to describe the size and texture of their nipples. If Simon was a scientist hoping to uncover the perfect sexual chemistry, Ian was a philosopher hoping to devise the ultimate theory of existential love.

By his own standards, Ian was still down on his luck near the end of Lent Term. Miranda, his fallen, statuesque ideal, continued to haunt him from afar by sending long apologias from London. Louise, meanwhile, his quiet, redhead figurine dream, had been so alarmed by his gift of goodies at the end of Michaelmas Term that she remained cool to his advances throughout the new year, which only encouraged him to write her tear-jerking billets-doux asking for her forgiveness. The net result of these double-barreled blows on his not inconsiderable estimate of personal self-worth was a slow, spiraling decline into the arms of self-pity. By late January, when the war started, he began to sleep late almost every day and skip fencing practice. By February, as the fighting worsened, he began to shower and shave less frequently and lost a bout he shouldn't have in the annual Oxford–Cambridge Varsity Games. And by early March, as the combat climaxed, he had lost all interest in Nietzsche, had stopped fencing all together, and had begun searching for clues to a solution of his romantic–identity crisis in cheap paperback editions of Barbara Taylor Bradford and imported copies of *Calvin and Hobbes*. "Maybe I should lift weights," he said. "My upper body is too small." "Maybe I should learn French." The occasion of the All-Clare Mardi Gras Bacchanal presented an opportunity for me to drag him out of his self-flagellating den and push him back into the courting circle.

"Let's go check out the clothes," I said, pulling him from hypnotic repose in front of the dartboard. "We're already past fashionably late."

We stepped out into the cool air of Old Court and slipped surreptitiously to the one spot in college with an unimpeded view of the Thirkill Room: the top of Clare Bridge.

"Can anybody see us?" Ian whispered. "I'm so embarrassed."

"Stop talking," I said. "You'd make a terrible spy. Just climb up on top of one of these balls and tell me what you see."

Ian put his right foot into my hands and maneuvered himself to the top of a ball, stretching his arms out for balance. Once he was steadied, he turned toward Old Court and craned his neck to see inside the room. A minute went by without any word, and then he suddenly announced: "Bloody hell. You're not going to believe this. Everyone's dressed in drag!"

The room was purring when we arrived—a jolly, cheerful, murmuring purr that hung over the outstretched glasses and upturned noses like a cloud of perfume smog. The light, like the noise, seemed to dance in the air, leaping from the pupils of the candelabra, twinkling from the lobes of every earring, and cascading from the chandelier—coccyx of the Milky Way—like endless ribbons of peach chiffon from the shoulders of the Queen Mum. Time had stopped (was this Clare or Versailles?); the party was cast (an all-star bill); and decadence flowed from every corner in a gushing fountain of braying laughter, tinkling wrists, sparkling white wine, and *eau de toilette*. At the center, on the edge, and flowing through it all was the chief socialite-impresario of Clare, Nigel Parkhill.

"Good evening, good evening, Ian and Bruce. I'm so glad you could come." Nigel, dressed in vivid green, came gliding across the pale floral rug and planted two kisses on both of our cheeks. "And don't you both look divine."

He tipped his champagne glass, dipped his head, and escorted us into the room. Inside, several yellow marshmallow sofas surrounded the second-story room, punctuated by uptight antique wooden chairs, and lorded over by giant mirrors in gilded frames and miniature sketches of croquet games along the banks of the Cam. Untrue to Ian's surveillance, none of the people upon closer inspection was dressed entirely in drag. True, most of the men had long hair and most of the women had short; most of the men wore slinky silk blouses and more women than men wore trousers and brogues. But every person seemed to boast in his androgynous vogue one distinguishing gender clue: the longer the earrings, for example, the more likely that ear belonged to a man; the more exposed the breast, the more likely that breast belonged to a woman. Among this rarefied chic clientele, Ian seemed perfectly male chauvinist in his baggy tweed jacket and slice of hairy chest and I, in my navy trousers, dark blue shirt, and bright crimson tie, seemed as much out of place as a Damon Runyon racketeer at an Evelyn Waugh garden party. Mind of a libertine; wardrobe of a hood.

"Come in, come in," Nigel said. "Let me get you a drink. But first let me introduce you to some of my friends."

He ushered us up to the central huddle and into the upright lap of one of his dearest pals, whose tight outfit and short hemline made her gender very clear.

"This is Chantalle," said Nigel. "Meet Ian and Bruce."

We smiled. She looked at both of us from head to toe, and settled her eyes on Ian. He stared, transfixed, at her.

"That's some dress," he said.

"It's the fashion," she said. "I borrowed it from a friend who's a psychiatrist."

"Is that spelled with a capital *F*?" I asked.

"Psychiatrist?" she said.

"No, fashion."

"Well, the dress *was* made in Paris—"

"And that's certainly with a capital *P*."

She simpered and pivoted back toward Ian. I wished him well and turned away. No sooner had I taken one step to my right than

I found myself face-to-face with a certifiably fashionable man with blond hair to his waist, a chartreuse morning coat to his knees, and one caramel espadrille poised slightly in front of the other. He was just resting his cigaretted wrist on his well-cocked waist and spinning his glass toward the ceiling when I arrived in earshot.

"So what do you think?" he said to several of his friends. "Is this classical or contrapposto?"

"I think it's tagliatelle," said one man.

"No, seriously," he huffed. "One foot forward and the other back. What is that?"

"Let's ask Nigel," said one woman, looking around for our host, who was at that moment just returning with several drinks. "Nigel dear, is this pose classical or contrapposto?"

"Neither," he said without batting an eye. "That's Ralph Lauren."

Nigel Parkhill, for all intents and poses, was a classic Cambridge Yah. His skin was as pale as custard, his hair was as fair as barley, his nose was as angular as the masthead on the flagship of Her Majesty's Royal Navy. He dressed only in suits or sweats (never jeans), wore matching ties and handkerchiefs (usually polka dots), and owned more pairs of wide-wale corduroys than I owned pairs of socks. He came to his own Mardi Gras gala, for instance, in a pink broadcloth shirt, white silk bow tie, and an oversized lime green three-button suit with a white kerchief dangling joey-like from its upper breast pocket. His accent, to boot, could best be diagnosed as severe nasal congestion.

Nigel, however, was not what he appeared. His clothes, his pose, even his accent were all careful affectations to disguise a less-than-noble birth. Of course, ambitious makeovers are quite common in Cambridge. The British class system, as I was discovering, was not as much a system, nor as closed a class, as most people inside it would like to believe. Yet even in that world of smoke and mirrors Nigel's guise was a sleight of some distinction, for he was not born in Essex nor in Surrey but in Jackson Hole, Wyoming.

In many ways it is easier to penetrate the English elite if one hails from rural Wyoming than from cockney Cheapside. Many of the most "Brideshead" characters I met in Cambridge, for example, actually came from abroad. There was the German lawyer in my course who wore a different-colored paisley ascot every day of the week. There was the French aristocrat I met from Peterhouse who was writing his M.Litt. thesis on homosexual overtones in Edwardian schoolboy literature. And of course there was Nigel, a graduate student in art history, who was writing his Ph.D. dissertation on a series of prose poems about Venice written by the Oxford high priest of letters, John Ruskin, in the late nineteenth century. All of these characters looked the part of a gentle Englishman, but their true genius lay somewhere else: they could act the part as well.

"Pegram," called Nigel from the center of the room. "Would you pour Chantalle some more champagne?

"Sy," he cried in the other direction. "You must meet my friend Bruce. He would love to hear about the George Eliot love letters you found in the basement of the U.L.

"Now, Bru," he said, pivoting back toward me. "You just *have* to meet my pal Rana. He's Indian—very rich—and wait till you hear what he had to do before he came up to Cambridge."

Already spinning from the merry going round, I accepted my drink—a mocha-colored concoction artfully concanted from Kahlúa, vodka, allspice, and cream—exchanged banalities about George Eliot, looked in vain for any rich-looking Indians, and marched through the middle of several charming circles to find the food table overlooking the Cam. Heaping bowls of fruit were perched on either end, sprinkles of sugar cookies dotted the tablecloth, and a porterly, rotund silver samovar was poised at the heart of the spread just beneath a marble bust of Lord Byron. I was looking at Byron's reflection in the face of the samovar when someone tapped me on the shoulder and reached to embrace me.

"Bruce," came a squeal from inside my arms. "I'm so happy to see you."

It was Susanna, dressed, unlike she was at the Crew Meal, in a dark two-piece pants suit. Since our first meeting in Michaelmas Term I had seen Susanna at many Clare events. With her bleached-blond hair and two dozen outfits, her whitened skin and broad toothy smile, she seemed to me a central figure in the social network of the college. In some ways I was right about her position; in others I was not.

"What are *you* doing here?" she said, squeezing her shoulders close to mine in conspiratorial fashion.

"I'm spying," I said.

"For whom?" she whispered.

"The proletariat."

My answer bounced flatly off her forehead and landed in her drink. She took a sip to mull it over, then changed the subject. "Hey, do you know that man who just walked in?" she said, pointing indiscreetly across the room. "The one with the funny jacket. He's so handsome."

"That must be Nigel's friend Rana," I said. "I think he's an Indian prince or something."

"Oooh," she said. "India. That sounds exotic . . . which reminds me, have you figured out what international relations is yet?"

"No," I said. "But I'm working on it. I have an exam next week, so I have until then to decide."

"The war must be providing you with all sorts of material."

"It should," I said. "But I wonder if it has. I don't think it's had much effect around Cambridge. The parties all seem to continue."

"Maybe," she said. "But I just came from the King's Mingle, and it just wasn't the same as last year."

"What's the King's Mingle?"

"Don't you know?" She took a quick sip of her drink, a cranberry cocktail with a fizz so powerful it looked like it came from Liquid-Plumr. "King's voted several years ago not to have a May Ball because they thought it was too elitist—can you imagine?—so now they have a big party every year at the end of Lent. This year they had to have special security because they thought it might be bombed."

"Did you have a good time?"

"It was a good laugh, I suppose. But Peter really wanted to come here."

"Peter!" I said, recalling as I did the bloody scene at our Crew Meal. "Are you still seeing him?"

"Well." She grabbed the back of her hair and diverted her eyes. "I know what everyone thinks. But I rather like him. He's not so bad, really. You see, I always wondered if I could ever have a healthy relationship with a bloke because I could never say no."

"Can you say no now?"

She straightened her back. "I did to Peter."

"And what happened?"

"I changed my mind."

As she spoke, Susanna recognized someone standing behind me. "Hillary," she called. "Hill. It's me."

A young woman brushed my shoulder on her way to double-kiss Susanna's cheeks. Like her friend, Hillary was wearing a two-piece pin-striped suit that seemed to stretch in a single line from the tip of her black suede pumps to the top of her soft blond bun in a striking effect not unlike an upside-down exclamation point.

"Do you know Hillary?" asked Susanna. I took her hand as if to shake it; she demurred as if to say, "Why don't you give it a kiss?" I let go.

"Hillary and I are starting a drinking society," Susanna said.

"Like the Lobsters?"

"Oh no," she said. "All *they* do is have a drinking party in the spring which anyone can attend if they buy a ticket. We're forming a new society, for captains and cuppers—you know, those who play intramural sports."

"And those who direct plays for the college," said Hillary. "That's how I get in."

"And what will you do?"

Susanna shook back her hair. "Every two weeks or so we'll have dinner with good-looking male societies from other colleges."

"Sharking, you mean."

"Flirting," corrected Hillary.

"What's the difference?"

"In sharking you have something in mind—an aim."

"Like getting someone into your arms?"

She stared at me coolly. "I mean into bed."

Hillary Prime was a first-year linguist in Clare, a first-time director of Oscar Wilde for the Clare Actors Society, and a first-class wordsmith. Several moments into our initial encounter, Nigel's friend, the George Eliot scholar, stepped up to the table where we were chatting.

"This is Simon," I said, by way of introduction.

"Actually," he interrupted, "it's Symond."

"Sorry," I stammered. "I must have misunderstood."

"Not to worry," he said. "It's an uncommon name. It comes from an obscure earl in a Shakespeare play."

"*Macbeth*," said Hillary. "Act Five."

"Why, yes," said Symond. "Nicely done."

"But I thought his name was Siward," she added.

His face fell to his shoes.

"Actually," he said, "it was. I'm afraid my mother can't spell."

He turned to the fruit. She turned toward the bar. I was left standing like a fool—in well over my head.

At many times throughout the year, and especially the times that I happened to hobnob with the yah and mighty, Cambridge often seemed to me a giant theatrical set. The weather was dank, the buildings were dark, the trees were heavy with age, but the student with a few pounds in his pocket and a surplus of free time could splurge on a life-style so grandiose it would make even marble Byrons blush. Liquor was the fuel that drove this class, sex was the fire that triggered its clash, but the one currency that sealed its exchange was the spoken word. For those peers in the realm of belles-lettres, words are like pearls one can dangle for display. Words are like swords one can wield for cachet. But above all, words become dialogue, dialogue becomes theater, and theater becomes the main display in an ongoing parade of wit.

Wit is not taken lightly in Cambridge: it is the lifeblood of the body theatric. Unlike NARGs, who treat conversation as imprecise word games, Yahs look upon even the simplest exchange as a chance to phrase a coinage. A typical Yah-like conversation goes something like this:

It begins with a question. "What is the difference between a nook and a cranny?"

Someone has an answer. "A nook is a niche, while a cranny is a crack."

Someone has a crack response. "Then why does a nook need a separate niche?"

Someone has a definitive theory. "Because a niche was once a nest, while a nook was just a corner."

Someone takes the theory and carries it to extremes. "You can't very well eat breakfast in a breakfast niche."

Someone returns with a *coup de grâce*. "And you can't find your nook in life."

All this took place in a gyp.

The longer I lived in Cambridge, the more I marveled at the cutting, almost divisive, role that language played in the lives of so many students. Much more than just words, language in Cambridge is about gamesmanship—scoring points off a verbal sparring partner. It's about artifice—maintaining a facade of total control, where nothing requires too much energy or too much concern. It's about inflection—delivering even the most casual remarks in a tone of voice that suggests utter humility while actually epitomizing complete condescension. And ultimately language is about class—using words to build a nest high up in a tree where birds of a feather flock together and where hedgehogs of a more mathematical bent are kept far away.

The gap in Cambridge between the literati and the numerati is hardly new. Soon after learning from Cyprian about the NARGs and the Yahs, I came upon a copy of a lecture by Cambridge physicist-novelist C. P. Snow on the chasm between scientists and humanists. "There seems to be no place where the cultures meet," he said in the early 1960s. "In fact, the separation is much less bridgeable among the young than it was even thirty years ago." Thirty years later this separation has not gone away, and the gap between Bernard's birthday bash and Nigel's bacchanal seemed to be wide enough for two novice crews to pass each other without even touching their blades. Fashion may contribute to this gap; snobbery may play a part; but ultimately what keeps these groups apart at Cambridge is that they speak different languages. Since the universal curriculum at Cambridge was abolished earlier this century, neither group has learned the necessary means to engage the other in meaningful conversation. Moreover, since the only way to be admitted to the specialized courses at Cambridge (and Oxford as well) is to pass specialized exams, students who wish to attend these schools study only their particular subjects, and a few related ones, during their years in secondary school. At exactly the same time they should be broadening their minds, young students in Britain are being told to narrow their course of study.

The result, at least in Cambridge, is a bipolar campus. As far as the humanists are concerned, science may be the meat and potatoes of industrial success, but what they learn in the humanities is the subtle spicing of wit—the true gravy of conversation. Wit, in this case, is much more than verbal pyrotechnics. It is an attitude, a life-style, an expression of confidence: "I'm young, I'm British, I'm at Cambridge, I am, by extension, on top of the world." True wit, in the minds of these people, is not something one can learn by reading a

Berlitz guide; it cannot be put on and taken off like a DJ and bow
tie. In fact, wit is not something you have or have not; it is simply
something you *are* or *are not*. The goal of the classic Cambridge
education is, simply put, to become British wit. Those who aren't
just disappear underground, while those who are just float through
their myriad conversations on a gossamer of literary illusions and
rhetorical pageantry that lifts them farther and farther away from
earth and into an artificial orbit.

After several hours the Thirkill Room seemed to be even lighter
than it was when we arrived. Nigel had dimmed the chandelier and
allowed the candles to frolic alone in their tender strobe. Ian had
managed to transcend his doom and was becoming increasingly
animated as he talked in the corner with Chantalle, his damsel in a
dress. Even I had downed one-too-many cocktails and was feeling
free of the pressures of international relations and interuniversity
romance. Somewhere after my third Kahlúa-vodka-allspice-and-
cream I found myself floating in front of the balcony in a lightly
salted conversation with Hillary, who it turns out was not a "maid,"
but, in Cambridge terms, a "matron."

"So tell me about your 'husband,' " I said. "I mean your boyfriend."

"His name is Dean," she said. "He's a vet."

"A bunny and hedgehog type of vet," I asked, "or a cow and
horse variety?"

"Definitely a horse vet. He's very much of a horsey person, you
see. He rides for the university."

"You mean he rides for some team."

"He rides for *The* Team," she corrected me. "That's with a capital *THE*. He's a member of the Polo Club."

I smiled at the successful exchange. She retrieved a cigarette case
from her bag.

"If he's a vet, he must be very busy?"

"Not really. I don't see him much during the day, but he usually pops round about nine. You could say we have a nine-to-five relationship."

"A working relationship."

"At times."

She rummaged in her bag until she found a silver lighter and handed it to me.

"You like talking about relationships, don't you?" she said. "That's very American of you."

"Why do you say that?"

"I find it difficult to talk with English men about my personal life."

"About your love life, you mean, or your sex life?"

"Oh, I will tell people about my sex life, but not my love life. I find it easy to tell someone that I went to bed with a man, but I won't tell them why."

"What's the difference?"

"Sex is something you have—it's physical. Love is something you are—it's personal."

A voice came from the other side of the room.

"Hillary, Hill, where are you? Help."

Peter came pushing through the crowd and began pawing at Hillary's shoulder. "Where's Susanna?" he said. "Have you seen Susanna? I can't find her. I have to find her." He turned to look at me. His eyes were glazed, his hair askew, his pupils reverberated in their sockets as they tried to focus on me. "He's not Dean. . . . Where's Susanna? Who the hell is this bloke?"

"It's Bruce," said Hillary. "Susanna's not here. She went to get a drink."

"A drink? I don't need a drink. I have to find her. . . ." He turned around in a circle and staggered back into place. His four-button tweed suit clung to his sinking shoulders like a slumped-over bag of potatoes. "He sure does look familiar. Haven't I met you before?"

He didn't wait for an answer but turned toward the door and walked away.

"Take Peter, for example," Hillary said. "I don't trust him at all. He's not personal, he's merely physical."

"He's unbelievable," I added. "He didn't even remember that I rowed in his boat last term."

"Apparently, he gets that way a lot," Hillary said. "It's how he reacts."

"Reacts to what?" I said.

She looked at me for a moment as if trying to determine if I was making a joke, then placed the cigarette on the ridge of her lips and smiled. "Drugs."

I jerked my thumb down on the igniter button, shooting the flame into my index finger and dropping the lighter in response.

"So . . ." I said, with a touch of forced grace after plucking the lighter from the rug and kindling it with two hands. "I guess that explains a lot."

"Bruce," she said, arching her eyebrows, "don't be so naïve. Half the people in this room are on something."

She blew a puff into my face.

"And how do you know that?" I said.

"Everyone gets his stuff from the same place."

"Which is where?"

"You don't know?"

"I guess not."

"The Buttery."

I laughed.

"The Buttery?" I said. "I've eaten dinner there almost every night this term, and I can tell you with a certain degree of confidence that there are absolutely no spices of any kind in that place."

"It's not the food, dummy. It's the servers." She poked my crimson tie.

"The servers are selling drugs?"

"Well, I don't know about all of them. But one in particular . . ." She took a step closer. "Everybody knows it, Bruce. You should just look around. I bet I can teach you a lot of things about this place that you don't already know—"

"Peter, stop it!" The words careened off the ceiling paint and dropped into the room. "Just shut up!"

"I'm not going to shut up until you tell me where you went. What were you doing with that Indian bugger?"

Peter was standing in the door with his arms waving in the air; Susanna was slumping with her back sliding down the jamb.

"Peter," she whispered through tightly clenched jaws, "everybody's looking."

"I don't care," he stammered. "I just—"

"Excuse me," cried one of the many who had turned in the direction of the fight. "Could you two speak up a bit? We're having a little trouble hearing you."

A gentle laughter rolled around the room. The guests turned back to their drinks. Nigel went sliding around the perimeter to hush over the row. But the damage had already been done. The guests in the interim had glanced down at their watches, felt the prick of embarrassment, and begun collectively to disengage, decouple, and ultimately deflate. The great balloon that is a cocktail party slowly returned to earth with a giant exhale of hot air.

I said good night to Hillary, who flicked her cigarette into my drooling champagne glass and accepted my kiss on her hand.

I said goodnight to Ian, who was unsuccessfully attempting to seduce Chantalle by comparing himself to Helen of Troy.

I said good night to Nigel, who put his arm around my shoulders and proclaimed eternal brotherhood.

I descended the stairs, ascended the bridge, and returned at last to terra firma—where my biggest personal tests of the year were now just days away.

XV

PRAYING

Church and State

St. Mary's tolls her longest chime and slumber softly
    falls
On Granta's quiet solitude, her cloisters and her
    halls;
But trust me, little rest is theirs, who play in
    glory's game
And throw tomorrow their last throw for academic fame.

> —Winthrop Praed
>   "Lines Written on the Eve of an Exam," 1826

The road on exam day was covered with bags—bags on the sides of bicycles that test takers rode to receive the exam, bags under the eyes of the untested toilers who had read too late into the night, and bags on the backs of the testy tutees that were filled with books long past overdue. The books in the bags were dry and stuffy—dry as the sand in an empty desert, stuffy as a room shut up in a storm. The stuff in the books was freeze-dried in the minds of the three score and seven academic road warriors who gathered in the halls of the Cambridge Centre of International Studies and prepared to collect a qualifying exam that would take them fifty-six hours—almost as long as a cricket test match.

"Good morning, students. Please step up to the table and collect your examination papers. Make sure you enter your examination number at the top of each separate essay and do not write your name anywhere on the paper. Above all, please remember that essays must be written in English, no Americanizations allowed."

Before receiving their *honours* degrees, undergraduates at Cambridge must pass a series of examinations that are known as a tripos, a term which originally described the three-legged stool on which all examinees were required to sit. Ph.D. students, by a different measure, are required to complete a dissertation of sufficient length and manifest originality. M.Phil. candidates, because of their respectless status between B.A.'s and Ph.D.'s, are required both to sit an exam and to write a dissertation. Unlike Ph.D.'s, who must write a free-standing tome of around eighty thousand words, our dissertations were required to be no more than twenty five thousand words; and unlike undergraduates, who must sit their exams in unventilated rooms within the perspirational sphere of smarmy neighbors and under the intoxicated glare of oft-plastered dons, we were allowed to pick up our questions at nine o'clock on Tuesday morning and return them along with four completed essays of ten pages each by five o'clock on Thursday afternoon.

At the first of the year that task seemed nothing short of insurmountable. After two terms I would be expected to write one essay in four of five categories—history, theory, strategy, economics, and law—four out of five of which I had no previous training in at all. At the end of first term, however, I began to view the assignment as much less of a burden—four essays, three days, an unlimited number of books, and all I had to do was write, something my friends kept telling me was the simplest profession in the world. But by the middle of second term I began to think that neither of these views was entirely accurate and that in fact the examination process was a giant test case in the psychological battlefield of international relations.

For starters there were the cryptic letters we received from the

Centre. The exam was not an exam, they said, but "Compulsory Essay Question Papers." We were not supposed to write one essay in four of the five categories, they said, but instead "answer any *four* questions, not more than one from any category." Next there was the relentless jockeying among the pupils themselves. The British students, for their part, claimed never to study: "Who, *moi*? Exams. I can't be bothered. These papers are merely necessary evils, like putting up with the weather." The foreigners, for their part, claimed only to study: "Exams. *Comme tragique!* I never leave my rooms. Cambridge is the hardest university in the world." Both of these lines struck me as equally absurd, but the self-professed disdain of the natives only seemed to heighten the self-induced delirium of the outlanders, especially those from the Developing World, many of whom mistook British arrogance for a thorough grasp of the material.

Finally, the strangest aspect of preparing for the exams proved to be the process of maneuvering through the academic mindfield of the U.L., the University Library. The library system at the University of Cambridge is the school's most prominent memorial to the nineteenth century and, I suspect, was probably the inspiration for Oxford don Lewis Carroll's mind-bending wonderland. To begin with, books in the library are primarily divided into categories not by subject but by size. That means that folio books on, say, the history of Japan are placed in one section—Fourth Floor, South Wing, Front—while quarto books on this same subject are located in a completely different section—Third Floor, Mezzanine, North Wing, Back—and octavos, duodecimos, and other odd sizes are kept on restricted shelves under lock and key and can only be obtained by receiving *written* permission from the head librarian. As if this arrangement were not enough of a disincentive, most students who use the library are forbidden to check out books. The authorities have tried to compensate for this inconvenience by allowing patrons to pluck any number of books they wish from the shelves, place these books on any table in the building, and with a simple signature reserve these books for their private use. The result of this policy is that during exam time there are often more books on the tables than on the shelves, and, as everyone except the librarians might have anticipated, the books in one subject, say international law, find themselves magically transported from their original location where other students might discover them and relocated to a totally unrelated area such as Arab nationalism or animal husbandry. Last and certainly least efficient of all, the number of hours that the library is open is only slightly greater than that of the average bank. Thus, if a student six weeks before an exam is clairvoyant enough to know the size of a book for which he is searching, and if that student is fortunate enough to find that book on the mostly uninhabited shelves, then that student will have the opportunity to peruse the pages of that hallowed tome to his mind's content—but only until suppertime on weekdays, only until lunchtime on Saturdays, and not at all on Sundays, when he should be reading the Scripture in church (Ground Floor, South Apse, Front Pew, Kneel).

Day One began in earnest. The first question I answered was in Section E, International Law. We had ten options to choose from; I chose Number 8: "Discuss the legal rules governing the use of armed force in international relations." The essay was fairly straightforward. "The use of armed force in international affairs can represent both the greatest failure and the greatest achievement of international law," I began. Using the current war as a case study, I walked through the various restrictions against invading another country as well as the regulations governing the use of force in the U.N. charter. Whenever possible I tried to mix in as many legal terms as I could, such as *jus ad bellum* (the laws that govern going to war) and *jus in bello* (the laws that govern warfare), and drop in as many official figures, such as the number of the Security Council resolution authorizing the Korean War (S/1501; 25 June 1950). To end I reached for a resounding conclusion: "At its best, international law is capable of endorsing armed conflict as a means of promoting peace and security; at its everyday worst, however, the law remains an impotent reminder of the lack of justice in international affairs." My style no doubt gave me away as a moralizing American, but at the height of that moment I actually believed what I wrote and, more important, at the end of the first day I started to believe that I might have learned something in the preceding months, despite having slept through most of my lectures.

Day Two began with a vengeance. I woke up early, threw my curtains open, and staring at the surprisingly sun-drenched U.L., dashed off a rapid two thousand words on "To what extent did the war in Korea mark a turning point in the Cold War?" Heeding the advice of our course director, who suggested in a preparatory session that the biggest mistake one could make on an essay was not to answer the question, I dropped the following sentence at the top of a paragraph about a thousand words into the paper: "Although the outbreak of the Korean War did not in itself mark a significant turning point in the Cold War, the conduct of the conflict did in fact have long-term significance." I was feeling so confident at the end of that essay that I went to the Buttery for a plateful of sausage and beans and late that afternoon sat down in my rooms to a screenful of "Strategic Studies," specifically "What are the main military problems for NATO presented by European unity?"

Day Three began slowly. In the field the deadline for escalation was rapidly drawing nigh and again the news from the real world seemed to encroach on the course. I opened my Compulsory Essay Question Paper to Section B, Theory of International Relations. I was frustrated. Some of the choices seemed too anachronistic: "What do you consider to be the major intellectual contributions to the idea of the balance of power prior to 1914?" Others too abstract: "To what extent are the differences between theories of decision-making really arguments about levels of analysis?" In my mind I was still struggling with the same issues that had emerged that night around the fruit bowl—namely, what was the relation between the outside world and what we learned in our Cambridge monastery? I chose Number 5: "Is realism right to deny the possibility of a harmony of interest among states?"

I began with a statement: "In international relations, war is considered the ultimate clash of interests. It is not surprising, therefore, that theory regarding the role of state interests in international affairs has undergone dramatic changes in the last century in response to major wars." Moving with a certain deliberation, I examined the changes in academic thinking in response to major wars. The First World War had spawned a generation of idealists who believed in the harmony of states; the Second World War had created a generation of realists who denied the existence of harmony. In recent years, however, realists have begun to admit that a harmony does at times exist. By the middle of the afternoon I had managed to turn the question on its head (not something the course director had advised) and was nearing the point at which I had to draw together the two worlds that had been haunting me for several months—the actual and the academic, the real and the theoretical. In a rush of adrenaline near the final deadline, I reached for a reconciliation. Since wars had in fact influenced academic thinking, then perhaps the lesson of the most recent war was that different states could at times act in harmony. "All states want to survive in a nuclear world," I wrote, "and all states need each other for economic development. These two concerns—survival and independence—are the only tenuous and common threads in international affairs. To achieve these communal ends, realists and idealists alike [NARGs and Yahs, perhaps?] must decide when to act in harmony with others and when to act alone. The need at times to harmonize with others can no longer be in doubt."

For a moment I felt wise.

"The children . . . haunt me most . . . at twilight . . ."

A single flame stepped along the white fence of candles illuminating the whispering mouths.

"Twilight . . . now turned . . . to blood seeping . . ."

The mouths lifted upward in a pleading song that touched the row of faces on the platform above.

"Through bandages . . . of cloud . . . wrapped tight . . ."

The faces breathed the shadows of the candles below and joined them in a human chandelier.

"Round . . . the earth's brow . . . as another . . ."

The chandelier floated within the dark chapel like a constellation of song and light.

"Wounded day . . . dies away . . . into the night."

The constellation disappeared in a gust of wind as the singers in unison blew out their candles.

It was ten thirty-five on Thursday night, hours before the end of Lent, and 150 students were gathered along the two-tiered mahogany pews that line the sides of Clare Chapel. The occasion was a student-led service, "Twilight (for the Children of War): A Lenten Compline for Peace and Reconciliation."

"Listen, listen," sounded a woman's voice. "I journey from the other side with a burden of chill truths. Why are you so afraid?"

The Chapel was the largest building in college. It protruded from Old Court in the direction of Trinity in a manner that left little doubt about its importance to the life of the college. Other clues reinforced the message. The chaplain of Clare was also its dean. The multipipe organ was its loudest voice. And just in case anyone missed the association, *The Clare College Student's Guide* made it manifest: "Clare is in origin a Christian foundation and the Chapel has always played a vital part in its corporate life." The connection between Cambridge and the Church of England goes back, literally, to the origins of both. In the 1530s, Henry VIII turned to the university to get scholarly approval to divorce his wife. Later, a Clare fellow, Hugh Latimer, was martyred by Henry's daughter Queen Mary for refusing to renounce his break from Rome. And by the nineteenth century, when both institutions were thriving, there were more churches per square mile in Cambridge than anywhere north of Rome, and a staggering two thirds of Cambridge graduates became clergymen.

This sense of allegiance continues today, albeit in a slightly altered form. Students may not go to chapel as often as they did in the past; other religions may now be tolerated; but the Church still plays a dominant role in setting the moral tenor of college life. Just as the chaplain held the only public discussion at the start of the war, so the students turned to the Church as soon as the war ended to contemplate its meaning. Ironically, in a community otherwise divided by language, the only true sense of community all year was provided by a conversation in church, on the subject of war.

After telling a story of a child haunted by dreams of bombers and death, the woman lit a candle in front of her face and walked from the antechamber to the center of the room. As she did, the guests passed candles through the pews and the choir began to sing.

"Thou shalt not be afraid for the terror by night; nor for the arrow that flieth by day. Nor for the pestilence that walketh in darkness; nor for the destruction that wasteth at noonday. A thousand shall fall at thy side, and ten thousand at thy right hand; but it shall not come nigh thee. . . ."

When the music stopped, a male voice called out: "In our time we need to hear within us the sounds of the earth crying."

And the voices of the chapel responded, *"We confess:*
"That we prostitute our science and knowledge in the cause of war,
"That we say 'Peace, peace' but do not make peace,
"That we have made this planet perilous for our children,
"That we have turned away our face from the face of the Lord,
"Lord, have mercy upon us."

When the recitation was done, the woman's voice returned, and with it a sense of eerie reflection. My exam had been an intellectual catharsis—a private consummation—but the service, in the communal tradition of Cambridge, proved to be a public confession.

"The old order of making war has gone," the woman said, "and the new order of making peace has begun. Fear not, go in peace into the world: you are reconciled with God and with one another: be the fellowship of reconciliation."

The choir and the congregants extinguished their candles and streamed together out of the Chapel and into the chill of the night.

She needed to see me.

In the days before the exam I had stayed close to home, calling Rachel to update her on my progress, writing her to keep me alert, but missing the opportunity to traverse the country for a rendez-vous. Now she wanted to meet me, and she didn't want to wait. So on that Friday after Lenten Compline, I rode my bike to the train, took a train to the bus, and rode a bus to Parliament Square, where I met Rachel at the same café where we had ordered sandwiches and soup at the end of Michaelmas Term.

She looked beautiful. Her hair was straight black; she was letting it grow. Her shirt was pure white; she was hoping for spring. Her beret was so purple she looked like a sundae with a plum on top. My exams were over, my vacation time was free, and when she sat down across from me and laid her cheek on my hand, I had never felt more in love. We ordered salads. Rachel was bursting with a story to tell. Over the weekend her ex-boyfriend had come to see her in Oxford. He asked her to forgive him; she told him she wouldn't. He asked her to come back; she steadfastly refused. For the first time in over a year, she said, she felt strong enough to stand up to him. "I will never forget what you did for me," she said. "You taught me to love myself."

I tried to smile. She sounded grave. Her story wasn't finished. Over the previous months, Rachel said, while she had grown more sure of herself, she had also grown less sure of me. When she saw me, she no longer smiled to herself. When we talked, she no longer felt warm. As she ticked off her list of grievances, an audible grum-ble built up in my stomach and I braced for the inevitable—"You're not a creative thinker." Other than her friend Melinda, I said when she had finished her speech, I'd never met anyone else who made me feel so inadequate. "Bruce," she responded, "I'm afraid to say it, but you are inadequate."

The last ball fell. Our salads arrived. I didn't know whether to laugh or cry. I thought back to our late-night trek and all my high-minded expectations: sure Catherine had branded Heathcliff a lout, sure Moby-Dick had dragged Ishmael halfway around the world, but somehow this scene hardly seemed the preferred outcome of a successful shark. I pulled back my hand. For several minutes we went back and forth in a sort of reverse endgame to our postcard romance: am not, are too; did not, did too; couldn't have, could've; shouldn't have, should've. I uttered something about acting on hope. She stated something about living with fear. I felt myself growing more agitated until I tried to claim the last word. "I'm not inadequate," I finally protested, "and it pisses me off that you think I am."

She sat back in silence. I huffed to myself. For a moment neither one of us spoke, until she started to smile. You know, you're really bad on the telephone, she said. You're much more candid in person. I took a bite of cucumber. Would you still read my essay? she asked. Rachel retrieved the paper on Virginia Woolf she had been writing since I had known her. She gripped her cheeks and held her breath. I began to read. The essay was about feelings—fearing the memories and remembering the fears that are buried deep within our bodies and deeper within our hearts. It was about time—thoughts in the present, hopes for the future—all of which seem to hide a past we unknowingly want to forget. The essay was brilliant. It made her cry. Like the characters she so adored, Rachel could not forget her past.

It was time to go. We got up to leave. Rachel clasped her arm in mine as we walked toward the Circle Line underneath Westminster Bridge. Once on the Tube we didn't speak. The train eventually came to a stop and Rachel stepped out, at which point she realized it was the wrong station and jumped back into the car. We started giggling. She held my hand. At the next stop—the right stop—I touched my finger to my lips and then touched it to hers. She walked out backward through the closing doors and watched as the train left Paddington Station, taking me to King's Cross. Rachel and I never saw Wales together. We were never together again.

EASTER TERM

XVI

READING

The Writing on
the Wall

Of all those arts in which the wise
  excel,
Nature's chief masterpiece is writing
  well.

—Duke of Buckingham
Essay on Poetry, 1682

The road was a jet stream, swirling with wind. The jet stream
was smoldering, choking with fumes. From the Channel, the
Atlantic, and across the Irish Sea, planes were pouring into Stansted
Airport and smothering the lowlands with clouds of smoke. Feeling
lonely as a chimney in a burning wooden house, I sat in the smoking
section of British Airways' coach class and stared out the window at
the M-11. At the end of Lent I had gone on a class field trip to
NATO headquarters in Brussels, then stayed over to eat chocolates
and waffles in Bruges before heading back to the Easter treats of the
Clare Buttery: pork vol-au-vents, beef-and-kidney Stroganoff, and
my favorite cross-cultural delicacy, chicken tikka pizza. All around

me the papers were crying that Britain was in decline. CHILDREN
DEPRIVED OF CULTURAL HERITAGE, wailed *The Telegraph*. INSPECTORS
ATTACK ENGLISH TEACHING, echoed *The Guardian*. The previous
day, on Shakespeare's birthday, the Prince of Wales had delivered
a *cri de coeur* attacking British schools for failing to teach basic liter-
acy. "I am no orator, as Brutus is," he quoted. "But as you know me
all, a plain blunt man." The country was moving from bright to
dim, he said, and the dimmer it got, the darker it seemed.

"Excuse me," said a young lady in a blue bow tie as I stood
moments later in the Baggage Claim Lounge and waited for my
luggage to disembark. "My name is Debbie. I'm from British Airways, and I wonder if I might ask you a few questions."

"Sure," I said, looking over her shoulder at one of those ads,
called adverts, that strike the new returnee as emblematic of the
place: TRY THE NEW MID CLASS FROM VIRGIN AIRWAYS. UPPER
CLASS SERVICE AT ECONOMY CLASS PRICE.

She looked down at her clipboard and began to read. "British
Airways are taking a survey of our most-valued customers in order
that we may determine how better to serve you in the future. I am
going to ask you several questions. First, would you say that your
flight with us today was a) extremely satisfactory, b) satisfactory, or
c) not satisfactory at all?"

I thought for a moment, then answered, "C) not satisfactory at
all."

She looked up at me, hurt. "Really?" she said. Catching herself,
she fumbled through several sheets of paper before finding the appropriate page and slipping it underneath the clip of her board.
"You have said that your flight today was 'not satisfactory.' I would
like to ask you several more questions that will help us understand
your dissatisfaction. Is that acceptable?"

"Yes," I answered.

"First, were you greeted at the airport today by a British Airways
uniformed representative?"

"Yes," I said.

"Would you say that representative conducted himself in a manner that was a) extremely helpful, b) helpful, or c) not helpful at all?"

"A) extremely helpful."

"Number two, were you met at the ticket counter by a British Airways ticket agent?"

"Yes," I said.

"Would you say that ticket agent served you in a manner that was a) extremely courteous, b) courteous, or c) not courteous at all?"

"A) extremely courteous."

"Number three, were you welcomed on board the aeroplane by a smiling British Airways flight attendant?"

"Yes," I said.

"Would you say that the flight attendant's smile was a) extremely genuine, b) genuine, or c) not genuine at all?"

I couldn't resist chuckling at this one. "A)," I said, "extremely genuine."

"Sir," the lady said after half a dozen more questions all of which I answered to the "extremely" degree. "You said that your flight was not satisfactory, but all of your answers indicate that you were extremely pleased with the service you received. What, may I ask, was unsatisfactory about your experience with British Airways today?"

"Only one thing was unsatisfactory," I said. "I am a nonsmoker, and I was forced to fly all the way from Brussels in the middle of a smoking section. That made my flight extremely unpleasant—"

"Are you American?" she said.

I dropped my arms in disbelief.

"What difference does that make?"

"Well," she said, "in this country smoking is still considered acceptable in public. I'll just change your answer to 'satisfactory' and we'll disregard your results."

She thanked me, smiled, and handed over a brochure: "British Airways: The World's Favourite Airline."

.   .   .

"Where have you been, young man?"

Terry stood up in the Porters' Lodge when I came through the door and pounded his fist into his hand.

"Term started several days ago," he said, "and you've been letting the post gather in your pigeonhole."

"I've been to Waterloo," I said.

He perked up his slumping shoulders. "Aah, Waterloo," he swooned with suddenly misty eyes. "The sun never sets on the British Empire."

"Terry, Waterloo's in Belgium now. The capital of Europe. Surely you've heard—"

"I know, but it's all because of Merry Olde England. Just remember, son. We saved their tails in two world wars—"

"And then we saved yours."

I stepped behind the counter to collect my mail, as Terry, well plucked, sat down at his desk and picked up his copy of the *Cambridge Evening News*.

"So, do you have a date for the ball?" he asked when I returned to my side of the desk. "You must be going with that fair young lass from Oxford?"

"I'm afraid not," I said.

"You're not?" he gasped. "What happened? Did she give you what we British gents call the old elbow?"

"An elbow, a shoulder, or something like that. I guess it's—how do you say?—back on the pull for me."

He let out a smoky laugh. "You're becoming quite proficient in our language," he said. "Did you see what Prince Charles had to say yesterday about young people not speaking English properly? He said most children in this country leave school without ever reading Shakespeare."

"The prince is becoming quite outspoken, isn't he?"

"It's true. The Queen would never have delivered a speech such as that."

"I wonder what she thinks of Charles's tirades?"

"Excuse me?" he said.

"I said, I wonder what she thinks when Charles makes his pronouncements on schools, architecture, and all that?"

"Son," said Terry, now standing once again and adopting his haughty, professorial air, "one does not openly wonder what the Queen thinks. And furthermore, let me give you one small piece of advice. When one is in polite company in this country, one does not commonly refer to Her Majesty with the term *she*."

"You Should Retain This Notice for Future Reference."

I sat on my bed several minutes later flipping through the mail that had gathered in my absence. There was a bill from the domestic bursar of the college, a receipt for two May Ball tickets, and a new term card from the Union Society listing upcoming debates, including the annual "American" debate at which I had been invited to deliver the opening address. But the weightiest item seemed to be the two-sided memo from the senior tutor of Clare, entitled "Summary of College Decisions, Periodic Review 1." It began with a declaration of purpose:

> At a recent Liaison Committee meeting the Junior Members suggested that from time to time the College circulates a review of recent decisions made and agreements reached. The review would have "official" status in that it would be expected, and could be assumed, that all Junior Members of the College would both read it and retain it for future reference; for this reason a copy would be provided by the College in the pigeon-hole of each Junior Member. This is the first such notice.

As I read through the list of sixteen "announcements and agreements," I thought of the many newspapers and books I had read in England, as well as the prince's speech about the state of the language. From the time I was a child, I had always heard that British

English was more elegant than its American variant, more graceful and precise. While living in England, however, I came across prose every day that seemed to me more a sign of obfuscation than elegance, more a tribute to verbosity than precision. Like its cousin the conversation, the written word in England today—especially the words writ by the elite—is often so high-minded as to be obscure.

As a self-appointed language explorer, I set out to map the local wordscape. In my journal I set myself this manifesto: It being apparent that I had taken up residence in the birthplace of the English language and that surrounding me at all hours of the day were shining examples of the writing of the Royals, it was decided by me that I should undertake a most thorough examination of the Queen's English today in the hopes that I might learn to write my way into the royal family tree. By spring several rules were becoming quite clear.

Rule Number One. It being incumbent upon the writer to give the "why" before the "what," always begin each sentence with a dependent clause. The Independent, in the third paragraph of its lead story on Prince Charles, provided a sterling example of this technique: "In a speech which may well prove to have even more impact on public debate than his assault on architectural quality—in which he criticised a number of modern architectural schemes, describing one as a 'monstrous carbuncle'—the Prince made a passionate plea for a return to basic skills. . . ." This delaying tactic is so pervasive in formal British writing that I took to monitoring the length of opening clauses in some of the worst offenders. On one page in Sir Harry Hinsley's *Power and the Pursuit of Peace,* the seminal work in our course, I counted 2 dashes, 3 semicolons, 7 commas, and 118 words—beginning with "Though not for the first time" and ending with "as well as in North America"—all before the subject. Royalists, I concluded, like to read sentences the way they eat baked potatoes, from the inside out. When it comes to writing down their thoughts, they split their idea down the center and serve up the fluffy parts first. Later they neglect the skin. Royalists, it seems,

never learned what my mother says: that the skin is really the heal-
thiest part.

*Rule Number Two. It is incumbent on even the most casual writer that
he begin most independent clauses with the word* it, *followed as closely as
possible by a form of the verb* to be. Announcement Number 13 in the
Summary of Decisions was the perfect illustration of this regulation.
"In the light of the University Safety Officer's advice, it will not be
necessary for every piece of electrical equipment brought to the
College by students to be tested." As far as I could tell, the sense
among Royalists seems to be, why ruin a good sentence with a
strong verb like "ruin," when "it is apparent that this sentence is
boring" will do the job just fine? Why make an announcement, or
announce a decision, or decide a question, or question a report,
when that report or question or decision or announcement can be
relegated to that central source of all news in Great Britain: the
tyranny of *it. It* is the most newsworthy subject in the British Isles.
In the course of one day, it is revealed, it is reported, it is recommended, it is confirmed, and, despite its multifaceted personality, it
is also understood. When *it* does not manage to do anything one day
that could be considered news, journalists feel so obliged to report
on its activities that they often just say, "It is interesting to note . . ."

*Rule Number Three. It being all the same, one choice or another, be
obliged that the passive voice should be used.* In the worldview of the
Queen's English, no one takes steps or actions or responsibility, no
one need dirty his hands. Instead, things either should be, will be, or
just simply are done; and when these things are completed, it is
somehow made known to the public at large. On the morning after
one of the biggest news events of the year, for example, the slaying
of an unpopular regressive tax, the tried and tired *Times* began its
story on the event with this impassive lead: "The death of the poll
tax was announced yesterday." In the speech to the Parliament
announcing the death, the secretary of state for the environment
and former president of the Oxford Union notified the country of
the change with a suitably evasive rhetorical flourish (employing

Rules One and Three): "In spite of the comprehensive system of income related rebates, and the reduction scheme we devised, the public have not been persuaded that the tax is fair." No one acted; no one reacted; no one complained. It was just time for a change.

Rule Number Four. In the event that one might be misunderstood, always clarify, repeat oneself, and say everything at least two times. On one hand it can be said that Royalists like their language used correctly. Grocery stores all across the kingdom, for example, have special checkouts for patrons purchasing 9 ITEMS OR FEWER. They also like their language to be delicate. A sign along the High Street in Cambridge, for instance, advises, DOGS MUST NOT FOUL FOOTWAY OR VERGE. But the biggest sin of all in English circles is to be ambiguous. "The review aims to be as short as possible," the head tutor wrote in a parody of himself, "consistent with the need for clarity." This problem is best solved by supplementing a simple statement with an explanation, an explication, and, if necessary, as it usually is, a healthy dose of extrapolation. A basic blue-blood motto seems to be: Don't make implicit what can be made explicit. The entire body of the Hinsley sentence, for example, which I had copied and taped to my wall as a Cambridge merit badge, exemplifies this technique:

> Though not for the first time, for there had been a growing disparity between Western Europe and other areas since the eighteenth century, yet more rapidly, more extensively and more directly than before—in Turkey's European provinces and in Central Asia from about 1870; in Turkey's North African possessions, in the Near East and Persia, in undeveloped Africa and the undeveloped Pacific from about 1880; in China and Korea from about 1885; in the New World, even, from about 1890 as the United States expanded from her continent into the Caribbean, undertook the Panama Canal and asserted her right under the Monroe Doctrine to be the directing Power in South as

well as in North America—the more developed states extended, were perhaps unable to avoid extending, their intervention and their control in areas where society and government were still as they had been in the European Middle Ages.

The British build sentences the way they build roads: a few motorways traverse the countryside and are linked together by a never-ending web of dual carriageways and narrow access roads that never meet directly in intersections, but come together in hundreds upon thousands of traffic circles that are called, literally, roundabouts. In England, it seems, the shortest distance between two points is around a circle.

Rule Number Five. If at all possible under the circumstances, never state directly, always suggest. Perhaps the most noticeable feature of the Queen's English is its all-around indirection. Unlike American English, which is straightforward, direct, and to the point (like a dead-end road), British English is loopy, roundabout, and generally understated. Even when it tries to be forceful, English worthy of the Queen's pedigree is always genteel. In November I snipped the instructions from an English firework. "Insert upright in soft ground," it advised. "Ensure firework will not fall over. Straighten fuse, light tip of free end at armslength and retire immediately." Just the thought of an American ten-year-old reading this instruction was enough to make me laugh.

At its worst, British indirection has all the bite of cold toast. My favorite sign in Cambridge, for example, was one on the front door of the Marks & Spencer department store that warned potential delinquents: SHOPLIFTERS MAY BE PROSECUTED. But at its best, this *stilus roundaboutus* can provide a sort of unintended poetry. The last letter I opened on the first day of Easter Term before going upstairs and checking on Simon was a one-page memo from the deputy director of the Centre of International Studies. Its contents would have made Wordsworth proud:

To: M.Phil. in International Relations course members

Re: Compulsory Essay Examinations

   i) As you know, I am not allowed to tell you whether you have passed the M.Phil. in International Relations written papers.

  ii) As you also know, you would have been informed by a certain date if you have failed.

iii) That date has now passed.

XVII

SEARCHING

Body and Soul

§♭

OUISA: How is [college]?
PAUL: Well, fine. It's just there. Everyone's
in a constant state of luxurious despair and
constant discovery and paralysis.

—John Guare
Six Degrees of Separation, 1990

"*I*t happened several days ago. . . ."

Lucy Fudge and I were sitting on a brown plastic sofa in the JCR. It was a Thursday night in early May. The pubs had closed for the night, and the Clare Late Bar was just filling up with midnight crawlers stopping off for a final pint or stepping out for a study break from their bibliotechal hibernation.

"As I was sitting there," she recalled, "I felt the Holy Spirit inside of me as I hadn't felt it for years. I used to be a good Christian— beginning when I was fifteen. I knew all the songs and prayed every day. But I haven't prayed in several years, so for me to feel that strongly was definitely something special."

"So why that night?"

She took a sip of cider, pulled back her blond hair, and crossed one leg beneath the other. Since January when Lucy started dating Simon, she had been cultivating a certain appearance, a kind of sultry-carpenter look, with manly brown pullovers, army green jeans, and the kind of thick-soled black leather shoes commonly worn by London punks and RAF officers. As her transformation became more complete, however, her attachment to Simon—a boyish prep to the bone—naturally began to splinter. As it did, she had sought me out to talk.

"I'm telling you," she repeated, "there was an evil spirit in the room that night. I'm convinced Henry was possessed. No one else could feel it, but I could."

"And what about Henry. Did he feel it as well?"

Lucy smiled. "The next day he came to me and said he was sorry, it wouldn't happen again."

Easter Term started differently than the previous two. After spending most of the first two terms in the pub or in bed, most students began spending more time preparing for their year-end exams. Simon, for one, added up the work sheets he hadn't done, counted the days until his exams, and made out a ten-page revision plan. (At Cambridge any work done in preparation for exams, even work done for the first time, is considered "revision.") Ian, for his part, had completed three essays for his course and had begun work on his last: a study of reason versus passion in Euripides' *Bacchae*. I, meanwhile, was freed of lectures and able to focus on my thesis topic: namely, why did the Allies rebuild Germany and Japan in the late 1940s instead of fulfilling their original plans and tearing them down? Most historians, viewing the two cases separately, had cited Cold War politics or superpower conspiracies as a reason for the change. I, by viewing them side by side, was focusing on faulty original plans. I had only several weeks left to make my case, however: my draft was due to Dr. Long just days before the ball.

In the interim I still had two of my Cambridge fantasies left to fulfill, since rowing was the only one I had achieved. The first of my remaining fantasies—the debate—was fast approaching and much of my time in the early weeks of term was spent preparing a "paper speech" for my Union debut. In early May, I even attended a workshop on how to debate "Cambridge style." "Don't be boring," coached one of the boy-politicos. "Don't read statistics. And, above all, don't preach. Some people say practice in front of a mirror. I say that's a bunch of crap."

Finally, and of much more pressing concern, I still needed a date for the ball. As a result, I began spending less time in the University Library and more time in the college pub. I was leaning up against one of the whitewashed pillars in the pub late one Thursday night when Lucy sat down beside me and started talking about the Holy Spirit. She was sitting on the beanbag chair in Simon's room, she said, when Henry, their fellow first-year pal who had earlier competed in the Pie & Pints relay race, knocked on the door. He came in, sat down in a chair, and asked her if she was psychic. Then he took off his clothes. "Henry, stop it!" Lucy cried. "I feel cold."

For a moment, she recalled, the two of them stared at each other—she from her knees, he from his seat. Then Lucy closed her eyes and began to mouth some words in a kind of silent litany. She had had to keep praying, she said to herself. She had to keep talking and channel her thoughts. So she talked and prayed and whispered and thought until her lips were speaking in tongues and her eyes could no longer see.

Then she smiled. "I dropped my hands onto my thighs," she remembered, "and Henry reached for his clothes." He began to redress: shorts, socks, trousers, and shirt. At last he slipped on his shoes. Moments later the spirit was gone.

"It's all part of a pattern," Lucy said when she had finished her tale. "I'm going through this big transition right now. In school I was always very straight. But in my year out I went to Milan and lived with this woman. She was wild. She had two lovers every week, she went out every night. After leaving her I went to stay with her daughter in Berlin. I started drinking. I kissed a rock singer on top of the Wall. I did drugs. . . ."

Lucy was a remarkably unpretentious person. If anything, she took pride in her forthright attitude toward herself and toward others. Once, after one of our late-night chats, she asked me if I would have sex with her in order to give her a few pointers. When I declined, she couldn't understand it and asked Simon why I wouldn't. He, in turn, couldn't understand her and asked me why she would.

"I had lived such a cautious life," she continued. "My family doesn't talk very much. My father is very hardworking and strict. I wanted a change. Youth is a time of excess, I thought, while old people work all the time. I decided to explore my body. Drugs. Liquor. Sleep deprivation. I thought it would be a 'one-off' experience, a one-time thing. But I liked it."

She told me a story.

"When I was in Berlin, I took acid," she said. "A friend and I went to see the Ninja Turtles and he asked me if I wanted to pop a tablet. It wasn't really a tablet, though. It was a piece of paper. I ripped off a corner and put it on my tongue. I didn't even use the whole thing. I chewed for several minutes, then swallowed. . . . The scary thing about acid is that you swallow this piece of paper and it's two hours before it comes up."

"Comes up?"

"Yes, the images, they come up. At first it was colors, an amazing display of violet and orange and green. And then music, whatever music you're hearing seems to linger forever in your ears. My friend and I had the same experiences. As we were walking home from the theater, he was smoking a cigarette, and he dropped it to the ground. It seemed to burn a hole into the road—a big red volcanic hole like fire burning through the earth. He knelt down to pick it up and then jumped back. 'Did you see that?' he cried. 'The ground opened up like *Alice in Wonderland*.' We were having the same trip."

"So you enjoyed it?"

She thought for a moment. "I guess so. But Simon doesn't want me to do it anymore. He blames it all on Hillary. . . . Do you know her, Hillary? I think you would like her. She reads a lot, like you."

"As you were saying . . ."

"Well, I guess I did enjoy it," she said, rubbing the back of her neck and shaking out her hair. "But then again, I've often wondered which is better, drugs or sex? Of course, I've only had sex with one person. But sex is better, I guess. It takes less time, but still lasts longer. The problem is you need a man to have sex, and they're unreliable."

I asked her if she meant Simon. She responded by telling me how they first met.

"I just picked him out," she recalled. "I was going through the matriculation photograph and looking for someone to teach me about sex. I picked Simon because he's a boy, because he's vulnerable. You know the first lover in *Madame Bovary,* the one who's charming, handsome, wealthy, and talented? I wouldn't want to go out with that man. I wanted somebody who's less perfect."

"And did you pick the right one?"

"I thought so. We started going out. We were great friends, we were lovers, but then something happened. Last term we were just enjoying each day as it came. There was no pressure. Now there's so much talk about the future—'What are you thinking?'; 'How am I feeling?'; and all those mushy things. I don't like that stuff. I don't think in words. I just want to feel. But he wants more. He wants to be in *love*. I don't want to be in love—I want to have fun."

A scuffle broke out at one end of the room, and a pint glass skidded across the floor and ruptured against a pillar.

"So which side is winning, your body or your mind?"

"Well, in the short term my body is winning, but in the future I'll choose my heart. I do want to have a family, you know. And I want to be a good Christian."

"So how will you explain what you're doing now?"

"It's a struggle. The devil shows you a good time before he tries to take your soul. Listen, I live next door to two leaders of the Christian society at Clare. They're always trying to convert me, to use certain lines on me, but they don't realize that I've used the same lines on other people. It all seems so shallow now. Being a good person is harder than that. Of course, I want to stop before I go too far, but to tell you the truth, I didn't know how hard it was to be good until I realized how much fun it is to be bad."

"Avert your eyes, Mr. Feiler."

Simon was sitting on the floor of his rooms in orange-striped boxer shorts clenching a Marlboro cigarette in his lips and staring at a square whisky glass on his thigh. He didn't look up when I stepped through his door a half hour before dinnertime.

"This is not the stiff British upper lip you're looking at," he said. "I do not like to be seen in this state."

"What's going on?" I said. "What happened to your revision schedule?"

"I'm not used to not getting what I want," he said. "I'm usually able to control myself, not to mention the people around me. I guess that's what the next three years is all about. My ego will take a bashing."

"That could do some good."

"Watch it!" he said, now looking up at me. His eyes were bloodshot and far away. "Don't patronize me today, Mr. Feiler. I haven't slept in two days and I've already consumed an inordinate amount of alcohol."

I grabbed the near-empty glass from his hand and set it on the table. He waved his arm as if batting a fly, then dragged the twisted plaid duvet from his bed and laid it across his body.

"Will you tell me what's going on?" I said, spreading the curtains, opening the windows, and finally taking a seat. "Why is everyone in Clare in this sudden state of frenzy?"

"It's the game, don't you know. The river, the grass, the flowers, the charming students in their B.A. gowns. And, of course, the pressure to perform."

"You're not making any sense," I said.

"Listen, I have a question for you," he snapped. "Is she a Christian, or not? Is she trying to get a First, or what? And then, just once, I want to know: does she love me, or not?"

For a moment neither of us spoke. He took a drag from the bottom of his cigarette and winced at the bitter taste.

"So that's it?" I said. "You're having romantic troubles."

"Troubles, no, we're not having troubles at all. Not for Lucy at least. She says that apart from several things—which of course she wouldn't mention—she would be perfectly happy to marry me. She also said that she wouldn't have to be madly in love with the person she marries. Can you imagine such a life? I can't. I couldn't stand that."

"You sound as if you're changing your mind," I said. "What happened to 'just being human' and all that?"

"Look," he said. "I'm not asking for much. I want an intellectual, a physical, and an emotional relationship. I know this thing started out as just a physical relationship. But now I want more. It always happens that way. Usually, it's the other person—my French teacher at school; Emiko in Japan. This time it happened to me."

"That sounds sort of encouraging."

"Encouraging, maybe. But highly embarrassing."

"Ah, the great British sin: being embarrassed."

"Stop it," he said. "Hand me my shirt." I picked up a short-sleeve checked shirt from his mattress and threw it across the room. "I'm an optimistic person, really," he said, "but somehow I'm finding it hard to be optimistic this time."

"Maybe you're changing," I said. "It could be worse. Instead of saying 'I am' or 'I'm not' all the time, maybe you should say 'I have been' or 'I haven't been until now.' "

"I don't like talking to you, Mr. Feiler. You're too precise. I want someone to massage my ego and tell me what to do. I want someone to tell her what to do as well."

"I stopped doing that long ago."

"Lucy asked Hillary to give me a lecture. Do you know her, Hillary? I think you'd like her. She talks a lot, like you. But she's a bit wild. I'd be careful if I were you."

"Thank you for the lecture. I'll watch my step. Now where were we?"

"We were in trouble. The problem is she just wants it to be convenient. If she doesn't see me for three days, that's fine with her. If she's busy, there's always tomorrow. But I want more. I want to be the last person she sees every day and the first person she sees in the morning."

"You mean you want to sleep with her every night."

"Not necessarily. I just want to be more important. I want her to act like I'm an important part of her life. Also, I don't understand this religious thing. Why doesn't she just think the way I do? I don't go to chapel. I don't read the Bible. But I'm religious. It's not what you do, it's how you act."

"Don't you think that in the long run—"

"I can't wait that long," he interrupted. "What am I supposed to say? 'Give me a call when you want to settle down.' In the meantime she's driving me crazy, especially with her work. She talks about it all the time, but she never seems to do it. I'm just the opposite. I realize we're all under pressure here. But I have become the negative of work for her; I have become a distraction."

"So what are you going to do?" I said. "You're not sleeping, you're not eating, and you're not even studying."

"Thank you for that reminder. Throw me my trousers."

"It sounds like you need some temporary arrangements."

"But what will everybody think if I suddenly reveal myself to be a sap?" he said. "What about my image? The bar? I have to live with these people for three years, you know?"

"That's true," I said. "We wouldn't want them to think you have a heart or anything, it might ruin your reputation."

"All right," he said. "You made your point. You Americans have a strange sense of humour."

"It's called sarcasm," I said.

"It should be called humiliation. Now close your eyes while I slip on my trousers. You really shouldn't see me like this."

XVIII

DEBATING

Young, Free, and British

Q: What's the difference between America
and a yoghurt?
A: Give a yoghurt 200 years and it will
develop a culture.

—A restroom stall
History Faculty, Cambridge

"So, Bruce, what's in the package?"
Terry handed me my post on a cold, rainy Thursday afternoon in early May as I came home from a meeting with my supervisor on the progress of my thesis.

"It's a tie," I said.

"Your old school tie, I guess."

"No," I said. "I didn't go to an old school. It's a tie with the design of the American flag on it."

"Aha," he said. "Old Glory. I know it well. But tell me, why do you need it on a tie?"

"It's for a debate," I said. "I'm speaking at the Union tomorrow night and I need to look my best."

"The Union?" he said. "That's impressive. But you'd better be mighty careful when you're out there on that floor. Those debaters like to humiliate upstart Colonists like yourself."

"I realize that, which is why I need a secret weapon."

"A secret weapon? What kind of tie do you have there, boy? Not a bow tie is it?"

"Why, of course."

"For a dress suit?"

"No, a DJ."

"Well, I'll be damned. In that case I'm afraid I won't be able to be of much assistance to you."

"What do you mean?"

He looked over my shoulder to make sure no one was approaching, then leaned across the wooden counter.

"Because there's something most people think I can do that I can't," he said.

"And what's that?" I whispered.

"Tie a bow tie."

"What?!" I gasped, nearly blowing his cover. "You've got to be kidding."

"No, sir," he said, straightening his back. "I don't kid. I'm afraid you've met an Englishman with a frailty."

"But it's just like tying a shoe," I said.

"I know, I know, but I can't do it. My wife, Jimbo, has to do it for me. And I'll tell you something else—it's all the more surprising since I have a fixation about cleanliness. I even clean the soles of my shoes." He balanced his hand on the countertop and showed me the sole of his shoe, which, as promised, was as clean and spotless as the top of his head. "But still, I can't tie a bow tie. It always comes out lopsided."

"Maybe I should teach you," I said.

He set down his hands on the countertop. "I would rather die."

I laughed out loud. "If you change your mind," I said, "just let me know. Perhaps you could learn something from a Colonist after all."

"Watch it," he said. "That's the kind of remark that could get you in trouble at the Union."

"Not tomorrow," I said.

"Why not?" he said. "What's the topic?"

"Resolved: This House Would Rather Be Young, Free, and American."

"In that case," he said, "I wish you all the best, and I hope you fall flat on your bum."

"Good evening, ladies and gentlemen, boys and girls, Yanks and Brits alike . . ."

The chamber of the Cambridge Union Society was stuffed from its underlying wainscot to its overhanging gallery when I stepped up to the lectern at a little past nine on Friday night and prepared to propose the motion. The lectern for our side—the proposition—stood approximately waist-high, just three feet across an elaborate oak table from an identical lectern for the opposition side. The table, known officially as the dispatch box, sat immediately in front of a three-tiered, double-armed presidential throne, which rested against the back wall of the two-story House. To the right and left of the president's perch, on either side of the dispatch box, members sat facing one another in long rows of pews like opposing parliamentary parties. As with the House of Commons in London, which served as the Union's model, the gap where the front benches met one another was wide enough so that if two combative members came to blows and decided to have a duel, their outstretched swords when fully drawn would not touch each other.

The Cambridge Union Society was formed in 1815 by joining existing societies from three colleges: Gonville and Caius, St. Catherine's, and St. John's, the last of which had a debating club called the Fustian Society, *fustian* being an ancient oratorical put-down that meant, in essence, "full of gas." The university disapproved of the new group, however, and decreed that it was improper for young gentlemen *in statu pupillari* (of student status) to discuss political matters of the day. After a contentious debate, the vice-chancellor eventually consented to let the students discuss political matters, but only under the condition that the matters discussed relate exclusively to the previous century. The students readily agreed to this provision, and promptly circumvented the problem by prefacing every remark with the saving phrase, "Fifty years ago . . ." In the end, student ingenuity prevailed over professorial prudence and by century's end the Union had grown to include some thirteen thousand members, which was widely believed to be the largest affiliation of any club in the world.

The Union today, like the university it embodies, has lost some of its previous luster as well as its claim to hold a central place in the intellectual life of the country. To be sure, hundreds of students still join every year and a dozen or so debates take place every term, such as "This House Believes that Private Schools Are Not in the Public Interest" and "This House Believes that a Man's Place Is in His Home." Also, the Union is still considered the best springboard for a career in Parliament. In the year that I was at Cambridge, for example, five members of the Cabinet were former Union presidents.

But for the most part, the Union these days has become a home for back-stabbing, social-climbing party hacks to train themselves in the timeless techniques of political sabotage. In each of my three terms, for example, a political "scandal" graced the front pages of the university tabloid. In Michaelmas Term the crisis involved the Conservative Party on campus, when a group calling itself the Blue Dawn slate accused its rival, the Disraelian slate, of subverting the party's constitution by reducing the number of meetings that members could attend. In Lent, the *crise de term* involved the Labour Party, when Mark Scott-Fleming, the bearded, ponytailed medic from Clare, abandoned the party's traditional boycott against the Union's alleged conservative bias and actually got himself elected president, to the horror of his party and the disgrace of the opposition. In Easter Term a candidate for the ruling Standing Committee bowed out of the election after an opponent leaked a story to *Varsity* that he had stolen a cassette tape of a previous term's debate in order to hide the fact that he had failed to deliver the minimum number of three speeches needed to qualify for election.

All of these internal machinations make the Union mostly inhospitable to foreign intervention, since few outsiders care enough about British inside politics to throw their necks into the ring and few insiders care enough about the outsiders to cultivate their votes or even stab them in the back. Despite these drawbacks, I still enjoyed attending the debates, if only to listen to the flights of rhetoric and wit occasionally on display. Also, I still wanted to participate in a debate, if for no other reason than to match blows in the shrine to Cambridge's Greatest Wits. At the end of Lent Term I put in an application, and in the beginning of Easter Term the Union president summoned me to his office and told me that I had been selected to propose the motion. Were there any restrictions? I asked. Two, he said. First, I must wear a DJ, and second, I must be funny. What about time? I asked. "Well," he answered, considering his response. "If you're funny, you can go on as long as you want. If not, seven minutes."

I paused to look around the crowded house, then launched into my preamble.

"With all due recognition of the pleasures of speaking before this not *youthful* society . . . with all due consideration for traditions established here generations ago and not *freely* changed . . . with all due British respect and a touch of American immodesty, please allow me to propose the motion, 'This House Would Rather Be Young, Free, and American.'"

From all corners of the room the five hundred or so members applauded and booed my opening remarks. In the past, members would have sat on the side of the House expressing the position they supported, but these days members sit wherever they wish. At the end of the debate those in attendance vote for the side of their choice by departing the chamber through one of three doors, marked YEA, NAY, or ABSTAIN.

"Now as I see it, our side of the House has a quite simple task ahead of us this evening. We must try and convince you in the course of the next several hours—"

The audience intervened with derisive laughter.

"We'll take as long as we need," I called above the clamor. This line was met appreciably and I, relieved, went on.

"We must try and convince you that, if given the choice, you would rather be young than old, rather be free than not, and rather be American than out of date, out of luck, and generally out of touch."

The cheers quickly turned to jeers; the laughter changed to whoops of disapproval. I couldn't have been more pleased. In Cambridge, where conversation is considered art, debating is considered the highest form of artful dodgery. The winner is not necessarily the one with the better argument, but the one who wields the sharpest wit and best evades the other sword. "[The English] all profess to hate public speaking after dinner," wrote Leslie Stephen, "in consequence of which we never have a dinner of a semi-official kind without half a dozen speeches." As a result, he concluded, the real value of the Union is that "it tests a man's possession of that most inestimable quality in youth, a perfect willingness to make yourself ridiculous in public."

I dropped my voice to a whisper.

"I must confess to you at the beginning that I feel sorry for the opposition, for they must try and convince you that, if given the choice, instead of being Young, Free, and American, you would rather be over the hill, up the river, and under the weather."

The audience growled. I picked up the pace. The tussle had begun.

"Let's take the first of these three choices: This House Would Rather be Young. Now I realize that things change slowly on this side of the Atlantic. The British invented the nineteenth century, after all, so why live in the twentieth? In this country, old is in. Everywhere you go: old buildings, old clothes, old teeth . . . which reminds me, Mr. President"—I turned to face the throne to my left as I had watched previous debaters do—"is it true that Brits keep a stiff upper lip in order to hide their teeth?" The president laughed. I swung back around. "In Britain, ladies and gentlemen, the only thing *new* is the potatoes."

For the rest of my time I continued this duck and nod with each remark in a kind of seductive waltz with the audience that was not unlike an elaborate shark: nibbling at every bait, maintaining healthy respect, and, of course, talking at all times.

"As a visitor in this country, it seems to me that the collective imagination of the British stopped about two hundred years ago. Brits, for example, talk about the Battle of Waterloo as if it were fought last weekend. Even the toilet cleaner that my bedder uses is called Waterloo. Cleans up like the Duke of Wellington. Wipes out those tough, Napoleonic stains.

"I'll tell you a true story. Last week I went to borrow a nut and bolt from the maintenance man of Clare College. As I was leaving, I said to the man, 'Thank you very much.' And in response he turned to me and said, "Hah, don't mention it. The things we do for you *Colonists.*"

The mere mention of the word brought sustained applause.

"Colonists," I repeated. "We haven't been Colonists since the last time Cambridge beat Oxford in rowing."

The applause turned to painful whimpers, as one of my two speaking partners shouted, "We're losing! We're losing!" I smiled more broadly with every jeer they tossed and every boo they floated. "Time to go to Britain, we say in America, time to set our watches back five hundred years. . . .

"So you see, ladies and gentlemen, it seems rather obvious to me that when you consider the evidence, most of us would rather be young. Youth, after all, is the time of hope, the time of joy, the time of sexual prime. Take the simple expression 'Put the bin out.' To an old man it means lugging the garbage to the curb and stepping in—how do you say?—*dog do* along the way. To a young man, however, to a *Cambridge* man who puts out his litter to keep his bedder away, the words 'Put the bin out' are the four sexiest words in the English language, for they mean he has something—or rather someone—to hide."

It took them a while to deconstruct this line, but eventually they cheered.

"Now let's move on to the second notion, 'This House Would Rather Be Free.' There are several ways the opposition might attack this point. First, they can say they would prefer to be *not free,* but in bondage—"

This line, to my complete surprise, brought virtually uncontrollable applause, so much so that instead of trying to finish my arcane joke about a politician who had been recently caught with a call girl in handcuffs, I decided to leave the audience to their kinky delight and skip on to my next point.

"Seriously, Mr. President, Cambridge University goes out of its way to restrict freedom as much as possible. Our colleges tell us *when* to eat (only at mealtime), *where* to walk (not on the grass), *what* time to be home (before 2 A.M.), and even *who* to sleep with. Maybe the opposition likes this, maybe they went to a school where the matron wiped their plates and their bums every evening. I, for one, don't call this freedom, I call it adolescence. I would rather be Young, Free, and American, ladies and gentlemen, than live in a world where I can't go on a date without written permission from my tutor."

Two sections complete. One to go.

"Having realized that we would rather be young and free, the only thing left for us to do is convince you that—by definition—you can't be young and free without also being American."

As the boos returned with a vengeance, I pushed on without pause. Starting afresh, I mentioned several countries that came to mind as alternatives to America, singling out Malawi and then Japan ("I, my friends, would rather be Young, Free, and American than live in a country where all the men look like they got their business suits free with a tank of gas") before finally settling into the main event: the United Kingdom of England, Scotland, Wales, and Northern Ireland.

"Most of you, I suspect, when asked to describe an American, would say that Americans are (and feel free to agree) loud"—the cheers concurred—"ignorant"—they grew louder—"materialistic"—they boomed—"and generally, brash."

"We're winning!" my partners cried in mock despair. "We're winning!"

"If asked to describe a Brit, on the other hand, you would probably say the British are witty, knowledgeable, understated, and polite." They certainly agreed with that.

"Well, I suggest to you that the first definition describes not an American, but an American tourist. While the second definition—gee, the only person it accurately describes is Alistair Cooke. I put it to you, Mr. President, ladies and gentlemen, that we should not be caught comparing Cambridge students to American tourists. I, for example, would rather be a Cambridge student than be an American tourist. But that is not the point. I would rather be a Cambridge student who is Young, Free, and American than anything else. And let me tell you some of the reasons why. . . ."

The chamber went silent as I let my voice trail off. I knew that I would wit or wilt with my final section. I had, in a way, been gathering material all year.

"First, food. British food comes in one flavor: brown. Brown meat. Brown potatoes. Brown gravy. You Brits like gravy a lot," I said. "You even invented Yorkshire pudding, which, as far as I can tell, purposefully has no taste at all in order to suck up the taste of the gravy. You even put gravy on pudding; you just call it custard.

"Before I get carried away, I will admit that there are vegetables here. Carrots, for one. And canned peas, for another. But to avoid eating these said vegetables alive, you cook them in the same way as the meat and potatoes: you boil them. In Britain, as you probably know, the most popular spice is water. I, my friends, would rather be Young, Free, and American than be from a country which has perpetual fog that comes from overboiling potatoes."

The audience alternated between laughter and applause, but at this point my mind no longer registered their response as I over-dosed on the adrenaline of performance and felt I could do no wrong.

"Next, weather. Weather is one of the great dividers between America and Britain. Weathermen in Britain look at their colleagues in America and get what we might call 'weather envy.' America is just so big, with so much weather to cover, they say. The only thing we have to decide in Britain is whether it will be cloudy in the morning and rainy in the afternoon, or the other way around. To compensate for this lack of variety, the weathermen in Britain try to convince us that different parts of the country actually have different weather. As a result, weather reports in this country go something like this: 'In East Anglia there will be showers in the morning, giving way to continuous rain in the afternoon. In the Midlands, there will be continuous rain in the afternoon, giving way to intermittent showers in the evening. Central England will have intermittent showers in the evening, giving way to wintry showers overnight.'

"Is there a difference between these things?" I shouted. "Never mind that all of these places are close enough to one another that they can fit under a single cloud. Never mind that all of these places, like every other place in the country, start off most days in gray, spend much of the afternoon in showers, and then end the night in fog. The weathermen say they are different, so they are. But the weathermen miss the point: the great thing about this country, Mr. President, is that you can experience all four seasons in one day."

In a month that had already seen rain, sleet, and snow, but no sun, this line worked especially well.

"But in the end, ladies and gentlemen, I must tell you that the greatest difference between America and Britain is the showers. Bathing in Britain is the ultimate example of intermittent showers. The water often doesn't come out at all, and, when it does, it either dribbles down the wall like custard on a spoon or goes spraying all over the room like a bottle of champagne. With all the rain in Britain, the only place one is guaranteed to stay dry is underneath the shower, in the dead of winter. Basins, of course, are no better. If you were Young, Free, and American, you could wash your face in warm water." I cupped my hands together and swung them left and right. "In Britain you have to keep running your hands back and forth between the hot and cold.

"Ultimately, this is the reason to vote in favor of this proposition: America is the land of the free and the home of the choice. If you're tired of only brown meat and brown sauce . . . if you're tired of only hot or cold water . . . if you're tired of only two types of weather— intermittent showers and continuous rain—then come to America where you can have a choice.

"I recently saw a comic strip that showed an American and a Brit buying ice cream. The American says to the man behind the counter, 'I'll take one scoop of mocha almond ripple, and one of vanilla butter crunch, with marshmallow and hot fudge sauce, plus sliced almonds on top.' Meanwhile, the Brit says to the man, 'Va- nilla or chocolate. Er . . . you choose for me.'

"Choice, ladies and gentlemen, is the nourishment of the young and the nectar of the free. And choice, above all, is the opposite of class, a system by which everything is done exactly as its always been done. If you were Young, Free, and American, just think of the choices you could have: you could have faucets that don't drip, and fireplaces that work . . . you could have rooms that are warm, and toast that is hot . . . you could have trains that run on time, and telephone numbers that all have the same number of digits . . . you

could buy a drink after eleven-thirty at night, and—most important—you could buy any appliance with the plug already attached."

The audience laughed knowingly and the president moved to the
edge of his chair.

"Ladies and gentlemen, in the words of a famous American: Give
me *liberty,* or give me death. Give me *youth,* or give me death. Give
me *America,* or give me at least a room that has some heat. The night
is young. The Colonists are free. Britannia rules no more. Mr. President, I beg to propose the motion."

He stood up, applauded, and looked at his watch. I sat down,
smiled, and looked at mine. I had spoken for nineteen minutes.

"Ladies and gentlemen of the House, I had intended to stand before
you tonight and refute the arguments before us, but I'm afraid that
we have not got many arguments from the proposition side of the
House this evening, so I am on my own."

Justin Davies leaned over the dispatch box on the opposition side,
tossed back an errant tributary of his well-greased hair, tightened the
knot on his black bow tie, and slipped his hand in the tiny crease
between his gold pocket watch and his paisley waistcoat. After my
initial proposition statement, the president had introduced the first
opposition speaker, a bumbling first-year historian from Trinity
Hall who promptly spilled a glass of whisky all over his index cards.
He was followed in turn by a short, dry speech from the proposition
and, after a brief set of comments from the floor, the grand arrival of
the savior in black, Mr. Justin Davies: a graduate of Eton, a third-
year lawyer from Peterhouse, and a man known throughout the
society as someone with prodigious talents, both loquacious and
libatious.

"At this stage of the evening I would like to make it very clear to
members of the Union in this House, tonight, that we are preju-
diced on our side of the House. And I happily quote to you from
H. L. Mencken, an American, from his book called *Prejudices.* 'The
American people,' he said, 'taken one with the other, constitute the

most timorous, snivelling, poltroonish, nay ignominious mob of serfs and goose-steppers ever gathered under one flag in Christendom since the end of the Middle Ages."

The crowd loved that quote so much it nearly burst into a spontaneous chorus of "Rule, Britannia."

"But seriously, ladies and gentlemen, let's look at the motion before us. We have been told by the opposition that, for a start, we should want to be young. Well, I'm not sure young is actually the heaven we have been told it is. For myself, I say give me a seat in the House of Lords any day. We were told about Wellington and the Battle of Waterloo. In the words of W. S. Gilbert: 'When Wellington thrashed Bonaparte / As every child can tell / The House of Peers throughout the war / Did nothing in particular, and did it very well.' That, I think, sums up the British way of doing things. We will go on doing nothing in particular and doing it very well."

The audience applauded approvingly.

"Let's look at the next word, *free*. I'm in favor of freedom, of course. But Americans carry this to extremes. We don't have a constitution over here because basically we don't need one to get along with one another. The reason they have one over there is so they can have silly amendments, like the Twenty-eighth Amendment, which says that Americans have a constitutional right to describe anything over twenty years old as historic. They also have the freedom to carry submachine guns, the freedom to watch sixty-two television channels, and, of course, the freedom to wear bad clothes. Why do Americans talk so loudly? you may have wondered. So they can be heard over their trousers. Just look at the cummerbund and tie of the gentleman opposite, Mr. Feiler, and imagine that every morning in America children have to salute that."

The crowd laughed uproariously at my expense, and, as they did, I began to appreciate a fundamental difference between Justin Davies and myself. Justin, unlike me, had not written his speech. He had not practiced in front of a mirror. In fact, he was making it up on the spot. To be sure, he had pulled a few devastating slurs from a book of familiar quotations and jotted down a few notes, but for the most part he was relying on my speech—the proposition—to provide the structure for his, and he was depending on his own quick tongue—loosened by the pint of lager he took with him to the box—to provide the gist for his riposte. I, on the other hand, had researched my speech for days with Simon and his friends, had written it out verbatim on my laptop computer, and later had tested it separately on Ian and Cyprian. Justin's technique, according to Simon, is what the British proudly cling to as "the Cult of the Amateur." Never work too hard. Never put yourself out. Never let them see you sweat. Above all, always pretend you're not doing your best: if you somehow fail, you always have an excuse; and if by chance you succeed, you seem all the more brilliant for your lack of effort and your gentlemanly indifference.

"Finally, ladies and gentlemen, I ask you, what is America? We have been hearing what is wrong with Britain. But let us compare the two sides of the House. We have the Royal Family—we're proud of them; you have the Kennedys. We have the great Bank of England; you have insider trading. We go to pubs; you go to therapists. You're not Young, Free, and American, gentlemen; you're young, free, and Colonial. We gave you the language, we gave you the government, we gave you the Rolling Stones. What did you give us?" His voice rose to a level of bemused derision. "Kentucky Fried Chicken. Thanks a lot, boys, we're very grateful.

"And you mention tourists. Let me tell you, ladies and gentlemen, I had the unfortunate experience that I don't think many of you will have had of being a tour manager for Thomas Cook in Egypt when a hundred and fifty Americans went on a cruise ship down the Nile. Now, to start with, two of them died on me—"

"Two of them died *under* you," I said, interrupting in upstanding Union tradition.

He looked down at me for several seconds, nodded and said, "Are you quite finished . . . ?

"Anyway," he continued. "We sailed from Luxor on the most fantastic and perfect evening. The sun was setting and we went out on deck, where someone said, 'Oh my gosh, what happened to Mrs. Schwartz?' We had to turn the boat round and go back to Luxor. As tourists, you are the worst. Once, I got woken up at half past three in the morning. The telephone rang in my cabin, and it was the only young American on the boat. 'Help, help,' she said, and I thought, 'My God, heart attack again.' I rushed down to her cabin in my dressing gown, thinking I had another disaster on my hands, and what had she done—Young, Free, and American? She had Super Glued her hand to the office door. It took me three hours with a pot of nail polish remover to get her hand off the door."

The story worked like a charm. The audience nearly fell off its benches.

"No, my friend, if given the choice, we would not wish to be Young, Free, and American. We would wish to be sent to Nirvana. We'd go to heaven, where the food was French, the government was run by the Germans, our sex lives were à la Italian, and the police were British. You look at America, which has about every nationality, and what have you got? The food of the Germans, the government of the French, the police of Italy, and the sex lives of the English. . . .

"I have to say to you, in conclusion, ladies and gentleman, that I am a Londoner, first and foremost. Secondly, I am an Englishman. And finally, I am British. And I think that litany is one of which to be particularly proud. It's the First World, and surely still the highest world. I'm glad America exists. I like to see Americans, being Young, Free, and American. It can be very entertaining. But to be it, no thank you. How, indeed, can we support a country that thinks it's the greatest country on earth because it has more than one flavor of ice cream? Instead of being over the hill, up the river, and under the weather, as they described us, I would say that Americans are— to change the phrase a little—overweight, overdressed, and, thankfully, over there."

As the audience roared with patriotic delight, Justin took a vale-dictory drink, walked over to shake my hand, and returned to the head of his bench. The president stood up, rang the bell, and let loose the rush of students to march through the voting doors. Sev-enty-five students followed their dreams and walked through the gateway to America; three hundred eighty-seven followed their birthright and opted to stay home.

XIX

CLIMBING

An Anatomy of Hip

In short, whoever you may be
To this conclusion, you'll agree,
When everyone is somebodee,
Then no one's anybody.

—Gilbert and Sullivan
The Gondoliers, 1889

"*E*xcuse me, sir, are you a somebody?"
    I tapped a bearded third-year on the shoulder as he passed me carrying a pint of Guinness toward the back of the JCR. It was late Thursday night, the common room was almost empty, and the fluorescent light above me had been shattered in a fight.

"A what?" he asked.

"A somebody," I said.

"I'm Nick," he replied.

"Then you're a nobody?" I said.

"I wouldn't know. Who's a somebody?"

"I wouldn't know either. But a somebody knows. I'm told that that's the first sign."

Lucy and Hillary nodded approvingly. They gestured for Nick to move on. I straightened my back like an upstanding pupil who had just passed the first of many tests on his way to becoming potty-trained in the anatomy of hip at Clare. The next test, they said, would be harder.

The night had begun slowly. Ian and I were wandering around the Clare gardens after dinner, talking about our problems with work and the difficulty of finding a date for the ball. In one last attempt before May Week—the annual exercise in indulgence, intemperance, and creative intercourse that follows the end of Easter Term—we decided to embark on a college pub crawl, a rather desperate invention in which we would go to various college bars, have a drink, and seek out sharks. At first we tried Emmanuel, but nobody was there. Next we tried Sidney Sussex, but only found bedders. Finally, we headed for Magdalene, home of Louise Rogers—Ian's phantom love—but all we found was a scruffy bartender reading a porn magazine. Dejected, we dropped off at Gardenia for a doner kebab and headed home.

On the way we ran into Louise. She was skipping across the Market Square when Ian, suddenly undejected, went darting after her. They kissed twice on the cheek. She tightened the bandana around her head. "So, did you enjoy your trip to the Leper Colony?" Ian was asking as I arrived. Louise Rogers was the kind of person who thrived on danger. She had visited Morocco over Christmas, gone to India over Easter break, and was planning a trek around the Thai Golden Triangle over summer vacation. She was tough, well traveled, hard at heart, but just soft enough around her eyes to make Ian go weak in the knees.

"Listen," he said, not wasting time, "I was just wondering . . ."

"Sorry," she responded, not waiting around. "I don't have time.

I'm off to catch a film. But hey, I'm having a drinks party Friday night. Why don't you two stop by?"

She kissed him twice, smiled blandly at me, and skipped across the square into the arms of a waiting man, who was one week unshaven, greased like a dipstick, and dressed, like her, in leather. We tucked in our tails and slumped off toward Clare.

"I didn't expect to find you here."

Ian was licking his wounds in the corner and I was having a drink at the bar when Hillary plopped down beside me several minutes later. She was dressed, as always, in a baggy red frock. Her hair, as ever, was stuck in a bun. Her hands, as usual, were fingering a novel: *Sexing the Cherry*.

"Why not?" I said.

"Because nobody comes here on Thursdays."

I looked around at the two dozen people scattered throughout the room.

"Nobody?" I said. "Surely there must be somebody here you know."

"Oh," she said. "I know everybody. And trust me, they aren't here."

Cambridge has a strange sociology. It's the only place I've ever been where fifty people can be nobody, and five people can be everybody. The Cambridge school of sociological linguistics goes something like this: somebody walks into a crowded bar, looks around for a moment, then declares definitively, "Oh, nobody's here." That somebody then walks into a near-empty bar and announces unabashedly, "Great, everybody's here." Perhaps this unique census technique has something to do with the lack of numerical training among the literary elite, or perhaps it's the general obfuscatory atmosphere of the average smoke-filled, dimly lit pub, but regardless, I was determined to unlock the secrets of this social code.

The first qualification for being a somebody, according to Hillary and confirmed by Lucy, who soon joined us at the bar, is that somebodies know who they are and nobodies have to ask. The next determinant, they said, is the number of people who consider a person to be a somebody. This led me to propose a formula. It happens that the only way to enter the Clare JCR pub is to descend a winding flight of stairs into the basement of B Entryway. As a result, whenever people in the bar hear footsteps coming down the stairs, they turn to see who is arriving. The longer people stare at the stairs before turning back to their drinks, I suggested, the higher the status of the person arriving.

"But that won't work," said Lucy, the more legalistic of the two and the one with bushier blond hair. "If a bunch of nobodies are sitting at the bar and a nobody comes down the stairs, then they will all look up."

"But that never happens," I protested. "Every time I come down here, the same group of people is sitting at the bar."

"That's because everybody always sits there," said Hillary, a linguist by training and a model by sight, whom Ian had long ago decreed was the most beautiful woman in college.

"So how many somebodies does it take to make everybody?"

"It's not the number of somebodies," corrected Hillary. "It's the absence of nobodies."

"I see. So five somebodies can be everybody if no nobodies are present?"

"Yes."

"And anybody can be somebody?"

"No."

"Only fifteen percent," added Lucy.

"You mean only fifteen percent of Clare College is somebody?" I asked.

"Maybe fewer," she said.

"So it's like getting a First. A set number of people become somebody every year."

"If they're lucky," said Hillary.

"And they're blond," added Lucy.

"Don't tell me," I sighed. "Somebodies prefer blondes."

Sooner or later, almost every conversation I had in Cambridge returned to a single theme: class. Class is to Britain what race is to America—a burden, an obsession, and a potential fatal flaw. As a child, I had always heard that America was a land of social mobility, while Britain was a land of social rigidity. What I found in England was a network of classes that was not only much more fluid than I expected but also much more venomous.

Having outgrown the division between "upstairs and downstairs," inbred and out, the British today have dozens of different subspecies of classes, which have literally hundreds of different names. The tortured titles the British assign their classes have become such a mouthful to pronounce that they often sound like names of teeth: upper-middle-lower bicuspids; lower-upper-middle canines. Cambridge—long home to the late-blooming, uppercut, wisdom-teeth set—in many ways embodies the social changes that the country as a whole has undergone. Until the twentieth century the university was dominated by a rigid class structure, with fee-paying upper-class undergraduates being waited on by a small number of lower-class sizars. In that system, for all its faults, a student's status was rarely in doubt. But these days, when fees are paid by the state and entrance is earned by exam, the student body has become more meritocratic, and, by extension, much more middle-class. Students, as a consequence, must fight for their status.

Of course, social jockeying is not a new sport at Cambridge. Yet its practice does seem to have changed in recent generations. When American Norman Podhoretz arrived at Clare in the late 1950s, he was surprised by the social climate he found. A working-class boy from Brooklyn who had won a scholarship to Cambridge from Columbia University, Podhoretz was amazed at the instant status he received upon matriculation. "As far as [the porters and servants] were concerned," wrote the future literary critic, "so far, indeed, as the whole of England seemed to be concerned—I was a Clare man and therefore a 'young gentleman' to whom amenities, privileges, and deference were owed as by natural right." Podhoretz came to believe that the biggest difference between American and British students lay in their attitudes toward ambition, which he related directly to the presence of a strict social order in England. The British system, he observed in his autobiography, "seems to set fairly predictable limits on a young man's future and discourages appetite and demand." The American system of social mobility, by contrast, "sets no limits at all, and tells a man his social identity is something to be earned."

I have no doubt that Podhoretz's observations were accurate; indeed, many students I met at Clare seemed to fit his description precisely. But for the most part, Cambridge in the 1990s presents a different state of social affairs. With the arrival of more students from state schools and the inclusion of large numbers of women, the cozy, clubby atmosphere of the past has given way to a new open social playing field. Simon was a perfect example of that change. His grandfather, a self-taught man, had worked his way through the civil service but had hit a glass ceiling because he lacked higher education. Simon's father, an only child, was the first member of his family to attend university but, after leaving Oxford, opted to work in a foreign company because he felt excluded from the true British elite. Simon, an only son, was sent to a prestigious boarding school and then moved on to Cambridge. But still his status was in doubt. He looked, sounded, and played squash like a Yah; yet he studied the NARGiest subject of all, engineering. His image was up for grabs.

Simon stepped aggressively into this void and spent his first two-and-a-half terms assiduously building a reputation. He went to the Clare pub almost every night; never had fewer than two pints but always stopped short of six; never borrowed money from others and always laughed at their jokes; and, above all, never talked about his work but always got it done just in time. In the spring, however, with exams in sight, Simon changed his daily habit. He made a rigorous revision schedule; started setting his alarm clock; and even purchased special study enhancers, including lucky pencils, jars of chocolate, as well as special glucose tablets called Dextro Energy, the "Official Energy Products to the British Institute of Sports Coaches." He also gave up drinking for a week, to make sure he wasn't an alcoholic. Here he ran into trouble.

"I can't believe it," he said to me early that week. "I'm totally embarrassed. Humiliated. Nine months of work lost in one episode."

"What happened?" I said.

"I ordered a Coke at the bar."

While it may be difficult to destroy a reputation with one errant night at the bar, the point of Simon's fear was all too clear: status, and, with it, class, is no longer given out free at Cambridge; students today must go looking to find it. I decided to give it a try.

"I want to be somebody for a day," I declared.

Hillary was sitting on the edge of her stool. Lucy was leaning against the brick wall.

"You can't," said Hillary.

"Why not?" I asked.

"Because a nobody can't be a somebody."

"But I'll learn," I said.

"It'll take time," said Lucy.

"And money," Hillary added.

"How much?"

"About five hundred quid a year for beer," she said.

"And five days a week in the bar," Lucy added.

"What about tobacco?" I asked.

"Nobody smokes his own fags," Lucy said. "A somebody nicks them from somebody else."

"In that case I probably should have some on hand. What kind do you recommend?"

"Camel Lights," Hillary said.

"But I know somebody who smokes Marlboros," I said.

She flung her wrist in mock repulsion. "Everybody used to smoke Marlboros," she said. "But then somebody changed to Camel Lights. They're much more healthy, you know."

Lucy laughed at the nick at Simon.

"Okay," I said, straightening up in my chair. "I think I'm ready. Where do I begin?"

"All right, then?" said Hillary. She licked her lips and smiled.

" 'Whenever you're ready,' " I said.

She shook her head disapprovingly. "That's no good."

"What's no good?"

" 'Whenever you're ready.' "

"Why not?"

"It's too eager."

"I don't get it."

" 'All right, then?' " Lucy interrupted. "It's a question."

"A question?" I said. "What does it mean?"

"How's your sex life?" said Hillary.

"Sorry?" I stammered.

"Perfect."

"What's perfect?"

" 'Sorry,' " said Lucy. "If someone propositions you with 'All right, then?' the correct response is 'Sorry.' "

"This is crazy," I said.

They looked at each other. "This is life," they agreed.

A young woman with her dark hair in a ponytail walked up to the bar from the JCR and ordered a lager and lime. Hillary and Lucy prodded me forward to take my next test. I stepped to the counter and bowed my head.

"Excuse me," I said to the woman, a first-year I had seen on the river. "All right, then?"

"Sorry?" she said.

"Oh well," I said, sensing failure. "Thanks anyway."

"No," whispered Lucy. "You're premature."

"Oh," I said, lifting my chin. "Um, would you like to nick a fag?"

"No," she replied. "But I do need some friction." She pulled a cigarette from her jeans pocket, and I, at wit's end, swung around for advice.

"She means a light," muttered Hillary.

"Don't blow it," whispered Lucy.

I swung back around and gaped at the fag dangling from her lower lip. "Sorry," I stammered. "I don't have any friction. I'm afraid I'm premature."

Later, when I was lying in bed next to Hillary, it seemed rather odd that I would be sitting beneath the Clare Chapel in an underlit, whitewashed, Camel-Lighted pub, trying to learn the lingo of the Oxbridge somebody class. When I first came to Cambridge, I expected that most of my friends would come from my course, from the supposedly elite group of people that the Centre for International Studies had gathered from around the world. But except for the occasional weekly lecture or a chance meeting in the U.L., I almost never saw my fellow students. When one of my classmates complained about this to Mr. Langley, he responded curtly, "What you are requesting is an American seminar. This is Cambridge. We believe in the tutorial system."

One by-product of the vaunted tutorial system in Cambridge is that students—both graduates and undergraduates—are so isolated within the confines of their own college that they find it almost impossible to meet people in other parts of the university. Simon felt so trapped in the social machinations of Clare that he had nobody to turn to outside of college when he began having difficulties with Lucy. Susanna, the rowing coach, felt so excluded from those same social circles that she wanted to start her own drinking society. For a foreigner, with no friends from home or from a previous school, the social networks are even harder to penetrate. Unlike Norman Podhoretz, I was not granted immediate status as a gentleman at Clare; in fact, I was kept away. Slowly, with the help of Simon and Ian, I did become friends with many members of Clare. By participating in events like rowing and Rag Week, I began to feel a part of the college. Still, it was not until the middle of Easter Term that I truly became eligible to become an insider.

The reasons were twofold. First, the color of my neckwear. By standing in front of five hundred people at the Union with a red, white, and blue bow tie knotted around my wing-tipped neck, I forever guaranteed my reputation—no matter how loudly my normal wardrobe protested—as a verified American eccentric. Even people who were not in the chamber came up to me for several weeks after the debate to congratulate me on my performance and ask me if I planned to wear the same tie to the Clare May Ball.

Second, and more immediate, the hair color of my friends. Lucy, Hillary, and their fellow first-year Jo were known collectively, and sometimes enviously, as "the Blond Posse." As I began to spend more time with them, and, more importantly, as they began to spend more time with me, my reputation soared. Their attention, no matter how fleeting, may not have been enough to secure me a spot in *Debrett's Peerage,* but when on that Thursday night in late May two of the women widely believed to be the most beautiful in college actually came down the stairs into the crypt bar and sat down next to me, it set off sparks in the ranks of Clare not unlike ones last seen in England when a group of similar Colonial eccentrics tossed bales of homesick British tea into Boston Harbor. Then, the British were enraged that a bunch of American nobodies would even contemplate splitting from the Motherland, not to mention the even less pardonable sin of dropping the tea into the water before the milk. Now, a little over two hundred years later (the average span of British short-term memory), the process was reversed, and the natives at Clare were equally enraged that an American nobody had come back to Cambridge—wet nurse of the Motherland—to drink freely from the Holy Grail and become, however briefly, a somebody.

"You need some work," Lucy insisted when I returned to the fold.

"You're too aristo," Hillary said.

"Too what?" I asked.

"Too aristocratic."

I pulled my hands from my blue jeans.

"You need more sarky," Lucy announced.

"What's that?" I pleaded.

"More sarcasm."

I wiped the frown from my face.

"And your hair," Hillary said, mussing my scalp with her fingers. "Too straight. Your face, too clean."

"Don't shave for a while," Lucy advised. "And get yourself a leather jacket."

"You could wear an earring," chimed Hillary.

"Or bracelets from Africa," her friend enthused.

"I suppose everybody's been to Africa," I said.

"And Amsterdam," added Lucy.

By this time in the evening the concentration of so much activity in one area of the bar had begun to attract a crowd. I was sitting in the corner, facing the stairs. Lucy, Hillary, and now Jo—a first-year art historian and cello player whose blond hair reached halfway to her feet—sat in front of me, facing inward. And Ian and several boys from the snooker table were standing just behind the Posse, staring quizzically into our circle as if they were trying to catch a glimpse of some exotic animal at a zoo. Mark, the Union president, was there, with his half-shaven, half-shaggy hairdo. Next to him was Kirk, whose hair was greased up atop his head like the rear end of a duck. And the final person was Nick, the third-year with the wiry hair I had spoken to earlier in the evening. Together, with their mohawks à la mode, they looked like a band of Indians displaced from their native land.

"So let me get this straight," I said. "You're telling me if I stop shaving, stop cutting my hair, start smoking, and start wearing an earring, that I can become somebody."

"With a little more practice," said Lucy.

"And if I do this," I said, "being too aristo is bad."

"Horrid," said Jo.

"And wearing leather is good," I repeated.

"Divine," said Hillary.

"But that doesn't sound like a somebody," I said. "That sounds like a thug. If I leave this place and go out into the world, everybody will think I'm a truck driver."

"That won't happen," Lucy assured me. "Once you're a somebody, everybody sticks together."

"I see. A somebody without everybody becomes nobody."

"That's right."

Hillary got up to go to the bathroom, which she called a bog. The other two immediately rushed to accompany her. As soon as they had disappeared, the curious boys descended on me. "How do you do it?" they wanted to know. "Why are they talking to you?" The irony of the entire escapade quickly became apparent. In order to become somebody at Cambridge, I didn't have to change my clothes and dress down. I didn't have to affect an accent and speak up. All I had to do was be myself and be the object of somebody's attention. All of which goes to prove that social standing in Cambridge is much more hollow than it first appears: not only does somebody separated from everybody quickly become nobody, but, even worse, nobody surrounded by everybody just as quickly becomes somebody.

"Desperately seeking somebody," I announced when the Posse had returned from the loo. "The package tour to Memorial Court will be leaving momentarily."

"Bruce, you can't say that," Ian muttered. "You can't announce that you're leaving alone and then take the chance that they'll let you go."

A somebody, he said, never exits alone, but always waits for everybody else. For a somebody, the correct response to "I'm leaving" is "Me too." "Are you going?" is best answered, "Are you?"

"It doesn't matter," I said, turning toward the stairs. "This body is ready for bed."

"Wait," one of the Posse shouted, or was it all three? "We'll go with you."

They stood, linked their arms together, and marched toward me like a giant blond Pac-Man, sucking me into the bonus zone of somebody-land—a place where lights sparkle like wine and wits twinkle like stars, and where one tries to postpone the inevitable dimming before the fickle arbiters of class parcel out status to some other body in order to avoid flickering away themselves into the penumbra of nobody's business.

XX

WALTZING

A Ball

𝒮𝒷

PEYOTE: Wot is this place, anyway?
ARTHUR: You are in what scientists now know
to be a black hole. Floating free, an airless,
lightless, dayless, nightless time-lock,
a cosmic accident called a Cambridge
College Ball.

—David Hare
Teeth 'n' Smiles, 1969

I woke up at noon—a somebody with no date. I had trod many
paths in the previous months in search of the perfect fit, but the
other shoe always seemed to drop instead of slipping on. Hillary, my
fickle first-year fling, was tending bar at the ball and didn't need an
escort; Susanna, my rowing pal, was going with a prince. As if my
predicament was not bad enough, my mother had called the previous night to say I'd have more fun with a date. But at this late date,
without a godmother, I feared I'd be dancing on no toes that night
and feeling like a heel.

"Remember the Alamo!" Terry said, although he didn't seem to
know what it meant. "Do it for the red, white, and blue!"

So that afternoon, with my thesis asleep in my laptop computer and the Ball Committee scurrying around the gardens wielding walkie-talkies and rainproof tape, I crossed the Clare Bridge and went into town for one last blind search for a date.

I headed for Magdalene.

"Excuse me," I said to the porter behind the counter. "I'm looking for a woman named Fuchsia."

"Fuchsia Dunlop?" said the man between the arms of his handlebar mustache.

"Yes, that must be the one."

"Go across the road," he said, "down to the river, up the stairs, and to the left."

Following his orders, I crossed the road, walked to the river, climbed up the stairs, and turned to the left, where I knocked on the oak nameplate: F. C. DUNLOP.

"Won't you come in. I'm sorry for the mess. Ignore the paté on the ceiling."

Fuchsia Dunlop opened the door of her top-floor rooms, pulled her robe around her shoulders, and, in a moment, invited me in. The previous Friday, at Ian's insistence, I had gone with him to Louise's for a party of the Belladonnas—Magdalene's first women's drinking society. While Ian tagged around after Louise, I sat on the floor drinking Indian beer and eating chicken curry with a group of charter "donnas." The following day I met the same group at Emmanuel, the day after we met in Caius, and in the process we had achieved a curious kind of Cambridge intimacy: we had become "May Week friends."

May Week is the perfect microcosm for the anthropology of Cambridge. It brings outs and exaggerates many of the latent trends—interpersonal, international, and interclass—lurking just beneath the surface of the university. For some May Week symbolizes love and romance. For others it epitomizes freedom and debauchery. But for an outsider it also typifies the British love of euphemism and nostalgia, for in deference to the national penchant for obfuscation, May Week isn't one week but two; and in accordance with the tradition of longing for things past, May Week doesn't fall in May but in June.

In the course of the first seven days of May Week, the party-goer has a veritable arklike menagerie of societies whose parties he can attend. There are reptiles (Gators) and amphibians (Tadpoles); marsupials (Roos) and arachnids (Scorpions); carnivores (Minks) and herbivores (Hippos); even an assortment of hypothetical beasts (Thunderbirds, Griffins, and Unicorns). Some of these groups require blazers for admittance, others require money, but most just require the guest to PBASomething, usually PBAB or PBAB SpWW. I was even invited to one event that said PBA_____, and the _____ had been filled with "Babe."

At each of the parties I attended, usually having brought or been brought by Ian, the talk was always the same: "I got so pissed at the last party. . . . I'm going to get pissed even worse at the next. . . . How many balls are you going to crash?" But in the end, when all was said and drunk, our purpose was not to get pissed or sharked, but to get a date. Ian, of course, had his classical quest and could only think of Belladonna Louise. (At the Wylies, an outdoor party where every guest brings a bottle of vodka that is then mixed with a hint of grapefruit juice and served from a watering can, the two of them were actually seen going toward a specially designated "snogging zone.") I, however, was much freer, and by the end of the main weekend of May Week I had grown especially close to the leader of the Belladonnas, who was taller than the rest of the group, with reams of curly brown hair and large Olive Oyl eyes. By the morning of the Clare Ball, I had learned her "Christian" name (Fuchsia), her subject (English), and her future plans (becoming a chef); but I hadn't learned the one piece of information that constitutes intimacy in collegiate terms—her surname. Once again I was saved by the porter.

Stepping inside Fuchsia's spacious rooms, I immediately noticed the clothes on the floor and the foie gras on the ceiling (from a party, she explained), but—more important—I also noticed no photographs of boyfriends on the walls. We started chatting—about the weekend, about exams, about Cambridge after classes. It was a real conversation—no NARGy pauses ("Oh . . . that's strange"), no Yah-like gasps ("Really!? How brill"), and no references at any time in the ensuing hour about how drunk we had been on the previous day, how drunk we would be on the following night, or how many balls we would crash. Finally, when the conversation did turn to balls, I took my mug by the handle, apologized in advance for my two left feet, and invited her to go with me that night to the Clare May Ball.

She said yes.

I smiled, and, avoiding the conspicuous male temptation to turn instantly and go away, I continued the conversation for a moment before mentioning the time, finishing my tea, and floating back to Clare. It was 4:30 P.M.

"Well, Terry," I said when I arrived back home. "If there is an award for the last person to get a date, I think I might have won it."

"Congratulations, ol' boy. I knew you could do it. What's the lucky girl's name?"

"Fuchsia," I said. "I've known her for less than a week, but she really has the right attitude."

"I should say so," he said. "Anybody who'd accept a date on the day of the ball must be what we call a free spirit. Anyway, as you Americans say, I hope you have a ball."

"Ladies and gentlemen, please step up to the registration table and hand your tickets to the hostess. Remember, there will be no readmittance to the ball."

May balls are the highlight of the Cambridge year and the climax of May Week. Since most colleges sponsor separate balls, a friendly rivalry has emerged among the committees to see who can come up with the most lavish food and the most outlandish entertainment.

With tickets averaging 150 pounds a pair, the committees have close
to a quarter of a million dollars to splurge on their conspicuous,
all-night affairs. Some colleges, like St. John's, opt for carnival fare,
hiring merry-go-rounds and Ferris wheels to fill their Gothic quads.
Others, like Trinity, choose Euro-chic, assembling casino tables and
faux nightclubs beneath their medieval spires. But Clare, for its part,
prefers fairy-tale romance—a preference that isn't always realized.

My evening started at six, when Simon (my wicked stepbrother)
came to my rooms in undershorts and starched shirt to have me bow
his tie. He was followed soon after by Ian, who was wearing not one
but two DJs—the inner one black, the outer one white—and who
also needed his one tie bowed. Lucy appeared not long after that
looking for someone to hem her dress, but she wisely avoided asking me: sewing is nothing like tying a shoe.

At seven we set off for the night: Simon and Lucy; Ian, still
dateless; and I, in self-bowed black tie, who broke off briefly to pick
up my date, who had managed to dress herself in a hand-sewn
purple gown. The five of us reassembled at a French restaurant
inexplicably called Michel's of Oxford (marketing geniuses, those
Brits), the kind of place where the boys order in French to impress
their dates and the waitresses don't understand. *"Filet d'agneau avec
sauce anglaise?"* "Oh, brown meat with brown sauce." After dinner
we joined the soggy stream of students heading to one of the three
balls being held that night.

"I heard that in the old days people from the town used to come
out during May Week to admire the gowns," I said.

"These days they just complain about the noise," said Ian. "Last
year some local residents objected that the colleges were shooting
off fireworks in the middle of the night, so the county council
passed a resolution saying no fireworks after eleven."

When we arrived at Clare, a short line of guests was gathered
outside Old Court, where the normally somber entrance to college
had been decorated like a florist's fantasy. A pink and white tent
stretched out from the gate, with branches of pine hanging from its

brim and garlands of flowers entwined around its poles. A wooden swing hung from a nearby plum tree, and a giant corsage of pastel-colored carnations was pinned on the gate directly over the sign that said WELCOME TO CLARE COLLEGE: NO DOGS, STROLLERS, BICYCLES, OR PICNICS.

Stepping into the entryway, we were met by a platoon of security officials. Two people took our tickets, checked them with a master list, asked us to sign our names on the back, compared them with our personal identification, stamped them with a rubber rose, then returned them with a warning not to misplace them as porters would be circulating throughout the evening and asking us for proof of entrance. Once through with the ticketing agents, we took two steps forward, where we were met by several more guards, who ordered us to raise our arms like surrendering soldiers. To the right, one guard forced into our hands a packet containing the program, meal plan, floor plan, and entertainment schedule, while to the left another person wrapped red plastic hospital identification bracelets around our wrists and clipped off the excess tails. The entire regimen took almost ten minutes and was far more rigorous than any airport security inspection to which I had ever been subjected. The only things missing from this totalitarian routine were a strip search and an X-ray machine: "I gotta dance. Know what I mean?" In Cambridge one need not PBAB to a ball, but one does need to PBA-Passport, -Visa, and -Immunization Card.

"Matthew Sargaison, Gundula Azeez, John Breknell, and Damian Thantrey welcome you to the Clare May Ball," said our six-page Program Guide, *"by kind permission of the Master and Fellows of Clare College."*

Cambridge, at its worst, is dreary and grey—not the polished grey of marble columns, nor the stately grey of war monuments, but the gloomy grey of wizened buildings with splotches of age and wrinkles of time splattered across their once seamless façades. Cambridge, at its best, is lively and green—not the artificial green of

Putt-Putt felt, nor the murky green of salted seawater, but the brilliant green of crew-cut lawns bedecked with an afternoon croquet game or the hand-holding naps of puppy lovers sprawled along the riverbank. But Cambridge on ball night is neither of these. It is red and blue splashed against college walls, bathing the stones with spots of color and reaching toward heaven with fingers of light. It is white marquees in every court, with yellow balloons and pink festoons arching and stretching from every hip joint. It is, in short, a rainbow of fantasies, spanning the void between rain and shine, night and day, final exams and unemployment.

Once inside Old Court, Fuchsia and I quickly became separated from the rest of our crew. With so many choices among food and drink, magic shows and music acts, we felt like Hansel and Gretel let loose in a giant gingerbread house with no need to get written permission from the Witch to indulge in any illicit behavior or stay up past 2 A.M. We decided to start at the entrance and make our way through the venues. First, we needed a drink.

Throughout the evening, you will find cocktails in Old Court, Bucks Fizz and Kir Royale on the Clare Bridge, Champagne in the Master's Garden and free beer and lager in the Cellars' Bar.

Slightly intimidated by all this American-style choice, we stepped up to the first table we saw and grabbed two drinks that looked as if they could have been served at Nigel's Yah Who's Who. They were green and sweet, with a yellow parasol, and on first ingestion tasted like a mixture of tropical rum, clotted cream, and pureed lime jelly beans.

With drinks in hand, we started walking. Each of the four plots of grass in Old Court was covered with a giant canopy: one for cocktails, another for snacks, a third for the eighteen-piece Umbrella Big Band, and the last for the waltzing guests. Further afield, each of the function rooms was set aside for a different program: comedians in the Latimer Room, a foot masseuse in the MCR, and even a "Beauty and Image Analyst" in the Thirkill Room. By the time we arrived in the Fellows' Garden, close to half an hour later, we were ready to eat again.

Strawberries and cream are available in the Master's Garden. Cakes, croissants, filled bagels and candy floss [the local Freudian slip-up term for cotton candy] *are served in Old Court whilst in the Fellows' Garden, salads, crepes, barbecue, spring rolls and fruit are available. Hot soup will be served in Hall from midnight.*

We opted for salads, stepped up to a cart, and in an instant were given heaping plates with three different dishes—potato, pasta, and fruit salad, each one more bountiful and zestful than anything theretofore seen in Clare College that year. As we ate and chatted and waited in line to have our portrait taken *("Representative of the Coe Colour Centre will be in the Garden throughout the evening to photograph couples"),* we suddenly noticed that dangling above our heads like manna from heaven were dozens upon dozens of chocolate-covered doughnuts. A May Ball, we calculated, costs not only 150 pounds but 15,000 calories as well.

Once we had thoroughly digested the surroundings and viewed the fireworks at 11 P.M., the night began to lose its shape and dissolve into a seemingly endless stream of exotic drinks, candied snacks, trumpet blares, and vaudeville acts. Attending the ball was like stepping into the otherworldly paradise of one of those snowy plastic souvenirs—just when you get bored with one scene, move to another pavilion, give the toy a shake, and the party is instantly reborn in a musical flurry and sugary high. As if to emphasize this point, the next several hours were a blizzard of encounters.

In the sunken garden, bobbing at doughnuts, we came upon Susanna, now a graduand—someone who has officially passed her finals but not yet graduated. After nearly two years with Peter de Clare—enduring his abuse, hiding her background, falling from his sink—Susanna had finally ended their affair and in his place had started dating Rana, the Indian prince from Nigel's Yah-fest.

"Nice speech at the Union," Rana said to me as he took a sip of Kir Royale. He was dressed in a formal olive suit with a high Nehru collar. His mustache glistened with drops of champagne.

"Yeah," said Susanna. "I was really impressed. You could've almost been English." She brushed back her hair and straightened her glasses. For the first time since I had known her, I detected a slight northern accent.

"But you forgot the most important point," added Rana. "Do you remember that part where you said Americans have choices— about ice cream, or weather, or toast? You missed the best thing about America: you have a choice about class." He put his arm around Susanna. "In India we don't have that choice. Our lives— even our families—are all arranged."

"So what are you going to do?" I turned toward Susanna.

"Well, the prince will go home and rejoin his family, and I—" She kissed him on the cheek. "I'm going to join the army."

"The army!?" I gasped.

"Why not?" she retorted. "I think it sounds rather exciting. And besides, at least one of us has to find out the *true* meaning of international relations."

In the cellars, dancing to Wolly and the New Cranes (*"A heady mix of jazz, folk, and pop"*), we bumped into Cyprian and his date, Isadora. After several songs Isadora split a seam, and she and Fuchsia excused themselves to seek out the seamstress in A Entryway. We sat down to wait.

"So how did you meet her?" I asked Cyprian. His ponytail was tucked inside his DJ. His red tie was store-tied.

"Well, you know, ever since Sophie left me in March, my blood's been boiling. I met Isadora at a classics party. I knew right away she was the right girl. She was Greek, and she had brown hair, brown eyes, and a big nose. I have a history of women with big noses. And besides, she was a Pisces."

"You could tell?"

"I guessed. I told her she was a four-one."

"What's that?"

He let out a sigh. "If you take out the X and divide the remaining letters of the alphabet into a five-by-five grid, the first column of the fourth row is a P. When she told me she was a Pisces, I told her I had guessed."

"She must be the right one for you," I said. "Anybody who would fall for that line must be pretty desperate."

"Very funny. Anyway, just listen to me. I've only known this girl for two weeks and already I'm saying I'm prepared to spend the rest of my life with her. It's a bit hubristic."

"It doesn't have to take long," I suggested.

"I knew after the first hour. Of course, this is the time when I'm supposed to be meeting the love of my life."

"According to whom?"

"My clairvoyant."

"Your what?"

"I went to see a clairvoyant several years ago after I broke up with my girlfriend. She knew many things about my life, like the fact that I love music. She made me write 'I will have more confidence' on a piece of paper five hundred times. She told me my life would undergo a dramatic change around this time."

"I can leave Cambridge now," I said. "I've heard it all."

Isadora and Fuchsia appeared on the stairs and started toward our table. Cyprian stared at them.

"So this is the one," I said.

"This is the one."

"I'm happy for you. It has a certain classical air."

"I guess you're right."

"And will she follow you if you go somewhere else to teach?"

"I'll follow her," he said.

"To Greece?" I asked.

He looked at me. "To heaven."

Several minutes later, on the makeshift ballroom floor in Old Court, we finally met up with Terry.

"Don't tell me," he said, as I went over to introduce him to Fuchsia and allow him to fulfill the last of his famous three rules, " 'Dunlop.' "

"How did you know?" I said.

"I spoke with this fine young lady this afternoon."

"When was that?"

Fuchsia stepped in. "I called about six to see if you were going to pick me up or if I should meet you at the restaurant."

Terry perked up. "I told her I had taught you how to be an English gentleman and that of course you would pick her up."

I dipped my head and accepted the sword tap on my shoulder.

"Yes, Mr. Feiler"—Terry glanced at my tasseled loafers—"you don't have the right shoes yet, but at least you're learning the manners. Now, Miss Dunlop"—he turned toward her and bowed—"shall we show our friend how to dance?" He stripped off his jacket, gave her his hand, and led her to waltz on the grass.

If the ball had ended there, in the wee hours of the morning, I—and many others—would have gone home refreshed, rejuvenated, and reawakened to the magical possibilities of Cambridge. The setting was magnificent. The music inspiring. The food anything but brown. "The ball is the highlight of the year," Terry had gushed. "It's Disneyland on the Cam."

But the Ball didn't end in the wee hours of the morning. It lasted until dawn, when all those left standing would gather in the garden for the "Survivors' Photograph." In the interim between midnight and morning, between "well enough" and "alone," the party slowly came undone.

It began with a punt. Somewhere between the dance floor and

the champagne bar we once again bumped into Simon. "Meet at the dock in half an hour," he said. "We have a reservation." After securing our last bowl of strawberries, we wandered down to the makeshift pier and waited with Simon and Lucy for our tour in a chauffered punt—the May Ball equivalent of a gondola ride.

When our time arrived, Simon and Lucy sat in the stern, while Fuchsia and I moved to the bow. A uniformed chauffeur with straw hat and silk sash climbed onto the steering platform and skillfully used the pole to propel us toward King's. "At the top of the Gibbs building you will see a round window," he said. "That's a bathroom where E. M. Forster used to entertain young boys." We headed for Queens'. "Next to that cloister is a room where Erasmus wrote love poetry for Henry VIII." Fuchsia and I were following the tour, but Simon and Lucy were not: they were quarreling. In recent weeks they had been doing that more and more. Simon craved attention and demanded more time. Lucy needed space and started retreating. Their clashing needs finally came to a head on the night before Simon's final exam, when Lucy walked into his rooms, shut the door, and announced that she was pregnant.

Simon froze. When he came into my rooms later that night, his face was as white as the fog in his eyes and his body was as still as a cartoon character who had just run over the edge of a cliff but had not yet succumbed to the inevitable fall. His whole year had been a struggle to stay unattached—first with his girlfriend in Tokyo, then his neighbor Triple K. But late in the year he had lost control—tripping first by falling in love, then falling even further by tripping up in bed. He took his exam the following morning but stayed indoors for most of May Week. And when, on the day before the ball, Lucy discovered she wasn't pregnant, it didn't seem to matter anymore. The relationship had caught its crab. The veil of youth was rent asunder.

"I want to punt," Simon declared, after we had turned around and were heading back toward Clare.

"But you're pissed," Lucy protested.

"You're right," he agreed.

After persuading the chauffer to take a rest, Simon left his seat in the trough of the punt and assumed a position on the platform in the back. He rested his pint glass on the slick wooden surface and began to push us home. His course was wobbly, his legs unsteady, and Lucy only worsened the effect by continuing her verbal abuse.

"Be quiet," he said. "I'm concentrating."

"Grow up," she said. "You're like a child."

Lucy turned abruptly with her last remark, pivoting from her seat in the belly of the punt and in the process knocking over his glass, thus spilling its contents all over the platform and propelling Simon, staring at Lucy, into a time-lapsed, back-first free fall directly into the arms of the Cam. Students come, students go, but the river never stops telling time.

Next came the climb. Ian had been absent for most of the night. In our backings and forthings across the Bridge, we had not run into him even once. Simon's descent into the river, however, finally brought us together at river's edge and since the sun was just appearing over the trees, I suggested we climb onto the roof of Old Court for the sunrise. Ian declined, but gave us his key.

Fuchsia and I climbed the stairs of D Entryway, stepped across Ian's overturned books, and crawled out his window onto the catwalk five stories above the ground. From that angle, King's Chapel looked like a giant bread box with a lace bonnet on top. The river meandering through the Backs seemed even more calm than usual. As we admired the scene and drank a toast, we heard someone shouting at us.

"Bruce, Fuchsia . . . down here!"

It was Ian, who at that moment was using a rope to pull himself up the outside of the Grand Marquee in the Fellows' Garden. The tent was at least twenty-five feet high and seventy-five feet long. When Ian reached the top, he balanced himself like a tightrope walker and brought his hands to his mouth.

"Louise!" he cried in the direction of Magdalene. "Louise, I worshiped you, I really did. You were all I ever wanted."

The presence of a screaming suitor on top of the Grand Marquee was more than enough to attract the attention of the goons at Security Central. Several porters came rushing to the scene, several dozen students came pouring from the tent, and for all we know several hundred townspeople could at that moment have been telephoning the police to complain of fireworks past 11 P.M. Ian, meanwhile, seemed unconcerned. Like Simon, he had reached the end of a year-long struggle, in his case the battle between mind and body. In the *Bacchae,* the hardheaded king of Thebes succumbs to the lure of Dionysus and passion triumphs over reason. In real life, or at least at the Wylies, Ian and Louise had ventured off into the snogging zone. For a moment—arm in arm, face-to-face—he was in bliss. Caution had been tossed to the wind, passion appeared to triumph. But when the sun came up an hour later and she invited him back to her rooms, he declined. When she invited him to go to the Magdalene Ball, he said no. At the end of the year, the end of the pursuit, the kiss was all he wanted. Ian could not succumb to the cult of pleasure: the bodily act might corrupt his ideal. The pursuit itself proved to be more important than the pursued.

As the guards started shaking the rope of the tent, Ian turned toward us for a final bow. He peeled off his outer dinner jacket, tossed it onto the canvas, and slid like a child to the lip of the marquee and landed, like a cat, on his feet. Tragedy had been averted. The hero was restored.

Last came the dance. Fuchsia and I climbed down from the roof and walked toward the Fellows' Garden. The ball was coming to an end; the Survivors' Photograph was drawing nigh; but first we wanted one last waltz. All through the night the music had been diverse: from Anita Chakraborty (*"The mistress of mellow music"*) to the Brand New Heavies (*"Giants of acid jazz"*); from SPAM! (*"The coolest* a cappella *crooning in town"*) to Root Jackson's Unfinished Business (*"Talented purveyors of punk"*); from Masquerade (*"Hip-swinging African music"*) to my favorite, Wolodomyr Dyszkant (*"Laid-back Ukrainian entertainment"*). The last band of the night on

the Main Stage of the Ball was Haji Ahkba and the Funk Ambassadors *("We raise the curtain—they bring down the house!")*.

Inside the marquee close to two hundred ball boys and girls were
gathered in front of the illuminated stage. Some of the boys had
discarded their DJs, many of the girls had ditched their high heels.
But for the most part the guests bumping and grinding on the portable parquet floor were in remarkably natty condition. The members
of the band, meanwhile—a short, fat, balding man with a mustache
(alias Haji Ahkba?), three backup singers with flowing brunette hair,
and an eight-piece eclectic electric rhythm section—could not have
been less concerned with dignified appearances. With each song the
main singer, Chubby Ahkba, would discard another article of clothing—first his lemon blazer, then his blueberry vest, next his flowery
tie—until he reached a one-piece lycra suit. "Purge me of my sex!"
he chanted. "Purge me of my love."

After several more thrusts, when a student came to the stage and
announced that the next song would be the last, Haji the Great
disappeared behind a bank of amplifiers and emerged seconds later
to a synthesized trumpet blare wearing nothing at all from head to
toe except for a black leather G-string that clung for its life around
his sizable waist and sprouted from its scanty frontal piece a five-
foot, flexible green plastic tube with a smiling yellow foam-rubber
head attached to its outer end. The crowd burst into a frenzy of
hooliganic hoots and howls as Chubby (and Hairy) Haji Ahkba the
Great grabbed hold of his squirming penile projection and began
shaking it back and forth, singing:

> "I like coffee;
> I like tea;
> I don't like fucking
> Pricks like me."

The crowd could hardly contain itself, as the three backup singers in
white unitards prostrated themselves on the ground as if genuflect-

ing to a king. Haji Ahkba himself, clearly moved by this spontaneous display of reverence, started lifting his prop erect into the air and
screaming, "Fuck Me! Love Me! Fuck Me! Love Me!" and urging
the students to follow his lead and purge him of his sex. And so they
did: at six o'clock on a misty mid-June morning, on the ninth day
of May Week, several hundred of the brightest young minds of
Great Britain, dressed in dinner jackets and wearing ball gowns,
strutting necks tied like shoes or trussed with fake pearls, gathered
alongside the banks of the Cam, underneath a giant white tent, and
shouted at the tops of their potato-fed, lager-sogged, smoke-filled
lungs, "Fuck Me! Love me! Fuck Me! Love Me! Purge me of my
sex!" while stamping their feet, shaking their bums, and waving
their arms high in the air in order to show any guard on patrol that
they were still wearing their red hospital tags. Roll over, Christopher Robin; make way for the modern Cambridge rain dance.

"Ladies and gentlemen, may I have your attention? Please stop
talking. Cross your arms in front of you, look directly at the camera,
and, whatever you do, don't move."

Minutes later, as we gathered beneath the wide-angle lens in the
last remaining patch of grass in the garden, I reflected for a moment
on the evening's activities. Like so much else at Cambridge, the ball
had started out all elegance and smiles but over the course of the
evening had degenerated into dissipation and debauchery. It was as
if all the guests were Cinderellas who reverted to their darker selves
when they stayed up past 11 P.M. Part of the debauchery, I'm sure,
came from too much liquor; part from too little sleep. But most, I
suspect, came from the character of the students themselves. At the
end of my year in the Empire of the Mind, I was left with the
overwhelming impression that Cambridge, for all its aged buildings
and storied past, for all its rigorous exams and strict regulations, is
still a world where the personalities of the students emerge through
the tradition and exert themselves on the place.

In many ways, the personalities gathered before the camera that morning were a remarkably isolated lot. All through the ball, those inside were not allowed out (at least if they wanted to get back in), and those outside were not allowed in (at least if they wanted to stay). In that sense the ball was a telling metaphor for Cambridge, with the students locked in, the town locked out, and the two worlds connected only by the fireworks that were shot from inside the college but landed in the middle of town. Not long after the ball I learned a revealing story about that gap. Two centuries ago Cambridge students invented a special term to describe the townspeople—"snobs." The swells, in those days, were kept in, the snobs were kept out. It was not until Cambridge graduate William Thackeray wrote the *Book of Snobs* in 1829 that the term *snob* came to mean a person of any social rank who displays vanity or vulgarity. Within a generation the term had been completely turned on its head and *snob* became an insult that people outside the university hurled at those within.

To my surprise, however, the true face of Cambridge is much less snobbish and much less uniform than its exclusive image might suggest. Far from an exclusive upper-class resort, Cambridge, with its open admission, has become a sort of social melting pot for brainy postpubescents. In this sense the university is the worst kind of club: it is a club anybody can join. And because the members realize how fragile their status is, they spend a lot of money to uphold it. SHOW BALLS SELL OUT TO CREEPING CLASSLESSNESS, wrote *The Guardian* several days after the end of May Week. "The guests are all just snobbish automatons living out a pose." The trouble, said one old boy in the article, "is that balls are just so *bourgeois*. Not enough nobs; too much riff-raff. The people that really matter are all having parties at the Little Chef [the English equivalent of Howard Johnson's]."

Perhaps the greatest irony of all is that while Cambridge traditionalists complain that their beloved institution drifts into classlessness (read: bourgeois hell), those outside still complain that the institution embodies class-based exclusion (read: aristocratic heaven). While those inside know the party is over, the rest of the world still looks at Cambridge and sees the privileges of the past. To these people Cambridge students will always be "the elite," "the snobs," or simply "them." "They are rich, complacent, self-loving, self-regarding, self-righteous, phoney, half-baked, politically immature, neurotic, evil-minded little shits," says the main character in David Hare's *Teeth 'n' Smiles,* a musical about an eccentric band (not unlike Haji Ahkba and the Funk Ambassadors) that is invited to play at a Cambridge May Ball. "Expect nothing and you will not be disappointed."

"Are you ready?" called the photographer, and the students all posed, teeth and smiles. "Three, two, one . . ."

"Cheers!"

After the Survivors' Photograph, I walked arm-in-arm with Fuchsia back to Magdalene and said good night, with a hug, at the door. Amid all the decadence and depravity, ours had been a fairy-tale romance—three days, two nights, one ball; no snogging, no shagging, no fairy godmother; just rapturous compatibility. I didn't even know her sign. With my DJ smelling equally of Cam water and strawberry juice, I headed back through town. Bicycle bells and traffic whistles filled the early morning air. I wandered past St. John's, erecting last-minute tents, and strolled past Trinity, pulling down its marquees. As I walked into Clare and across the Bridge, I noticed an object in the champagne-soaked grass behind the sign NO MOORING ON THE BANKS. Curious, I stepped into the garden, reached under a napkin, and discovered a memento that somebody had left as they hastily fled the ball and returned to earth: a single black velvet high-heeled shoe.

XXI

GRADUATING

Port and Prejudice

As soon as the University authorities had settled in
Cambridge, they built their schools and drew up a sylla-
bus for the students. Everything, the University said,
was to be done by degrees. That is why things change so
slowly at Cambridge.

—C. R. Benstead
Alma Mater, 1944

The garden on graduation day was a bouquet of blooms—rosy
round mums with blush on their cheeks; dandy lean dads with
lions on their ties; and budding young siblings with wide iris eyes.
The bouquet of blooms was a strange menagerie—goose-necked
tourists with cameras quacking, batty students with winged gowns
flapping, and owlish dons with their pupils squinting as their students flew away. With parents, porters, and packs of French school-
girls looking on from the bridge, the graduands of Clare College
gathered in the garden, processed slowly through Old Court, and
disappeared into the marble belly of the Senate House, where they
were asked to bend down on one knee, grip the pinkie of the

vice-chancellor, and humbly receive their *honours* degrees. After the fleeting ceremony, the newly suffixed graduates emerged from the building and returned en masse to Clare, where they were allowed for the first time in their careers to walk unaccompanied on the grass.

"Are you sad to see them go?"

I stood underneath the main archway of college watching the students picnic in the court and discussing the day's events with Terry, who was dressed for the occasion in his three-piece regalia with a freshly brushed bowler crownlike on his head. He gripped his drooping pipe to his chest like a teddy bear.

"They're good kids," he said. "They always are."

Only undergraduates are allowed to participate in the degree ceremony held in June, and, in any case, I wouldn't be eligible until after my oral exam. Earlier that day I had walked over to the Sidgwick Site to meet Dr. Long. Our fourth and most important meeting of the year had been shorter than any of the previous three. "Well done," he had said, as he handed me my thesis, "Winner Take Some: The Politics of Reparations in Japan and Germany, 1945–1948." It was 109 pages long, and, as instructed, had footnotes at the foot of the page, a bibliography at the back, and was written as best I could entirely in English English. "Better than most. Quite good, actually. I never expect much from these M.Phil. dissertations, but this one was quite readable. I'll be curious to hear what your examiners say. They ought to be quite pleased." He reached toward his cupboard. "A glass of port to celebrate?"

I looked at Terry as I recalled the incident and realized I had probably received more one-to-one tuition from him than anyone else.

"I understand that the fellows of Clare had a meeting last evening and decided to allow visitors into the college today."

"That's right," Terry said. "And just between you and me, those fellows are a bunch of bloody fools."

"That's pretty strong language," I said.

"We are in the business of education," he declared. "And for one day a year I think we should be considerate to the third-year students who are graduating. We should at least keep the tour groups out of the college. We are not Notre Dame or the Eiffel Tower. We are an institution of higher learning." He nodded his head defiantly, then added, "Oh, I told them what I think."

"At the meeting?"

"Oh no! They don't invite the likes of me to those meetings. It's a true port-and-sherry affair. But I said to one of the fellows today that tourists don't respect our traditions. Why, I remember a time last week. I went up to a man in the garden and asked him to leave. He told me he was a member of the university. 'You're lying,' I said to him. 'If you're a member of the university, then I'll put feathers in my bum and fly around the garden. You're no more than a bloody tourist.' Well, he took exception to what I said. And then he got violent. It's always the liars who get violent. 'Young man,' I said, straightening my back and smoothing down my tie. 'I don't believe that a member of this university would strike a porter. I will ask you again to kindly remove yourself from the premises of this college.' He spit on my feet as he left."

The following day I went walking in the garden and discovered the limits to the college's open-door policy. Simon, who would soon be returning to Japan for the "long vac," was hosting his father's boss from Tokyo and asked me to come along and translate. The boss, Mr. Horie, who was visiting his son in London, wanted to take a tour of Cambridge and drove up the M-11 for the day with his wife, daughter-in-law, and two-year-old grandson. After gathering for tea in Simon's rooms, we headed down the path toward town, stopping briefly for a detour in the Fellows' Garden, which showed no signs of the Grand Marquee that had shaded its lawns a week earlier.

By chance we were the only people in the garden that morning. Although tourists are requested to stay out, many still climb over the slagging garden chain at the entranceway. Members of the college are allowed in at all times. After admiring the flowers and taking a few snapshots of the bridge, the six of us wandered back toward the path. As we approached, I noticed one of the porters, a tall, thin man with an aquiline nose, walking briskly across the bridge in our direction. I had never seen him outside of the Porters' Lodge in Old Court.

Continuing on, we stepped up the low stone stairs onto the pathway that led from Memorial Court to the river when the porter came to a huffing stop directly in front of me and said, with tilted head and raised eyebrows, "Are they with you?"

I looked at the kid on my shoulders, his grandparents a step behind me, and his mother, along with Simon, several feet behind them. "Yes," I said. "Is that all right?"

"Well, uh . . . I guess so," said the porter. "You see, I just received a phone call from the master, who said he saw some *Japanese* in the garden and that I should get them out."

I looked at him with disbelief—was it worse that the master had made such a call or that he had just repeated it to me?

"Is there a problem?" asked Mr. Horie.

"No," I said. "There isn't a problem. It's just time for us to leave."

During the time that I lived in Japan, my friends and I used to play a game. The game involved trying to answer a riddle: "If you put a Japanese, a Chinese, and an American into one room— and assume there were no language barriers—which two would become friends?" For those most familiar with these three cultures, the answer was nearly unanimous: the Chinese and the American. After my year in England, I began to turn the question around: "If you put a Japanese, a Briton, and an American into one room, which two would become friends?" To me the answer had become surprisingly clear.

Slowly, reluctantly, and to my great astonishment, over the course of my year at Cambridge I began to see great similarities between the British and the Japanese. I resisted these impulses at first, thinking them the product of the fact that I had spent most of my years outside of America living in these two cultures. Later, when I felt more strongly and first mentioned these ideas to friends—British, American, even German—my friends not only summarily rejected this notion, but acted gravely insulted, as if I were somehow committing a heresy by comparing the land that produced Shakespeare with the land that produced the Walkman, the country that fought off the Nazis with the country that attacked Pearl Harbor. Chastened, I retreated and rethought. Still, after numerous more coincidences and encounters, including the one in the Clare garden, I became convinced that comparing Britain to Japan was far more valuable and far more suggestive than comparing either with the United States.

To begin, the two countries share a remarkable number of structural similarities. Both Britain and Japan are island countries, slightly removed from their continental mainlands. They are roughly the same size (Japan has 50 percent more land than the United Kingdom, but it's mostly uninhabitable; its population is twice as large) and have roughly the same weather (in Japan, unlike Britain, the sun does shine at times—at least on the flag). Moreover, both are constitutional monarchies, with symbolic royal families and bicameral parliaments, and both are leading industrial nations that within the last century have both seized and lost colonial empires. Both require driving on the left.

Beyond these structural similarities, the two nations share an even larger number of underlying cultural resemblances. Both Britain and Japan, for example, have largely homogeneous populations (Britain has fewer than 5 percent nonwhites within its borders; Japan has fewer than 1 percent non-Japanese) and both have unifying national religions (the Church of England and Church of Scotland are both state institutions; Shinto, formerly a state religion, now melds with Buddhism into a national creed). Both have languages with similar emphases on courtesy, hierarchy, and indirection, and both have diets with similar, simple, nonspicy foods (just as most Japanese could not imagine an evening meal without rice, so most Brits are bereft without potatoes: in Britain, a day without potatoes is like a day without rain). More important, both countries boast a powerful national pride that verges on the xenophobic. Both Japan and Britain, for example, have gone out of their way in recent decades to avoid immigration, integration, and other ways by which alien elements might intrude on their national heritage. In many ways it was not surprising that the master of Clare would think the Japanese had invaded his garden. In the year that I was a student at Clare, the college had no blacks, no Indians, and only one half-Japanese, half-English student in an undergraduate population of over three hundred. If Cambridge, one of the leading centers of liberal education in the country, is that exclusive, imagine the corridors of power.

While these cultural similarities were everywhere apparent, one episode more than any other convinced me of the uncommon affinity between Britain and Japan. In early spring I was waiting on a train platform in London with an American friend. We were reading down the row of adverts along the Tube tunnel when we came across one by British Rail. IF YOU SEE SOMEONE GETTING CAUGHT WITHOUT A TICKET, the ad said, WOULD YOU LOOK AT HIM? THINK ABOUT IT. Later, inside the train, we saw another ad in the same series. HAVE A GOOD LOOK AT YOUR FELLOW PASSENGERS. IF YOU'RE CAUGHT WITHOUT A TICKET, THEY'LL HAVE A GOOD LOOK AT YOU.

"What are they trying to say?" my friend asked. "I don't understand." His comment forced me to reread the slogans, which I realized were similar to many I had seen in Japan that appeal directly to one's sense of public embarrassment, or shame. In Britain, although it is a Christian culture, this sense of shame is rampant. Embarrassment, I had often teased Simon, is the national religion. Whereas an American transportation authority would probably use the threat of prison—a policeman with a giant gun, a police dog with a vicious bite—the British politely encouraged people to purchase a ticket so that they might avoid being looked at by others. TRY DISAPPEARING INTO A CROWD WHEN THE WHOLE CROWD IS STARING AT YOU, said the last of that series, which I spotted on a kiosk at Cambridge. JUST THINK WHAT YOU SAVE WHEN YOU BUY A TICKET. You save your image, the adverts suggested, you save your reputation. In short, you save face.

Having discovered such a strong cultural affinity between Japan and Britain, I was left at the end of my year with one nagging question, which was similar to the thought I had when I began my journey: namely, if these two cultures are so alike, why is Japan at century's end on the rise, and Britain at the same time in retreat—or at least in remission from irreparable decay? Again, I suspect that the answer to this question has partly to do with structural reasons. Britain, which was more industrially advanced at the start of the twentieth century, was on the winning side of both world wars and, as a result, believed it had little reason to change course. Japan, on the other hand, was literally and psychologically destroyed in the Second World War and thus forced to remake itself. Also, the diverging paths of these two countries have partly to do with social differences. Britain has never expressly overturned its outdated class structure, but instead has allowed its classes to tear one another into pieces in a bloodless civil war. Japan, meanwhile, explicitly outlawed its feudal class structure earlier this century and has moved to create a new model of a communal state.

Unlike what some people suggested to me, neither of these trends was predetermined: it was not somehow written in the stars or passed down through the blood that Japan would pull itself together in the twentieth century or that Britain would pull itself apart. Rather, these outcomes owe more to government policies and national attitudes toward their country's one dominant and inexhaustible national resource: people. Britain and Japan, in the final analysis, have vastly different perspectives on the role of education in their land. At the elementary level Japanese students go to school more hours every day and more days every year than their counterparts in Britain. At the secondary level Japanese students continue their education longer and in greater numbers, with proportionally twice as many people staying in school until they turn eighteen. And at the highest level more Japanese students pursue further education and more companies demand it: 40 percent of Japanese students go on to university or college, while in Britain the number continues to languish at the lowest level among major industrial nations: 17 percent.

While in Japan I learned to evaluate the role schools play in the success of a country not solely in terms of the "Three R's"—reading, writing, and arithmetic—but in terms of a broader gauge, what I call the "Four C's"—curriculum, character, communication, and citizenship. This same measurement of how schools prepare their students for their role in life can be applied to higher education as well. While it is not possible to understand the entire, multicontinental, cross-generational rise and fall of the British Empire by examining merely its chief brain trust, the Oxbridge colleges, these institutions have played a central role in British society and thus can provide clues to its current condition. As my Blue Badge Guide to Cambridge might have put it: Oxbridge is England's past; the past is the present; and the present holds the key to the future.

Curriculum. The curriculum is the pride of the Oxbridge system. Students are admitted to a college after demonstrating proficiency in only three or four areas, and then, once they arrive, they narrow their already diminished course to one subject. The university argues that this system produces experts rather than amateurs. My experience at Cambridge convinced me otherwise. In the area of history, for example, which was my major at college, undergraduates at Cambridge may know *more* history than their counterparts in American universities, but they are certainly not *better* historians. If anything, one could argue that Cambridge student-historians are worse off than their American counterparts since they have less knowledge of parallel and perpendicular fields, such as literature, psychology, even maths. Instead of producing broad-minded thinkers, the Oxbridge system more often than not produces narrow-minded specialists. After twenty-one years of the Great British Education, for example, Ian the Classicist could easily read ancient Roman texts in the original, yet he could hardly keep score in a game of darts. Simon the Engineer could factor equations and equate factorials even after four pints of lager, but he had no books—*no books!*—anywhere in his rooms, only papers and worksheets and music magazines scattered about his four empty bookshelves.

Even more than narrow-mindedness, the Oxbridge curriculum has engendered a greater problem: an antibusiness bias. For centuries the English elite maintained a cool attitude toward industry because it was considered "dirty," and this prejudice was reflected in the country's leading intellectual retreats. In the nineteenth century fewer than 10 percent of Oxbridge students came from business families (compared with 42 percent at Harvard), and only 4 percent went into business after leaving. Thus, even those who came to university predisposed to business were turned off to the idea during their tenure. Cambridge, much more than Oxford, moved to embrace the practical sciences in the twentieth century, but still a royal commission found in 1922 that "science teachers [at Oxbridge] are too few, their accommodations insufficient, their students lamentably small, and the output of work less than should be expected from universities promising such great appointments." The number of students going into industry rose briefly in the 1930s, but dropped off quickly after the war. Today, fewer than 8 percent of Oxbridge graduates go into industry (compared with two-thirds in Japan), with the majority becoming doctors, lawyers, accountants, or consultants. In effect, by creating an academic elite who don't wish to clutter their minds, Oxford and Cambridge have produced a ruling class who don't like to use their hands.

Character. One of the things that surprised me most while reading about Cambridge was how many famous people who spent time there actually did not like it. "I was not for that hour," wrote

Wordsworth, "nor for that place." A few, such as novelist and don Kingsley Amis, did not like the setting. "[Cambridge] is a town whose most characteristic images—King's Chapel, say, at dusk in a thin mist—seemed cold and lonely, a setting more appropriate to an unhappy love-affair than the bustling exchange of ideas." But most, such as E. M. Forster, complained that the students were too elitist. Many of the boys coming up to Cambridge, he once wrote, have "well-developed bodies, fairly developed minds, and under-developed hearts."

Today the student population at Cambridge is no longer drawn from an exclusive social set. Yale, with its high-priced tuition and rarefied standards, seemed far more elitist than Cambridge. But Cambridge students still seem far more conscious of status. This attitude is best exemplified by the pressure surrounding exams. It is a Cambridge tradition—and a surefire mark of a shame culture at work—that exam scores are posted publicly outside the Senate House and, for third-years, are printed in the newspaper. Officially, Cambridge gives each student one grade based on the cumulative results of his or her year-end exams. These grades are divided into three classes: Third Class (for a few stragglers), Second Class (for the vast majority), and First Class (for the top 10 percent). In practice, however, most faculties divide the Second Class degrees into two categories, 2.1 and 2.2. Moreover, they divide these categories into even more arcane divisions, such as a "high 2.1" or a "low 2.2." The result of all this academic gerrymandering is widespread confusion and deep-seated anxiety.

As with class, when one brings up the subject of exam results, everyone has a story to justify his or her position—especially those in the middle. One person says he studied too hard; another confesses he worked too little. A friend of mine who earned a 2.1, for example, claimed he got Firsts on his first two sections but then slept through the final part and received a Third. I was unsure how to respond to this story. Was I supposed to think he was a genius for getting two Firsts? Or was I supposed to think he was a fool for failing to set his alarm clock? In fact, what I thought was how sad it is that so many people at so great a place allow their identities to be caught up in such a mindless way. Instead of learning to count their blessings and be generous toward others, Cambridge students are learning to quibble over rankings and compete among themselves.

Communication. The general breakdown of the old social order in Britain is nowhere more apparent than in the area of language. Traditionally, language patterns have mirrored class structure. Writer Nancy Mitford divided all speech into "U and non-U language," for upper-class and non-upper-class. Leslie Stephen believed the differences could be traced to schooling. The world could be divided into two classes, he wrote, "those who have and those who have not received a University education." For generations, members of the British ruling elite were educated in prestigious schools, where they were expected to learn the lingua franca of enlightened conversation. In turn, these people were expected to use their learning to lead the country. As George Orwell realized, to his dismay, no revolutionary change could happen in Britain without the leadership of this educated class. "In almost any revolt," he wrote, "the leaders would tend to be people who could pronounce their aitches."

Like so much else, this rigid order in language no longer exists and has been replaced by a creeping classlessness. Cambridge today offers a stunning example of the changing patterns. Speech at the university can be divided into "S and non-S language," for student and nonstudent speech. Among the nonstudents—the administrators, the professors, even the porters—language still follows the old rules. Clare College communicated with its members under the false assumption that we all spoke the same language. Announcements were filled with such enigmatic terms as *placets* and *non placets* (votes of yea, "it pleases," and nay, "it pleases not"), *absits* (letting a student be absent during term) and *exeats* (letting him leave when term is done), as well as a host of hierarchical distinctions, such as *procancellarius* (one who grants degrees from the university) and *prae-*

lector (one who grants them from the college), and—most important of all—*Cantab* (for degrees earned by hard work at Cambridge) and *Oxon* (for those just given away at "Awxford"). As if these were not enough, every night before dinner in Hall, a fellow would stand on the raised platform that supports the High Table and attempt to read a prayer in Latin, even though the language went out of general use over a millennium ago.

Students, meanwhile, no longer speak the rarefied language of the Conversation. Because of their varying social backgrounds and specialized courses of study, the only common language students share these days consists of pub-speak, pillow talk, and street slang they picked up from the telly, which they were all watching when they were young in lieu of studying Latin. The headlines of the Clare *Procrastinator* demonstrate the true level of intellectual discourse among students today: GET PISSED, CLIMB ABOUT A BIT, AND STEAL SIGNS WITH PETER; EIGHT BALL: AN ORGY OF SPITE, VENGEANCE, HOPELESSNESS, DESPAIR AND SEXUAL PERVERSION; and, a weekly feature in this esteemed journal of higher angst, the PRETENTIOUS BASTARDS' CORNER.

Over the last several decades the old order seems to have broken down and been replaced not by a new order, per se, but by a general free-for-all, and in some cases a complete turnabout. When Norman Podhoretz arrived at Clare in the 1950s, he was surprised (and pleased) that a lower-class kid from Brooklyn was given a room with a fireplace; was waited on night and day by a gyp, who woke him with a cup of tea every morning at a time of his choosing; and, most shocking of all, was called "sir" by the porters. When I arrived at Clare in the 1990s, I was given a room with a red lightbulb for heat; was woken up in the middle of a dream by a bedder who said she would arrive at the same time every day whether I liked it or not; and, most significantly, was made aware that I should call the porters "sir." The chickens, my lord, have come home to roost, and they have laid a scrambled egg.

Citizenship. Without a doubt, the greatest contribution that Oxbridge made to the rise of the British Empire was the production of a steady supply of well-educated, well-mannered men who could steadfastly steer the ship of state. These men, with their common language and upstanding characters, became the backbone of what is known in Britain as "the Great and the Good," a kind of Who's Who of Upstanding Citizens. After the Second World War, however, the Empire quickly began to implode. Given the central role that Oxbridge graduates played in the buildup of the Empire, it seems fair to ask what role these distinguished alumni played in its demise. Noël Annan poses the question directly in his book *Our Age,* a sort of collective biography chronicling the lives of the Oxbridge elite in the twentieth century. Annan, the former provost of King's College, acknowledges that Oxford and Cambridge did not prepare its students to revolutionize the British economy after the Second World War. He admits that government leaders were unable to diminish seething class tensions. And, after remarking that many of these changes might not have been possible under the economic circumstances of the time, he accepts that Britain did not have the leadership from Oxford and Cambridge the times demanded. Comparing Britain to Germany and France (and perhaps unwittingly thinking of Japan), Annan concludes, "Sadly enough the humiliation of defeat teaches men better than the vanity of victory how to revive and inspire their own dear country."

By restricting access to their elite conversation fraternity at Oxford and Cambridge, the Great and the Good had convinced themselves of their own invincibility. Annan says that the greatest achievement of the Oxbridge ruling class was the peaceful dismantling of the Empire; their greatest failure, he asserts, was the decision not to join the European Community at its beginning. The members of that class were able to accept the failings of their imperial past, but were unable to embrace a new vision for the future. In a way, this mirrors what happened at the two universities. The greatest accomplishment of Oxford and Cambridge since the Second World War has been to throw off the yoke of exclusion and accept a much broader cross section of the population; their biggest failure has been their insistence on maintaining a high-minded isolation and thus not encouraging students to play a leading role in forging a new social order in the country. Cambridge bends over backward to teach its students to be good scholars; yet it fails to raise even a finger to encourage these students to be good citizens—of a country in need, a continent coming together, or even the world at large. The result today is an institution—Oxbridge—that takes young people headed for a glorious future and isolates them for a spell within the high walls and sequestered courtyards of its own vainglorious past.

"Come in, Mr. Feiler. Have a seat. I'm afraid you're a little bit early today. Your examination will begin in a moment."

Richard Langley, M.A., was seated in a rotating black leather chair, thumbing through a copy of my dissertation. His hair was suitably silver, his jacket characteristically tweed, even his tie was stereotypically maroon. But his trousers, to my surprise, were inexplicably denim, and his shoes were shamefully white—sneakers, to be precise. As he sat beneath a faded portrait of Lord Palmerston and tapped his foot on the floor, Mr. Langley looked like a cross between a rare-book librarian and a member of the Mickey Mouse Club.

On the day after my meeting with Dr. Long, I had printed out two copies of my dissertation, carried them to the Board of Graduate Studies at 4 Mill Lane, and placed them on the counter. Two women stepped forward. "Are you submitting two copies of your dissertation?" the first woman asked, to which I replied, "Yes, ma'am." "He's submitting two copies of his dissertation," she repeated, to which her comrade responded by checking the first line of a multilayered form that appeared, from my angle, to have about the same number of pages as my thesis. "Have you signed a supplemental sheet declaring that your dissertation does not exceed twenty five thousand words?" she asked; again I responded affirmatively. "He has signed the sheet declaring that his dissertation does not exceed twenty five thousand words," she repeated; and again her compatriot made an affirmative mark. This process continued for about two dozen more questions, at which point the second woman signed the form and slid it to the first woman, who signed it and slid it on to me, who signed it and slid it back. "The Board of Graduate Studies now have your dissertation," the first woman said. "We will pass it on to the Centre of International Studies, which will then pass it on to your two examiners, who will then submit their evaluation. When this is complete, we will notify you that it is time for your viva voce exam. Do you have any questions?"

"Well, yes," I said. "How long will that take?"

She patted me on the hand with a sudden friendliness. "Oh, don't worry, honey," she said. "We have plenty of time. We've got a whole year to finish."

A week later, after escaping to London, I was summoned to St. John's.

"We would like to ask you a few questions of fact," said Mr. Langley after his deputy, Philip Toole, the one with the (Oxford) D.Phil., had settled in beside him and they had dispensed with perfunctory pleasantries. "First of all, you say in your first chapter, page nine, that in 1921 John Maynard Keynes resigned from the government."

I nodded my head in agreement.

"*Lord* Keynes, Mr. Feiler, was never part of the government. In point of fact, he worked at the Exchequer."

I looked at him blankly.

"Sorry," I said. "It's an American mistake."

"Indeed," Mr. Langley replied.

"Quite," Dr. Toole agreed.

"Moving on," Mr. Langley continued, reading down his list of

prepared questions. "On page ten, you state that Prime Minister
Lloyd George went to the Paris Peace Conference in 1918 intent on
imposing a strict reparations settlement on the Germans."

He turned to the page in his copy of my dissertation and nodded
ominously at Dr. Toole, who nodded equally ominously back and
tapped the offending line in his copy of the thesis in a manner that
reminded me of the similar tag team I faced when I turned in my
dissertation at the Board of Graduate Studies. I crossed and un-
crossed my legs. I loosened the collar of my shirt. Had I made
another factual error? I wondered. Was Lloyd George not prime
minister? Was this examination going to continue at this pace for
another hundred pages?

"Mr. Feiler," said the director of the Centre of International
Studies, University of Cambridge, who a little less than six months
earlier had invited me to a private, chummy lunch in his rooms.
"Are you aware that in this country we don't say 'Prime Minister
Lloyd George,' we say '*the* prime minister, Mr. Lloyd George'? "

I mumbled my reply, "I see."

"And that reminds me, Mr. Feiler," said Dr. Toole, showing no
resistance to hitting a man when he's down. "On page eleven you
mention that in 1909 a young British journalist named Norman
Angell wrote a book called *The Great Illusion*."

I nodded apprehensively.

"I wonder if you could tell us what exactly you mean by the
word, *young*." he said. "In 1916, Mr. Angell was thirty-seven years
old. Do you consider that to be young, or were you just trying to
flatter your examiners?"

The two of them giggled in delight. I felt my swallow swell up in
my throat.

"Sir, I'm sure I didn't make it up," I said. "I must have made an
error."

The two of them looked at each other. Mr. Langley took off his
glasses and rested them on the plastic dustcover of my dissertation.

"I'm sure you didn't make it up either," he said. "But still, I trust that you will want to correct these oversights before we deposit your thesis in the University Library."

I sat back in my chair. They returned to their notes. The examination continued apace.

For the next half hour, as Mr. Langley and Dr. Toole proceeded through their separate lists of errata, peccadilloes, typos, solecisms, and assorted American boo-boos, I began to grow increasingly frustrated—not unlike what I felt the previous year during my admissions interview. Then it was: "Why did you get a B+ in French?" "Did you say 'please' when you asked for admission?" Now it was: "Why did you say 'Central Europe' when you really meant 'Southwest?' " "Did you say 'thank you' for our considering giving you a degree?" In both of these interrogatory encounters—the bookends of my Cambridge experience—the emperors of the mind seemed more interested in discussing my typing skills and grammatical manners, in pointing out the differences between the "intellectual correctness" of England and the mental barbarism of America, than in eliciting any ideas I might have had that were related to my course of study.

At the end of my year at Cambridge, I had been feeling disappointed with the general quality of academics I witnessed but pleased with the quality of people I had met and the quality of work I had done. Now, just days after accepting a toast from Dr. Long, that work was being mocked in an examination that wasted almost three quarters of its time wallowing in introductory chapters before even arriving at the central topic of my thesis—the Allied occupations of Germany and Japan. In retrospect, the reason seemed simple: neither Mr. Langley nor Dr. Toole knew much about my topic, nor were they able to find anyone who did. Instead, they were both British historians and, as a result, homed in on the one part of my thesis that dealt with British history, even though this was the one section for which I did no original research. The main body of my dissertation, the main thesis of my work, they completely ignored.

To be sure, I had made some minor errors in my introduction; I had made some typographical errors in the body of the work. But that hardly seemed worth riding fifty miles from London—nor even walking five minutes from Clare—just to sit through a thirty-minute lecture on the virtues of the English use of the definite article. Rather than viewing the exam as a rite of passage before receiving my degree, I began to see it more as an exercise in humiliation designed to remind me—as well as my friends, who related similar experiences—of the hierarchy within the university community. Instead of treating me as an adult, as they had promised at the beginning of the year, they treated me as a child, reminding me at every turn of their eminent authority.

"Well, Mr. Feiler," Mr. Langley said as the examination dragged to its conclusion and he handed me both copies of my dissertation. "I believe you have a little more work to do."

"What exactly does that mean?" I gulped.

"Oh, your degree is not in doubt," he said. "In fact, your dissertation is quite exemplary—especially your conclusion. If you'll just take a few minutes this afternoon to clean up those errors, we will notify the Centre of International Affairs, which will notify the Board of Graduate Studies, who will inform the praelector at Clare that you have satisfied the academic requirements for the M.Phil. degree."

They shook my hand and turned toward each other. I took my papers and left the rooms. Two days later I received a letter from the University of Cambridge informing me that the Board had approved my degree and that my name had been officially removed from the Register of Graduate Students. I had finally reached the end of the maze. It was time for me to go down.

EPILOGUE

GOING DOWN

Brideshead Visited

§℔

We drove on and in the early afternoon came to our destination: wrought iron gates and twin, classical lodges . . . , open park-land, a turn in the drive; and suddenly a new and secret landscape opened before us. We were at the head of a valley and below us, half a mile distant, shone the dome and columns of an old house.

—Evelyn Waugh
Brideshead Revisited, 1945

"So this is it? You're going down?"

The day after receiving my M.Phil. I stepped into the Porters' Lodge to say goodbye to Terry.

"Back to America," I said.

"Well, then," he said, rising from his chair and lifting the swinging top of the counter. "Why don't you come in and have a chat before you go? One more for the road."

I stepped behind the counter and for the first time all year sat down beside Terry's desk. He began to reminisce, recalling the first day that we met and telling me how after thirty years of service he deserved the O.B.E., Order of the British Empire. After a while he worked his way around to a request.

"I want you to do me a favor," he said. "When you get back to America, don't tell people what it's really like here. Tell them what they want to hear."

"Why's that?" I asked.

"Let me tell you. When I meet people and they find out how I earn my stipend, they are fascinated. But if they knew what the typical undergraduate life was like on a rainy day in January, they would be disappointed. If they knew that the student rolls out of bed in the morning, fixes himself a piece of burnt toast, then hurries off in the freezing air to be ten minutes late for lectures—well, they just wouldn't believe it. They think we wear the 'Oxford Bag'— forty-two-inch trousers, bow ties, straw hats—and go punting up and down the Cam singing the 'Eton Boat Song.' Of course it's like that some of the time, but it's not what we call the normal way of life, fifty-two weeks a year."

"So how would you describe the normal life at Cambridge?"

He hesitated for a moment. "It's what we call 'the Game,' " he said. "It's gone on longer than Wimbledon and will go on for another century to come. It's not normal, but it doesn't have to be. It doesn't change, and then why should it. We like it the way it's always been."

I stood up to go. I thanked Terry for his kindness, turned in my key, and submitted my pledge of obedience that said I hadn't put tape on the walls.

"There's one more thing I have to ask you," I said, as Terry walked me through the Lodge and reached to open the door.

"What's that?" he said.

"Did you make me into a gentleman?"

He stopped and appraised me from head to toe, as he had done the first night we met.

"Well," he said, twisting his mustache. "All I can say is that I made you a little smoother around the edges. No more squirrel guns and raccoon caps for you. I can take credit for that."

"Yes, you can," I said. "And you should."

I bowed my head as he liked to do. He reciprocated and stuck out his hand.

"Now go on," he said, "and Godspeed—from a common man, from a friend."

"I've decided," Ian announced. "I'm going away."

The day after my farewell with Terry, Simon came up from a brief stay in London and we headed away in a "hire car" toward the region that road signs in England refer to as THE NORTH. The first stop on our farewell tour was Sheffield, a once-thriving steel town, where Ian was competing in the World Student Games. We watched the following afternoon as Ian—in full form—danced and dodged and eventually defeated a Hungarian and an Italian, before being dislodged himself by a one-armed Canadian. The next day, with Ian in tow, we drove farther north to our true destination, to Castle Howard, the country's most prominent—but least likely—memorial to Oxbridge elegance. This grandiose mansion, begun in 1692 by the 3rd earl of Carlisle, has become a Mecca for middle-class Brits to pay their last respects to the aristocracy, ever since it starred in the 1980s television series *Brideshead Revisited*. For me, however, it proved to be not so much a tribute to the past as a sign of the times.

I went to Castle Howard at the end of my year, as I went to Cambridge at the beginning, expecting to be overwhelmed by the grandeur and the sophistication. Instead, I was surprised by its garishness and vulgarity. The earl's descendants, forced to accomodate the hording public after World War Two, have used their *nouveau* riches to buy a squadron of paddleboats with swans on their bows and a platoon of trolley cars with circus lights on their roofs to escort guests around the estate and shuttle them off to the Adventure

Playground, where they can ride the plastic water slide and play pin the tail on the obelisk. Disney has not only invaded the Cam, but with this "Six Flags over the Realm" has all but co-opted the Crown.

That afternoon, before driving to the station to drop off Ian, who was heading back to Sheffield, and Simon, who was going home to Tokyo, I suggested we have a farewell drink. We were sitting in the Castle's Refreshment Centre, not far from the overflowing Coach Park, when Ian wrapped his fingers around a cappuccino cup and announced that he was giving up the law and going on a trip instead.

"But where?" I asked.

"Greece," he responded.

"But why?" Simon wondered.

Ian smiled.

When I met Ian at the beginning of the year, he was uptight and upset, upbraiding me and everyone else with his most recent book-learned idea. Simon, for his part, was just the opposite, upbeat and upright—but with little or nothing to back him up if he should take a tumble. By the end of the year the two of them had changed roles. Ian, the scholar, was abandoning the academy and leaving his beloved books behind. Simon, the dilettante, had succumbed to his twenties by purchasing a Filofax and even composing a summer reading list. His first book, which he brought along on our trip and revealed at our coffee table, was Nietzsche's *Beyond Good and Evil*.

"No!" Ian howled when he saw the title. "Don't you know that philosophy fucks you up? Don't you know that it takes young minds and turns them into ideologues? You should stop before it's too late. You should stop before I did."

Simon was nonplussed. "It helps me get to sleep," he said.

Ian was not impressed. "It will make you stay awake. Listen, think back on this last year. I bet you remember what happened to your body as much, if not more, than what happened to your mind. If you stay in school long enough, you begin to believe you can separate the mind from the body. But it's not true." He turned to me for support. "Think of rowing," he pleaded. "Think of Rachel."

"I think that was a fantasy."

"That's not the point," he snapped. He sat forward in his chair, rattling his cup in its saucer. "The point is that life isn't two separate spheres—wisdom and desire. It's a fusion of the two. There's a great quote from Aristotle. . . ." He pinched the bridge of his nose for a moment, then snapped his finger in remembrance. " 'No one who has not tasted true love is truly knowledgeable.' "

Ian slumped back in his chair. Simon picked up the clue.

"So that's what you're going to Greece for," he said, "*true* love?"

"I'm going because I don't want a life that ends, 'Game Over, Low Score.' I want to win big." He took a sugar cube from the plastic bowl and placed it on the table. "You see this cube," he said. "That's a note. Middle C, let's say. In Western music you take this note and build on it. You develop it, embellish it, cultivate harmonies around it. But there's a problem: in the end, you always come back to the same note."

He took another sugar cube and placed it on the table beside the first.

"This is also a note," he said. "But it's an Arabic note. In Arabic music, the more you develop, the more you stray from the original source. I have both of those notes in me, both of those voices. So now I'm going to stray for a while, to break away from all the harmony."

I sat forward, about to interrupt.

"I know what you're thinking," he said. "But don't worry. I promised my mother I'll come home in a year. I still want to be successful. I still want my life to end on a major chord."

Simon leaned across the table and smiled.

"Would that be a one-handed or a two-handed chord?" he asked.

Ian grinned at both of us, then popped the cubes into his mouth. "Two."

· · ·

I headed north.

During all the time I had spent in Cambridge, I had never taken part in the one true English obsession—walking. Walking is to the British what driving is to Americans: a tradition, a birthright, and the most efficient way to avoid other people. Americans invented drive-ins, drive-thrus, even drive-by shootings, while the British invented the Proms (a popular summer concert series in which participants walk around during the performance), the Wellington (a fashionable rubber boot for walking in the mud), and the pelican crossing (a type of crosswalk into which any person can step and instantly claim the right-of-way). With only one afternoon to walk, I drove to a recommended spot in the Yorkshire Dales, picked up a map from the local pub, and headed out under overcast skies in the direction of a nearby knoll. Despite my year in England, however, I was unprepared for the rain.

Out on the dale the landscape was varied—hard rock in some places with a sharp edge, rolling fields in others with classical over-tones. A series of homemade paths cut across the fields, through a minefield of live sheep droppings and over a matrix of meandering stone fences. The smell of lamb musk and fertile soil blended in the air into a kind of English stew. As I stepped and climbed and sniffed and walked (walking, that is, on the grass), I could not avoid the temptation to lose myself in my farewell scene.

Britain had been a continual surprise to me. When I first moved to Japan, five years before Cambridge, I expected to be different, an American abroad. But I soon discovered that even though I looked like an outsider, when I opened my mouth and spoke Japanese, I could sound, even act, like an insider. In England I had the opposite experience. With several exceptions (the most notable being my straight American teeth), when I walked into a room, I looked like a native, but as soon as I opened my mouth, I would reveal myself to be a Colonist and, by extension, a secondary being. At first this bothered me. I wouldn't talk to store clerks or chat with barbers for fear of being prejudged ("We English don't easily forget"; "Don't forget to look both ways"). Gradually, however, I changed my mind as I adjusted my view of my hosts, as well as my view of myself.

Like many Americans, I came to England with a nagging sense of intellectual inferiority. England, in my mind, was not only older, but wiser as well. As a child, I was surrounded by the symbols of English eminence. The spokesmen on serious television commercials always had English accents, while the McDonald's spokesman was dressed like a clown; the marmalade my mother spread on her toast was "Made in England," while the Pop-Tarts I ate were made in Illinois; my father's favorite television show was *Masterpiece Theatre*, while I preferred *Gilligan's Island*. Like an adolescent craving parental acceptance, I felt at times as though I could never be intellectually validated until I proved myself to be as cultured as the British.

A year in Cambridge cured me of my inferiority complex. Not only could I do the academic work at one of England's ancient universities, but my American interdisciplinary background made the task easier. Not only could I comprehend the famed subtleties of the Queen's English, but my straightforward American style proved more versatile. Not only did I gain a certain self-confidence at Cambridge, but I did so while remaining young, free, and American. And, like Ian, once I had realized my pursuit—once I had proved myself *to* myself—I didn't need the approval of my pursued anymore. I could leave Cambridge, secure.

After several hours on the dale, I began to lose my bearings. I was still heading in the same direction—up the path I had followed so closely, away from the flatland and toward the hills. It had begun to rain, lightly at first, as if watering the grass, then harder and harder like an incoming storm, until water was streaking down my neck and splashing up my legs. I was growing disoriented. Looking at my map, I decided to abandon my quest for the lake and turn toward a paved road off to the east. I hurried in that direction, hoping to follow the road back to town, or maybe catch a ride. The rain was heavy. Night was falling. I was feeling cold. Arriving at the edge of a field, I scrambled to the top of a shoulder-high fence and was preparing to leap onto the road, when a car came speeding up the hill to my right, slammed on its brakes, pressed on its horn, and came to a stop in the exact location where I was about to jump. I looked at the driver, then down at the ground, where I saw for the first time what he had seen and what might have saved my life: a small white lamb, walking on the water, which flowed like a river, and making its way, like a wayward child, to the other side of the road.

AFTER CLASS

*U*nlike preparing for a Cambridge degree, writing a book requires a one-to-many tuition of the most exhaustive kind. Using my best American-style English, I would like to thank the many who stand behind the one whose name appears on the cover.

First, I would like to express my appreciation to some of the numerous people at Cambridge who offered me friendship and support: Anne, Christopher, Elizabeth, Fuchsia, Jamie, Kirk, Richard, Rob, Sean, Sophie, Stephen, Terry, and my friend and adviser from beginning to end, Christopher Reohr. The people closest to me, of course, knew I was writing a book, although everyone I met did not.

Meanwhile, back at home, my agent, Jane Dystel, never wavered in support of this project and always managed to cheer me up. My editor, Jonathan Karp, never failed to improve the manuscript and always did it with style. In addition, many other people assisted along the way, by offering support, answering a question, or simply providing me an excuse to get out of the house. These include: Peter, Katherine, and especially Margaret Bergen, Ruth Ann and Justin Castillo, Karen Eastman, Ben Edwards, Jan and Gordon Franz, Ivan Held, Jessica Korn, Fred Lane, Katherine and Will Philipp, Dee Brock and Linda Resnik, Alex Beers and David Shenk, Jeffrey Shumlin, Max Stier, Jane von Mehren, and Dominic Ziegler.

Finally, I would like to pay special tribute to the members of my family, otherwise known as my "editorial board." My parents, Jane and Ed Feiler, not only read each draft and approved each revision, but also built my desk. My uncle Henry Meyer proved that wit is not exclusive to England; it also thrives in Mississippi. My sister, Cari, in addition to frequently lending her advice and even more frequently her car, managed in the midst of my failed sharks to meet, date, and marry Rodd Bender. My brother, Andrew, despite having attended the "other place," poured mind and soul and more than several pints of red ink into this book and shares in its authorship. But leading the way, both in years and in class, was my grandmother Aleen Feiler, who has long been the first to read, encourage, share, and lend. It was she, ten years ago, who first allowed me to travel, and this book, an overdue thank-you, is dedicated to her.

Learning to Bow, my book about life in small-town Japan, was published a month after my return from Cambridge. Within a month of that, I had received three letters: one from a woman in Japan requesting a date; one from a man in Arizona requesting a job; and one from a woman in Wisconsin who said that my book had inspired her to move to Japan and who thanked me for including a bibliography for further reading.

On the outside chance that that woman has now returned from Japan and is considering a move to England, I offer the following brief list of works about Cambridge. This survey is not meant to be

exhaustive, but rather to include only those books I found particularly helpful (and ones that are available in the United States).

Fiction. *The Literary History of Cambridge,* by Graham Chainey (U.
of Michigan), lists 111 works of fiction published between 1844 and
1984 that relate in one way or another to Cambridge. Of the ones I
read, the two I enjoyed the most were *Jacob's Room,* by Virginia
Woolf (Harcourt), and *Maurice,* by E. M. Forster (Norton). The most
obvious book to read that is not on the list is *Brideshead Revisited,* by
Evelyn Waugh (Penguin), which is nominally about Oxford, a distinction that is irrelevant to everyone in the world except those who
attended one or the other and who love to exaggerate the differences
between the two in a vain attempt to satisfy their own sense of
individuality. Lastly, perhaps the best novel I read about Cambridge
was written by an American (gasp!), in American English (ya-hoo!).
The book is Bruce Duffy's *The World as I Found It* (Ticknor & Fields)
and it describes in loving, fictionalized detail the lives of philoso-
phers Ludwig Wittgenstein, Bertrand Russell, and G. E. Moore.

Nonfiction. Sadly, there is no general-interest nonfiction portrait of Cambridge, and even if there were the author would have
been hard-pressed to produce a work half as good or as witty as Jan
Morris's *Oxford* (Oxford U. Press). Meanwhile, for pure historical
background, I found many books invaluable, among them: *A Social
History of England* by Asa Briggs (Penguin), *British Society Since 1945*
by Arthur Marwick (Penguin), and *The Decline and Fall of the British
Aristocracy* by David Cannadine (Yale). For a readable history of the
social impact of Oxford and Cambridge, I recommend Noël
Annan's *Our Age* (Random House), a "group portrait" of English
intellectuals in the twentieth century.

Finally, to my friend in Wisconsin, if you do make it to England,
be sure to pick up a copy of Clive James's *May Week Was in June*
(Picador), which is not only an amusing look at Cambridge but also
one of the funniest books I've ever read. Otherwise, the train leaves
from King's Cross, the cost is twenty quid, and don't forget to look
both ways.

ABOUT THE AUTHOR

BRUCE FEILER is author of the highly acclaimed *Learning to Bow: Inside the Heart of Japan* (Ticknor & Fields, 1991), a humorous, first-person account of life in a small Japanese town. A graduate of Yale, he has also studied at universities in Osaka and Oslo and holds a master's degree in international relations from Cambridge University. He has worked as a reporter with the Kyodo News Service in Tokyo and has written for newspapers and magazines across America and Asia. A native of Savannah, Georgia, and frequent lecturer around the country, he now lives in Washington, D.C.

ABOUT THE TYPE

This book was set in Bembo, a typeface based on an old-style Roman face that was used for Cardinal Bembo's tract *De Aetna* in 1495. Bembo was cut by Francisco Griffo in the early sixteenth century. The Lanston Monotype Machine Company of Philadelphia brought the well-proportioned letter forms of Bembo to the United States in the 1930s.